Jane Stork was born in Albany, Western Australia, in 1945. She spent her childhood and early adult life in Western Australia and New Zealand. She has lived in India and the United States of America. She now lives in Germany.

Breaking the Spell

My life as a Rajneeshee
and the long journey
back to freedom

Jane Stork

Jane Stork, Breaking the Spell: my life as a Rajneeshee, and the long journey back to freedom

Copyright © Jane Stork 2009

The moral right of the author has been asserted.
All rights reserved.

ISBN-13: 978-1986754200
ISBN-10: 1986754200

To my parents

Dulcie and John Paul

"And the question whether we are to judge the act by the result and approve the bad act because it was needed for the good result - that is life too. Life puts such questions as these and they cannot be answered with a long face. Only in lightness can the spirit of man rise above them: with a laugh at being faced with the unanswerable, perhaps he can make even God Himself, the great Unanswering, to laugh."

Thomas Mann (1875-1955),
Joseph and his Brothers

Prologue

An apparition in white came through the door. Hands joined in greeting, a soft smile playing on his lips, he moved towards the chair placed there for him. He seemed to float towards it. Silent tears of joy filled my eyes as I gazed on the vision of celestial beauty. I was sure I was in heaven and God had come to speak to the assembly. Bursting with pious devotion and honoured to be among the chosen few, it was inconceivable to me that everything I felt and saw was simply a projection onto the pristine white screen standing before me.

If someone told you that they would willingly give away their freedom, you would shake your head in disbelief. But that is exactly what I did. As a young Australian wife and mother of two small children, I happily handed over my freedom to someone else. In doing so, I entered into a prison of my own making in which I was both guard and prisoner and all the while the deception was so complete that I thought myself to be an independent and free individual making wise decisions for myself and my family, and for the good of mankind. It was not until I was locked into a physical prison with high stone walls and metal doors that clanged when they were shut that the extent of my self-deception slowly began to dawn on me.

This is the story of how I came to relinquish my freedom, of what it took before I realised what I had done, and of the years that followed as I faced the devastating consequences and struggled to win back the priceless treasure I had recklessly thrown away.

Decades have passed since the story began. I am a grandmother now who keeps house, tends the garden and bakes with her grandchildren when they come to visit. All stories have a timing of their own and mine has taken long. It spanned many continents. There were no short cuts and it was necessary that I walk each and every step of the way.

Australia

1

In my family I am the fourth born. Rosemary is the first born, Susan the second, and Mary Lou the third. My mother always said I was the spirit of my grandfather. When my grandfather died, my father made the long journey to the home of his parents to bury him. My father loved his father very much. The evening he returned, he lay in bed with my mother and wept. She comforted him, and in doing so they joined their bodies together. I am the child of love conceived on that night of sadness and loss.

Six weeks after I was born, the deadliest conflict in human history ended. One of the estimated sixty million people who died in that war was my mother's brother, Jack. The night before his twenty-fourth birthday Nan, my grandmother, woke up crying that Jack was dead. In a dream she had seen his plane come down in water near a place where the houses were flat-roofed and white. Two men climbed out of the plane as it floated on the water and stepped into a small inflatable raft, but Jack was not one of them. As the men paddled away, the plane sank beneath the water.

After the war was over, the two men Nan had seen stepping into the inflatable, returned to Australia and visited my grandparents. They told them that they were the only surviving crew members of the first mission Jack flew. He had just completed his pilot training and was flying a bombing mission to Tunis in north Africa. Just short of their objective, and before any bombs were dropped, the plane was shot down into the sea. It had happened as Nan had dreamed it.

I think my parents thought I would be their last child and so they called me Jane, which is the feminine of John, my father's name. I represented my absent brother, the crown prince, for five years until, amid great rejoicing, he joined the family. He was baptised John, and our family was complete.

We lived in Albany in the south-west of Western Australia. Albany is on the coast, so that next to the warm smell of my mother, one of my earliest memories is of the salt breeze coming off the Southern Ocean. We lived on Melville Street, on Mount Melville. A little further uphill the housing stopped and the magic world of rocks, bush paths, orchids and rabbits began. I never tired of watching the tadpoles darting back and forth in the shallow rock pools. Sometimes we took a jar with us and caught a few to take home. We put them in the old concrete sink by the veranda. Over the next few days we would monitor with great interest their transformation from tiny tadpoles to big fat tadpoles to almost little frogs. We never really saw them as frogs as it seemed the moment the metamorphosis was complete they hopped off to see the world. Grandma Paul had the same kind of little frogs in the well in Busselton where we vied with each other to pump water for her, pumping madly as we primed the pump and listening expectantly to the gurgling in the pipe that heralded the approach of the first gush of water, and with it a couple of bewildered frogs.

Wandering along the paths, investigating rabbit burrows and chasing after tiny lizards, was a source of constant delight, which reached new heights when the orchids began to appear. Cowslip orchids were bright yellow; they grew low to the ground and looked like pockets of sunshine in the grass. If you tickled a trigger orchid with a piece of grass its trigger sprang open. Once it was open it didn't close again and it was always a challenge to find ones that were still cocked. There were delicate spider orchids, clumps of yellow-brown donkey orchids, and shiny royal blue enamel orchids. Aunty Dorry, Mum's oldest sister, painted pictures of elves and fairies in a magic world filled with orchids where elves reclined on toadstools while conversing with snails. Aunty Dorry was my fairy queen.

We had chickens in Albany. They lived in a large wire pen in a corner of the garden, with perches for sleeping and laying boxes near the entrance. The laying boxes were filled with shell grit. One of my favourite things to do was to collect the eggs. Except, that is, when one of the hens was clucky and she fluffed up her feathers and clucked menacingly at me, refusing to leave the box. Then Dad would come and lift her off so I could reach the eggs.

Sue loved playing the piano. She showed a natural talent and would get up early in the morning and go off to piano practice before the rest of us had rubbed the sleep out of our eyes. Mum and Dad wanted to buy a piano so Sue could practise at home and we could all enjoy her playing, and maybe even sing along. But a piano is an expensive instrument and hard to afford on a teacher's salary.

It was Dad who had the idea about the chicks.

'We already have a couple of dozen chooks,' he said, 'so how about we get a hundred day-old chicks and fatten them up for Christmas dinners?'

'A hundred day-old chicks!' said Mum. 'What would we feed them on?'

Dad said he had given the matter some thought and he would talk to a farmer friend. Over the next few days he extended the brooder and added more light bulbs. And suddenly there they were. Boxes and boxes of fluffy yellow chicks. I spent every spare moment in the shed with my arms hanging over the great wooden box, gazing in at the cheeping yellow life moving about in perpetual motion there. Soon the chicks were no longer fluffy little balls, they were small hens with brown feathers and red combs on their heads. And some were cocks that crowed loudly in the early morning. Dad moved the young birds to movable cages he had made. Every couple of days the cages were moved to another part of the garden. The copper, usually only lit on Monday for the washing, was now lit every day. Mum boiled up bags of bad-smelling potatoes and musty grains to which Dad added pollard before distributing the finished 'bird porridge' in bucketfuls to the hungry birds. Orders for fresh Christmas-dinner chickens were taken around the neighbourhood. The orders were recorded in a special notebook, and we were very excited the day the hundredth order was pencilled in. One night at dinner Dad said the birds were not to be fed the next day. When Dad was going to kill a chicken for Sunday dinner, he took it from its perch in the henhouse on Friday night and put it under a wooden box. That was so it wouldn't eat anything else and the crop would be empty by the time he killed it on Saturday afternoon. So when he said the chickens were not to be fed we understood that they were about to become Christmas dinners.

A day later the killing began. It was an all-day affair. One by one the moveable cages and their inhabitants were moved to a spot outside the laundry. With practised skill Dad reached in, took hold of a pair of legs and pulled out a protesting bird. With one motion he swung it against his knee and, with a lightning-swift movement of both hands, broke its neck. An axe blow, and the head was separated from the body. The carcasses were laid on the grass where Mum collected them three and four at a time. She dunked each carcass into the copper of boiling water and then handed it on to Rosemary and Sue for plucking. Mary Lou and I helped by pulling out feathers stuck to the wings and legs. The laundry stank of blood and wet feathers and steam. When all the cages were empty Dad joined us. He set up a small table at the end of the production line and there he gutted one hundred chickens. Heart, liver and cleaned crop and feet were returned to the empty cavity. Mum wiped each bird down with a tea towel as it was finished. In the afternoon and evening people arrived to pick up their orders. Everyone looked pleased and said 'Happy Christmas' as they left.

Not long afterwards a piano appeared in the house. Sue sat at it every day after school and played and played. Sometimes Mum would stand with her hand on Sue's shoulder and sing softly while she played and I would lay my head against the shiny wood and feel the vibrations or climb up on a stool and open the top to watch the white shoes popping out to strike the wires. One day, I thought, I will learn to sing like my mother, and Sue and I will give concerts together. Sue still has that piano.

From our house on Mount Melville we looked down over King George Sound, the vast bay that is the Albany harbour. Fishing was part of our lives. Family tradition has it that I caught my first fish when I was two years old. The walk down the hill in the cool greyness of early morning was filled with anticipation. We kids would run past the woollen mills holding our breath to avoid even the faintest whiff of the unbearable stench, not stopping until we came to the railway tracks, where we waited impatiently for Dad. Then we scampered across the wooden sleepers and jumped down into the sand dunes on the other side. Already the smell of seaweed and the ocean made me dizzy with happiness. A couple of small sand dunes and we were on the beach.

Dad had his own dinghy. Well, it actually belonged to Jack McBride who was a fisherman and a good friend of Dad's. Jack fished at night and when he came back in the first light of dawn he would stow the oars in the boat and pull it up clear of high-water mark. Whenever we went down to the beach, it lay there near the sand dunes waiting for us. Dad dragged the boat across the sand to the water. We dug a few handfuls of cockles from the wet sand, and then he lifted us smaller children in and held the boat steady in the shallow water as the others waded out and climbed in. Dad was the oarsman. He always jumped in last, set the oars in the rowlocks and rowed with strong steady strokes out to the edge of the weed bank.

It was a pleasure to watch Dad row. He was a tall, thin man who rowed with surprising power. To look at his wiry build you would not have suspected it of him. When he rowed he fell into a rhythm that was as graceful as any dancer.

At the edge of the weed bank Dad tossed the anchor overboard and peered down into the water to see that the boat was lying over sand, not weed. Satisfied that all was as it should be, he secured the anchor line and stowed the oars away. Then he reached into his battered old bag and distributed lines to everyone.

Cracking cockles was a messy, dangerous business. I didn't like it at all. When you put them on the big bait board and cracked them with the smaller board, they squished in all directions and the broken shells were sharp and cut your fingers. So Dad cracked them for me. He would line up three or four naked cockles on a bait board and lay it down within reach. Having carefully baited the hook, I would lower the line over the edge of the boat and let it glide down to the sandy bottom. On a still day I would look down through the water and watch the weed bank undulating back and forth to some mysterious command, and the whiting nosing around the defenceless cockle impaled on the hook. Whiting cannot resist cockles and it was just a matter of time before one of them would dart forward to gobble down the bait.

Pulling in a fish without tangling the line was a skill I learned very early in life. Hand over hand, hand over hand, was how it was done, with the slack line laid in loose coils to one side. You had to be careful when the fish was swung in over the side that it didn't fall into those neat coils. Sometimes it happened. If the resulting tangle wasn't too terrible, Dad would take it out right away; but sometimes it was one of those tangles that kept him busy for an hour or more on the back step on a Saturday afternoon.

By the time I had swung the fish over the side, Dad would be holding open an old calico flour bag he had dipped into the sea. As I swung my fish into the bag he caught it by the head. Holding the flapping slippery form firmly in his hand, he removed the hook and carefully handed it back to me. As I grew older I learned to take off my own fish. I would slap my catch against my thigh to steady it and use a spare flour bag to get a good grip on the fish before taking out the hook. My trousers would get slimy and covered with scales but I didn't mind. Those scales were trophies.

On the row back to shore everyone counted their fish and the champions of the day would groan at the number of fish they had to clean. On shore each of us would take a bait board and a dull fishing knife and begin scaling. You had to hold the fish firmly by the head and scale it from tail to head. As each fish was scaled, Dad ran his sharp knife over it one more time, and then cut off the head. A quick downward stroke and the belly of the fish lay open on the board. With practised fingers he plucked out the entrails and flicked them aside, scraped the silver–grey lining from both sides of the belly flaps with his knife, and laid the fish on a bag at his side. Then he scooped up a bucket of sea water and tipped the cleaned fish into it. One by one, he took the fish from the bucket, ran his thumb-nail down the exposed backbone in the open belly, picked off any last bits of entrails clinging there, rinsed it vigorously in the bucket of water and laid it carefully upon a clean fish bag.

Then bait boards were washed in the shallows and laid back under the seats, and the knives plunged into the sand to rid them of any last clinging scales, before finding their place back in the line bag. A final check that the boat was clean and no stowaway fish still hid under the floorboards, and Dad would drag the dinghy up the beach to the sand dunes. The moment we left the seashore the seagulls descended on the feast of heads and entrails in a screeching cacophony of sound. The walk back home up the hill was always long, but I was comforted by the knowledge that there would be fresh fish for lunch. I know of nothing sweeter than a King George whiting tossed in flour and fried in butter, so fresh that the tail curls right over as it cooks.

Sometimes Mum came fishing with us, though more often she took advantage of our absence to do undisturbed work at home. Like

Nan before her, Mum sewed all our clothes, most of them on a treadle Singer sewing machine. She made our dresses, underwear, hats and coats, and knitted our cardigans and pullovers. When the collars of Dad's white work shirts wore out, she took them off and reversed them. She made our fancy-dress costumes, the curtains and the bedding. The sheets were made of unbleached calico. I loved the smell of new sheets. They were a creamy brown colour and smelled of hay and grass and were pleasantly scratchy. After a while of being boiled in the copper every Monday and hung out in the sun to dry they lost their fragrance and became softer and whiter, but I always liked them best when they were new.

In winter pink woollen quilts were tossed over the blankets on each bed. They smelled of lanolin and were wonderfully warm. On winter evenings we huddled around the fire in the lounge room to read, or be read stories. When bedtime came we would rush from the cosy hearth and jump into bed. The quilts were pink on one side and a white lacy fabric on the other. Throughout the winter the wool filling gradually rolled itself into lumpy balls.

In summer Mum undid the stitching and took the quilts apart. We would sit around the table teasing the wool balls out into soft fluffy fibres again, dropping them into the laundry basket where they soon piled up like white fairy floss. The covers were washed and ironed and the pink side laid out on the table. The fluffy teased wool was distributed evenly over it. Then the lacy side was laid on top and, using a large needle and woollen thread, Mum made a big stitch through the whole thing and back out again, pulling the threads to draw the two sides together, before tying them in a double knot. The process was repeated over the entire quilt until the wool filling was anchored with evenly spaced knots and the whole thing had taken on a quilted look again. The quilt was then taken to the sewing machine where the sides were stitched shut. As each quilt was finished it was wrapped in unbleached calico and laid in the linen cupboard ready for winter. Unwashed, unbleached calico kept the moths away.

It was Mum's belief that children should learn to cook, especially girl children. To that end we were always allowed in the kitchen. We learned to cook from an early age, in much the same way as children learn language. The Golden Wattle was our cookbook. Interspersed between recipes for sheep's head broth, kangaroo tail soup, fricassee of rabbit, mock cream and Australian plum pudding, there were instructions for things like invalid cookery, how to chop suet, and laying and lighting a fire. Instruction for setting a table began with the advice to have 'clean hands and an apron'. Oven temperatures were 'cool', 'moderate', 'hot' or 'very hot', reflecting that it was written at a time when most people cooked on wood stoves, without thermometers.

The royal agricultural show was an important annual event in our lives as we girls always took part in the cooking competition. Throughout the year we practised baking the things we planned to enter on show day. The day before entries closed, the kitchen was filled with delicious smells and focused activity as we concentrated our best efforts on producing perfect examples of rock-cakes, scones, decorated cupcakes, Swiss rolls, lamingtons and decorated sponge cakes. Mary Lou's speciality was sausage rolls. She made the best sausage rolls in Albany. I say this on the authority of the show judges who awarded her the first prize year after year.

Christmas was one of the most exciting times of the year. Dad would come home with a large branch off a pine tree and we would help decorate it with crepe paper. The night before Christmas the family all went to midnight mass. On our way to bed in the wee hours of the morning we peeked in to see the Christmas tree hung with stockings and packages and could hardly sleep for anticipation. Mum made each of us a Christmas stocking, a tradition she continued for many of her grandchildren. The stockings were made of red net with a red crepe paper frill stitched all the way around. The foot would be filled with little bags of Turkish delight, pink and white coconut ice, caramel twists and fudge Mum had made.

In between the shredded cellophane paper filling the leg, our stockings held surprises like balloons and coloured pencils, paper whistles that rolled open when you blew them, a little toy like a biscuit cutter in the shape of a star or a mould to make a plaster-of-Paris pony, a cotton reel with four nails for French knitting, a hair ribbon or a doll's dress. Sticking out the top was a tin whistle with a big tassel. There was also a present for each child under the tree. It was usually a special dress or cardigan Mum had made us.

Christmas dinner was always a plump roast chicken with roast vegetables, peas and gravy. Dad stood at the head of the table and carved the chicken, distributing the delicate slices of white flesh onto our plates, and placing a spoonful of stuffing from the chicken with each serve. Mum arranged the vegetables around it and poured gravy over the meat. We ate quickly, in anticipation of the plum pudding with brandy butter, custard and whipped cream to follow. Mum made the plum pudding weeks in advance. It was tied in a floured cloth and boiled for hours in the big preserving pan, before being hung in the pantry until Christmas. On Christmas Day it was boiled again. Then it was freed from its cloth cocoon and turned out onto a plate. The thick rubbery skin was doused with brandy and lit, and the great brown marvel with its dancing blue flames was carried in triumph to the table. As Mum cut each serve there was deathly stillness at the table as our ears strained to hear the chink of her knife against a coin. The plum pudding contained threepences and sixpences! Coins that were found were nibbled clean and arranged like medals around the rim of the plate. Later Dad traded us new ones for old and when Christmas was over and all the pudding eaten, he washed and boiled the coins and put them away for the next year.

During school holidays we went to see Grandma Paul in Busselton. Dad and we girls went ahead, leaving Mum at home for a 'rest'. She joined us a week later. Visiting Grandma Paul was always a real adventure. It took all night to get there on the train. We had a compartment with four bunk beds. No sooner were we under way than we unpacked the supper Mum had made for us. There were homemade pasties, still warm from the oven, lemon barley water to drink and apples to clean our teeth. We sat in dreamy silence, chewing contentedly like the cows in the fields that flashed past the window. The conductor came by to punch the tickets Dad proffered from his coat pocket. After eating we washed our hands and then played clock or rummy, or read our books, or just looked out the window at the lengthening shadows cast by the eucalypts dotting the landscape. As darkness fell the conductor came by again to fold down the sleepers. With a few deft movements he transformed the railway compartment into a bedroom with four cosy beds made up with crisp white sheets and grey railway blankets with red stripes at each end. When he had left we changed into our pyjamas and brushed our teeth. The carriage smelled of leather and woollen blankets and wood panelling, and the smells and confinement were both comforting and exciting.

 I slept on a bottom bunk, end to end with Mary Lou. Dad tucked us into bed and gave us all a kiss goodnight, before climbing into his bunk, where he read by the dim glow of the overhead light.

I would lie there in the swaying train listening to the clickity-clack, clickity-clack of the wheels on the tracks and dreaming of the faraway places with strange-sounding names Mum sang about.

'Tea and toast in the dining car. Tea and toast in the dining car.'

The sound of the conductor's voice broke into my sleep as he walked through the train chanting his wake-up call. The blind was raised and the subdued light of early morning shone feebly through the window. Dad was already up and dressed.

'Come on sleepyheads,' he said, 'tea and toast in the dining car.'

We were allowed to go for tea and toast in our pyjamas. We walked down the corridor to the dining car like so many drunks after a night on the town, swaying and staggering and trying not to lose our balance as the train sped along. It was just plain old toast with butter, no honey or jam, but train toast tasted absolutely delicious.

We were all awake now and laughed and giggled and bounced off the walls of the corridor on our way back to the compartment. We wiped the crumbs from our lips and the sleep from our eyes with the wet flannel Dad handed us, and dressed quickly. A last check under the pillows for books and dolls and handkerchiefs, and Dad would fold up the sleepers and pack away the pyjamas in the overnight bag. Soon the train would stop and we would climb down and follow Dad along the platform to a different train. The next train didn't have bunks for sleeping, just seats. Now the time went fast. Soon we would be at Grandma's.

Grandma was a big woman with a big lap to sit on and big arms to wrap around you. She was soft all over. I liked to snuggle up against Grandma's leg as she stood by the stove, and bury my head in the folds of the long dark dresses she always wore. There was something strong and dependable about this jovial woman that made me feel perfectly safe. She lived in a small wooden group-settler's cottage. It was a square house divided into four equal-sized rooms, with a veranda back and front. We girls slept in the big, creaky, saggy beds on the front veranda. The house had no insulation, and in winter the wind whistled through the cracks, and the rain drummed on the tin roof fit to wake the dead. I would lie there in the dark in that saggy bed that folded itself around me like a hammock, and listen to the rain on the roof. My deep satisfaction at the sound of rain pelting on a tin roof to the orchestration of thunder and lightning remains forever a part of my secret treasury of joy.

A fire was always burning in the grate in Grandma's kitchen. In the morning Dad made our toast on the coals left from the midgie nut he had laid on the fire before going to bed the night before. Midgie nuts are the seed cones of the banksia tree. A green midgie laid on the fire in the evening will be an intact glowing red ember in the morning. Dad would bang it with the toasting fork to break it up into a bed of coals to make the early morning toast, before building up the fire again. Soon the kettle would start singing and the porridge would begin to bubble. Dad put a piece of butter into each plate before pouring in the porridge. We added sugar and milk, and I would wait expectantly for the little butter bubbles to rise to the top and float on the milk before I began to eat. There were mulberry and fig trees in Grandma's garden so there was always jam to spread on our toast.

The sound of a horse clop-clopping down the road and a muffled 'Whoa' as it held at the gate was my early morning wake-up call at Grandma's. There followed the metallic sound of the lid being lifted off the milk can, followed by the sound of a little water-fall as milk was scooped out of the big can and poured into the smaller one the milkman carried to the house. The creak of the front gate opening, the dull thud of running footfalls on the path, the lid being lifted off the billy and the chink of the money being taken out. Again the sound of milk being poured, and lids being replaced. The thud of running footsteps. The clang of one milk can banging on another. The snort of a horse. 'Gee-up!' The clip-clop of horses' hooves and the chink-chink of milk cans fading in the still morning air. It was the same every morning and I delighted in it.

There was no running water in Grandma's house. Water was brought in in big enamel jugs from the rain-water tank behind the house. Saturday was bath day. Water was pumped from the well and heated in the copper in the laundry shed. Dad carried the hot water by the jugful up the back steps and into the bathroom and poured it into the tin bathtub. A jug or two of cold water from the tank, and the bath was ready. We girls went first. It was cold in the little bathroom on the back veranda. The water cooled quickly so we didn't linger; a quick scrub and we were out, wrapping ourselves in rough towels before running in to stand by the fire where our pyjamas were warming on the fire screen. It was so delicious to climb into warm pyjamas. Then we curled up in the two great old easy chairs by the fire, wriggling like a bag of worms, and Rosemary would read to us while first Grandma and then Mum and then Dad had a bath. Another jug of hot water from the copper was added when the water got too cold. Dad was always the last, but he didn't mind. He once told us that in the years he was at boarding school he had taken a cold shower every morning. How awful! I had made a mental note to avoid boarding school.

Whenever we were at Grandma's, Dad chopped wood every day, filling the wood shed, the old tanks laid on their sides and the space under the house. He grew up in Greenbushes where his father did the books for the timber mill. Dad is said to have chopped down his first tree when he was ten years old. He and his brother Bob would chop down a big tree at the start of the school holidays and then spend the rest of the holidays chopping it up into firewood and bringing it home to stack in the woodshed. Dad loved to chop wood. You could see it in the way he honed the axe blade, rubbing it on the whetstone in small, rhythmical circles and holding it up again and again to check its sharpness. He was quiet and concentrated then, in a contented kind of way. Watching him chop wood gave me the same feeling of joy I felt when I watched him row the boat. With one hand he set the chunk of jarrah down on the chopping block, automatically reading its lines as he did so. Effortlessly he swung the axe into the air and brought it down with a thack that split the hard jarrah in two as though it were a stick of celery. Many years later, at the age of eighty-nine, on a visit to my home in Germany, Dad took his axe to beech tree logs drying in the yard. He filled a room in the cellar with firewood enough to keep us warm for the next three years.

Dad and Bob were very athletic when they were young. They rowed eights for their school; they starred in the inter-school athletic meetings, and they played tennis and cricket and football. Bob was a good bare-fist boxer and liked nothing better than a good fight once in a while. When they were studying at university and the mood seized him, he would seek out Dad.

'Come on, Jack,' he'd say, 'I feel like a bit of a fight,' and the two of them would walk down the Terrace in Perth, stopping likely-looking characters and asking them if they wanted to fight, for a purse of course. Eventually someone would agree, and as it was all very illegal, they would move off into a side alley. Dad's job was to find spectators, who would bet on the fight, thereby providing the purse for the winner. His secondary duty was to watch out for policemen.

'There's a fight. There's a fight,' he would mutter between his teeth, standing at the entrance to the alley as people passed by.

Soon a crowd would gather, and the fight could begin. Bob usually won, but he was always happy after a fight, no matter which way it had gone.

The year John was born, Dad and we girls left for Busselton right after Christmas. Mum and baby John joined us a couple of weeks later. It was a hot summer and we spent most of our time at the beach, an easy walk down King Street from Grandma's. There we built fantastic sandcastles, with moats and towers and bridges made of driftwood. We walked along the beach collecting pink fan shells and deep blue mussel shells, little black limpets and cockle 'butterflies' to decorate our masterpieces. We collected the bleached backbones of cuttlefish washed up on the shore and turned them into excellent boats to send out to sea with seaweed sails flapping bravely in the wind. We lay in the shallows and watched the ebb and flow of the water draw patterns in the sand between our arms. The braver among us practised putting our heads under water and doing dead-man's-float until we thought our lungs would burst. They were halcyon days and even the thought of the train ride home did not ease the sadness I felt at having to leave Grandma and Busselton, where life was so perfectly wonderful. It was 1951 and I was to begin school.

But before I could start, my tonsils flared up and Hanni, our doctor, said they had to come out. Hanni had been present at the birth of all five of us. He vaccinated us, attended to us at home when we were sick, set broken bones and performed all manner of surgery. It was Hanni who operated on the stomach ulcer that prevented Dad going overseas when war broke out in Europe. Dad spent the war in Albany, teaching and helping organise civil defence, which was lucky for us three younger girls who were all born during the war. Dad had a scar like a great zip from one end of his torso to the other from that ulcer operation. I was five years old when Hanni took my tonsils out. I still remember the cloth placed over my face in the operating room, the sickly smell and a disembodied voice telling me to repeat what it said as it counted backwards, the split second of panic when I couldn't get enough air, just before I swirled into a long tunnel with a light at the end.

No sooner was I home again than I developed pneumonia. Blood from the surgical procedure had seeped into the lungs and infection had set in. Hanni came and said I must return to hospital.

I lay in a big bed in the corner of the ward feeling hot and sick. I wanted to go home but I didn't seem to have the strength to get out of bed. A soft, sweet-smelling hand stroked my cheek and forehead. My guardian angel was smiling down at me. Actually, there were lots of angels. In fact, I had never seen so many angels all at once. They were waving their wings ever so gently, like butterflies, creating a gentle breeze that cooled my hot forehead. They were so beautiful and they were all smiling at me. I knew that soon I wouldn't feel so hot and sick any more and could go and play with them. Knowing that made me feel very happy. From far away I could just make out Mum's voice calling urgently,

'Nurse! Nurse!'

Now I felt really sick. My angel friends had gone. It was dark all around.

'Jinny, my precious.'

It was Mum. At the sound of her soft voice I started to cry. Mum wiped away my tears with her hand.

'It's all right Jinny, it's all right,' she crooned. 'I'm here. It's all right my love.'

'I want to go home,' I sobbed, although I noticed I couldn't just jump up and throw my arms around Mum's neck as I would have liked to. My body was terribly, terribly heavy and it hurt all over.

'You're very sick, sweetheart,' crooned Mum, 'and Hanni says you must stay in hospital until your body feels better.'

'Sing to me Mum,' I whispered and that beautiful voice rose and fell softly: 'Greensleeves was all my joy, greensleeves was my delight . . .' and I slept.

When I woke I felt Mum's hand enfolding mine and I didn't feel so frightened any more. My mouth was so dry.

'Mum, I'm thirsty,' I said, without even opening my eyes. A familiar squeeze of my hand. I felt better already.

'Nurse,' called Mum's voice quietly. I opened my eyes. It was light in the ward. There was a funny kind of transparent box over my bed and I wondered what it was. A nurse in a white dress and white hat came through the door.

'She's thirsty,' said Mum.

'Good,' said the nurse, 'she can drink a little water, and I'll take her temperature again.'

She reached through a hole in the wall of the box and slipped something cold under my armpit and then lifted my head so I could drink, and Mum held a glass to my lips. The water tasted awful. I lay back on the pillow and the nurse took the thing from under my arm.

'Her temperature is down,' she said, 'we'll ask the doctor if we can remove the oxygen tent when he does his rounds.'

Later that day, after they had removed the oxygen tent, Nan came with Teddy. Teddy had golden fur and when you pressed the round disk on his back he spoke bear language. 'Baaaaa,' he said at our first meeting, which meant, 'Hello Jinny. Glad to see you're feeling better.' But what was so special about Teddy was his very smart blue polka dot overalls and matching cap. Nan scolded me for having put my tablets in the pillowcase instead of swallowing them. They had been so bitter though. As soon as the nurse had turned her back, I had taken them out of my mouth and buried them in the pillowcase. Nan said I had almost died and that if Mum hadn't noticed the little stash of tablets when she did, I would be dead by now. I only half listened. I was looking at Teddy. I knew Nan was not really angry with me, she was just pretending, the way she always did when she had had a fright. She stopped scolding.

'I dressed him up for you,' she said. 'You need a good-looking chap to look out for you. Gave me a fright you did, princess.'

She hugged me, knocking Teddy's cap askew. I laughed and set it straight again. He was so handsome, and he had beautiful brown eyes. It was love at first sight. From that day on he went everywhere with me, except fishing. He might have got wet in the boat.

I sometimes wonder if I hid the tablets in the pillowcase because I didn't want to face the anguish that was about to envelop our family.

2

Dad was an early riser. First thing in the morning he would bring a cup of tea and a piece of toast to the bedside of everyone in the house. Except on Sunday when we all went to mass. In those days you had to fast before receiving communion. Dad used to tell us the story of waking late the day he was to make his first communion. He ran all the way to the church. It was a long way and by the time he got there his lips were parched and his mouth was dry. Without thinking, he ran to the rain-water tank outside the church and took a drink of water. Too late he realised he had broken his fast and could not receive communion! Bringing us tea and toast in the morning was his way of waking us up for school, or piano lessons, or just because it was time to get up. He continued this practice throughout his life, although in later years it became more of an early morning greeting than a call to rise. Until he died, Mum and anybody else in the house would be brought tea and toast in bed at six o'clock in the morning.

While I was convalescing from the pneumonia, Sue came down with scarlet fever and Rosemary and Mary Lou broke their arms. Our house was beginning to look like a lazaret. When Sue was well enough, she and I were sent to the Keoghs' for some wholesome farm cooking and healthy activity in the fresh air. The Keoghs were Dad's cousins. Frank and Terry worked the farm together and their mother ran the household. There was butter and jam and clotted cream on the table at breakfast every morning. It was heavenly.

Sue and I spent most of the day outside with the animals. We fed the chickens, collected the eggs, sat on the rails watching the cows being milked, and went riding around the farm with Terry in the horse and buggy. The horse was a good-natured animal called Gypsy. She was our favourite animal of all. Terry showed Sue how to handle the reins. She was good at it and he let her drive us wherever we went. Afterwards Sue would help brush Gypsy down while I scampered around on the bales of hay, scaring mice right, left and centre. The smell of fresh hay still evokes in me untroubled playful days.

One night on the farm I dreamed I was walking along the beach at Busselton with Dad. It was one of those perfect days when the sun is deliciously warm and the blue sky is mirrored in the clear sparkling water. We walked hand in hand and I felt deeply happy and content. Suddenly Dad disappeared. I looked around for him but he was gone. I was alone on the beach. I ran around frantically looking for him. The sky began to cloud over and the wind came up. I ran desperately along the sand, first in the direction we had been going and then from where we had come. He was nowhere to be found. I woke up crying. I was very disoriented and afraid. It was dark and it took me some time to realise that my pillow was on the floor and my head was at the foot of the bed. I slipped out and crawled into bed with Sue. She hardly stirred. Her warmth was comforting but I was filled with a deep sense of foreboding.

That morning, while Sue and I were at the farm, Dad brought Rosemary her tea and toast as usual and found her unconscious in her bed. He telephoned Hanni, calling out to Mum as he ran to the phone. Hanni arrived within minutes. He asked whether Rosemary had been unwell.

'No,' said Mum, 'but she has been very tired lately. So tired that she has been lying down and sleeping when she comes home from school.'

A couple more questions and Hanni was on the phone calling the ambulance. His diagnosis: TB Meningitis. When the ambulance arrived he told them to take her to Perth, fast! Perth was two hundred and seventy miles away – a trip of ten hours in those days. Dad went with Rosemary in the ambulance. Years later Mum told me that as the ambulance drove away she went into shock. For three days she lay on the bed in a catatonic state. Only with enormous effort did she manage to get up to feed and care for eight-month-old John, and for Mary Lou, going through the motions like a zombie, before collapsing onto the bed again. On the evening of the third day she gradually became aware of a loving presence in the room. She recognised it was her brother Jack. In that moment her energy rushed back in. She got up off the bed and walked purposefully out of the bedroom. She felt strong and ready to face whatever came.

For the first five years of my life I was the baby of the family. When our brother John was born I lost that place. Mum was busy with the new baby and so I turned to Rosemary. It was the natural thing to do. She was the eldest; she was reliable and I could count on her to help me adjust to the new situation. She was loving and playful with me and always had time to take me on her lap for a cuddle. But then suddenly she disappeared. When Sue and I came back from Keogh's farm she was nowhere to be found and Dad was missing too. Mum said Rosemary was very sick and Dad had taken her to hospital. I could tell Mum was very sad and I felt afraid and confused. I needed Rosemary more than ever, but she wasn't there. I settled down to wait for her. I waited and waited and waited. It seemed like eternity and I began to feel angry with her for taking so long, especially as Mum was so sad the whole time.

The ambulance delivered Rosemary to Royal Perth Hospital where she lay in a coma. The doctors confirmed Hanni's diagnosis. They told Dad there was no known cure. There was nothing they could do. Rosemary would die. Dad went to see the director of education and asked for leave of absence.

'Jack,' Blue Robinson said, 'if I give you leave you'll go crazy. I would rather transfer you to a school here in Perth. That way you and Dulcie can be close to Rosemary and you will have your work to keep you grounded.'

Dad was given a position at a school in Claremont and the family moved to Perth. All, that is, except me.

I went to live with Mum's sister, Bess, and her husband Bill in Bruce Rock, on the wheat belt. Mum explained to me that because Rosemary was very sick I would be having a kind of holiday with Aunty Bess and her family. Bess and Bill had two daughters. Judy was the same age as me, Kathy was two years younger. Mum and Bess were always close and, before she married, Bess often spent her holidays in Albany helping Mum. Mum and Dad knew I would be in good hands. And I was. Aunty Bess treated me as her own. Judy had started school at the beginning of the school year and I joined her, quickly catching up on what I had missed. We were inseparable. We did everything together; we played with our dolls, drew and coloured pictures, did our homework, and picked everlastings and pressed them in books.

Over the years I cherished the memories of those months in Bruce Rock, feeling grateful that Aunty Bess's loving care had spared me the trauma of being in Perth, where the family was struggling with the terrible situation of Rosemary lying deathly ill in a coma. Fifty years later, the truth of how I really felt at that time crashed in on me and I felt again the heartbreak I had experienced at the separation from my family. I missed them all desperately. With all my heart, with every cell of my body, I had wanted to be with them.

Rosemary would spend ten months in hospital and in time my grief turned to anger as I slowly came to the conclusion that my family didn't want me. Deep inside, defiance replaced sadness. If my family didn't want me, I didn't need them. I could do it by myself. I didn't need anybody! This misunderstanding by my six-year-old self retreated into the darkness of my unconscious, from where it was to profoundly influence my decisions and actions for a very long time to come.

In Perth Dad went to early morning mass every day to pray for Rosemary. Back home he brought everyone tea and toast and made breakfast and school lunches while Sue and Mary Lou got dressed. Meanwhile Mum fed and took care of baby John in readiness for the caretaker who would come soon after Dad and the girls left for school. Mum said it broke her heart every morning to hear John crying as she walked to the front gate on her way to catch the bus to the hospital where Rosemary lay fighting for her life. She knew he needed her too, but she felt compelled to go to Rosemary. There she sat with her, holding her hand, stroking her, speaking to her, singing softly to her, willing her back to life. After school Dad arrived to sit with Rosemary, and Mum would take the bus back home where Sue and Mary Lou and John were waiting for her.

One day the doctors told Mum and Dad there was a new experimental drug they wanted to try out on Rosemary. It was a glimmer of hope. They agreed. Four months after falling into a coma Rosemary opened her eyes and looked around. She did not know Mum and Dad and remembered nothing of who she was or where she had come from, but she was alive. She was also deaf. It would soon be understood that the drug had destroyed the hearing centre in her brain. Rosemary was still not out of danger. She faced months of debilitating illness and innumerable painful spinal taps. It would be summer before she was well enough to leave the hospital. We celebrated Christmas in the house in Perth, and then the family returned to Albany. We were so relieved to be back home. Rosemary was alive and we were a complete family again. And yet it was not the same, and it would never be the same again.

Rosemary turned fourteen during her illness. When she left the hospital she was so thin and frail that Dad had to carry her around like a baby. One of the first things she had to do was to learn to walk again. With time she remembered odd snippets of her childhood – holding baby John on her lap and being annoyed with her younger sisters – but to all intents and purposes it was gone forever. For her, and for us, it was as though she had just been born. She was not the same Rosemary who had fallen ill and been rushed to hospital. She was a stranger to me. It was as though my sister had died and someone else had come to take her place. When I approached her she sometimes took me in her arms and gave me a big affectionate squeeze, but just as often she would push me away and laugh derisively at my confusion. Her voice was a harsh monotone, the result of not being able to hear herself speak. She was like a wild animal that suddenly finds itself in captivity, and she ran away a lot.

Hearing voices at night I would crawl out of bed and look through the darkened dining room into the brightly lit kitchen. Mum and Dad would be talking to their friend, the sergeant of police, and I would know that Rosemary had run away again. On one such occasion I woke in the middle of the night to find Rosemary climbing into my bed.

'Ssh,' she whispered, 'don't tell Mum and Dad I'm here,' and I lay there listening to her rhythmical breathing, knowing Mum and Dad were worried sick about her and feeling torn between loyalty to my big sister and love of my parents. Dad found us curled up there asleep when he brought the tea and toast in the morning.

Mum and Dad did everything in their power to restore normality to us all, but Rosemary's illness was like an explosion that shattered the cohesion and harmony in the family forever. Try as they did to bestow their affection on all their children alike, Rosemary's needs continually demanded our parents' time and attention.

The family never talked about what was happening. I am sure Mum and Dad talked about it together, but it was never discussed in our hearing. I guess they thought they were protecting us by not speaking about it. Whatever the reason, we three younger girls developed a tacit conspiracy of silence, which I for one never thought to question. We went about our business trying to be as good as possible and, in a way, as invisible as possible, so as not to trouble our parents. We pretended to ourselves and the world that everything was fine. In those days in the country there was no recognition of special needs, or professional help for parents and families of children with special needs. We were on our own. It was an impossible situation. The illness had erased Rosemary's childhood and damaged her nervous system. And she was deaf.

What must it have been like to be suddenly deaf? Unable to hear the voices of your family, to see everyone around you talking and laughing and not understanding, not hearing when someone approached you, or the sound of your sister's piano playing, or the sound of the cock crowing and the kookaburra laughing? No sound. Only silence.

As time went by we learned to look at Rosemary when speaking to her and to exaggerate our pronunciation so she could read our lips. With the help of the local community attempts were made to find a niche for her where she could learn a skill and perhaps settle into a job. But she remained a wild thing and I lived in fear of her strange unpredictable ways.

That summer I developed appendicitis and my appendix was removed. Again the cloth over my face, the sickly smell, whirling down the tunnel with the light at the end, and waking up in the now familiar ward. After two weeks in a hospital bed I could hardly walk. The soles of my feet felt as though they had sponges attached to them. The following year I got rheumatic fever. When I recovered Hanni told Mum and Dad I needed to recuperate in a dry climate. I was sent to the preventorium in Kellerberrin. It was the year I turned nine. For the second time I was sent away from home. Although Mum explained that I needed to go to a warmer climate for my health, my suspicion that my family didn't want me grew, particularly as this time I was not with lovely Aunty Bess and her family. This time I was in a kind of prison.

The preventorium was run by nuns, for children who had been ill. It was in an isolated spot in the country. Here there was no tea and toast to wake up to in the morning. Blinding lights came on and harsh claps told us it was time to get up. After breakfast we were bussed to the convent school in town, where prev children received a second mug of hot milk at morning break 'because they had been sick'. I was in the habit of being a good kid, but there were so many rules I had to be constantly on guard lest I break one of them and be kept inside at playtime or my pocket money be confiscated.

When I was there we were eighteen girls and about the same number of boys. We ranged in ages from six to sixteen. Boys and girls only came together at mealtimes, which were eaten in silence.

All the boys slept in a dormitory on one side of the prev, and all the girls slept in another on the other side of the building. It was strictly forbidden to speak in the dorm. I still remember lying in bed whispering to my neighbours in the darkness when the lights suddenly came on and the talkers were ordered to the bathroom. It was late and the bathroom was cold. We lined up for a whipping across the back of the legs with a stick before limping back to bed with smarting legs. I did not cry. I never gave the nuns the satisfaction of seeing me cry. Instead I withdrew to a secret world inside myself, far removed from the reality of that unhappy place so far from my family, and the ocean, and my beloved Mount Melville. Although I missed everyone terribly, I pretended I was fine and didn't need them, and the shell I had begun to build around myself when Rosemary was sick hardened with each day of the year I was there.

I have just two happy memories of the prev. One is of the fragrant pink quinces that appeared as dessert in autumn. The other is of the gardener. He was an old man with a magic vegetable garden. I would slip through the gate in the wall to watch him weeding and watering his vegetables, and he would talk to me about the plants as though they were his friends. One day I was called into the office and forbidden to go into the garden again. From then on I just held my breath until I could go home. On the day I was to leave, the school bus was not available and my bicycle was too awkward to fit into the car that would take me to the train station. So while the car took my suitcase, I rode my bicycle. On the way I got a flat tyre but I took no heed of it. I was determined to get away from that place and pedalled with all my might into town. The tyre was irreparably damaged, but I was free at last.

3

The year after I returned from the prev, Sue went away to boarding school in Fremantle. She wrote regular letters home, always emphasising that she was happy and well. 'Don't worry about me. I'm fine,' was the message contained in every letter. Home for the school holidays she let slip that her appendix was hurting and that it had been hurting at boarding school too. She had emergency surgery in the nick of time, just short of a ruptured appendix, and septicaemia. It was typical of Sue not to want to bother Mum and Dad with her aches and pains, but her silence nearly cost her her life.

Unable to hear herself speak, Rosemary was losing the ability to project her voice, so Hanni arranged for her to go to the rehabilitation centre in Perth to learn to speak again and perhaps to learn typing or some other skill with which she could get a job. She was seventeen and would live-in at the centre. The absence of Rosemary and Sue left a gaping hole in the family. Although I was relieved not to be confronted with Rosemary's unpredictable ways every day, I found I missed her and felt strangely lost without her and Sue.

The following year the remainder of the family left Albany. Mum and Dad had been there for twenty-one years, but they would never return. At his request, Dad had received a transfer to Norseman, on the eastern goldfields, where he took up the position of headmaster of the junior high school. Mum had developed asthma since Rosemary's illness and Hanni thought a warm, dry climate would help. Norseman was inland and hot. It was flat and dry and dusty, a far cry from Mount Melville and the green of rain-drenched Albany. Many's the time the cry would go out 'Willy-willy!' and we would rush to bring in the washing and close the doors and windows against the rapidly approaching spiral of penetrating dust. And yet Norseman was a haven. Mum's health improved dramatically, which may have been due to the climate but perhaps also to the fact that she knew Rosemary was safe and doing well at the rehabilitation centre.

Life became more settled. We kids went to the convent school just up the road, and Dad went next door to his school. On weekends we rode our bikes out to Pink Lake, a great dried-up salt lake with a glistening pink hue. I missed the ocean, but in the late afternoon the Esperance Doctor would come in. That was the name given to the sea breeze that began on the coast in Esperance and penetrated all the way inland to Norseman. It had warmed up by the time it got to us but was always a welcome guest. Knowing it came from Esperance, I always imagined I could smell the salt in it.

Sometime around Rosemary's eighteenth birthday she wrote a letter saying she was getting married and inviting Mum and Dad to the wedding. She had met Tony at the rehabilitation centre where he was learning to walk again after a bad motorbike accident that had smashed his leg. Mum and Dad were distressed at this unexpected turn of events, for they knew only too well Rosemary's impulsive behaviour. They went to Perth and met Tony and his parents for the first time. Dad recognised Tony's father immediately. He remembered playing football against him in opposing school teams and felt somewhat cheered. When they met Tony he felt even better.

Rosemary and Tony began their married life together in a one-room house with a curtain hung across the middle to separate the 'bedroom' from the 'kitchen/living room'. Tony pumped gas at the local petrol station and went to night school to do his matriculation. They had a son, Peter, and Tony moved on to work for a company that made bakers' ovens, while he studied engineering at night. A daughter was born and they named her Kerry. When he received his engineering degree, Tony bought fifteen acres on the outskirts of Perth, put a big shed on it and began producing bakers' ovens of his own design. He screened off one corner of the shed for the family to live in, the noise of production not disturbing Rosemary in the least, while he built a house for them next door. The business thrived and Tony's ovens found their way into bakeries all over Australia. Rosemary retained her wild streak but the stability Tony afforded her, and the responsibility of caring for her husband and children, allowed her to build a creative new life out of the ruins of the old.

After only one year in Norseman, we moved still further inland to Kalgoorlie, the heart of the eastern goldfields. Dad became the headmaster of Eastern Goldfields High School, the only senior high school in the area. Mum had been born in Boulder, the town adjoining Kalgoorlie, and Dad in nearby Bulong. Bulong had been a lively gold-mining town at the beginning of the 1900s, but when we moved to Kalgoorlie in the mid-1950s all that was left were a few chimneys standing bleakly to mark the places where houses had once stood.

Dad's parents had been publicans in Bulong. Grandma would tell us children stories of how she had hidden miners in the cupboard when they were sought by the police for not having paid their mining fees. Grandma was of southern Irish descent. She had a strong sense of fairness and a lively mistrust of the police, whom she always felt to be on the side of the powerful. It was due to Grandma's Irish heritage that we were Catholics. Granddad had Scottish ancestors and was a Protestant. The year he turned seventy-five he was baptised a Catholic. He may have been hedging his bets, but it was probably to please his wife, for in those days couples of different religions could not be buried together. His good friend and next door neighbour was in the same boat. When Granddad told him what he had done, Harry said,

'If it's good enough for you Bob, it's good enough for me,' and went off and had himself baptised too. Granddad died not long afterwards.

Mary Lou and I went to the local convent school. None of the convent schools I attended offered science subjects for study, the tacit understanding being that we would grow up to be wives and mothers and wouldn't need science. The truth was that most of the nuns were themselves poorly educated. Many were country girls who had joined their order with only a basic education, and then left for 'the missions' without further ado. Their primary job was to attend to the spiritual wellbeing of their charges, instilling in them a healthy fear of God and giving them a strong grounding in the teachings of the Church.

I wonder how the young Irish nuns who entered the convent in Ireland with the intention of going to 'the missions' felt when they found themselves in the parched landscape of Australia. In those days when they left for the missions it was a one-way trip. They said goodbye to their families, never expecting to see them again, and then sailed off to Australia, only to find themselves in some remote place like Norseman or Kalgoorlie or Coolgardie. Hot, dry and dusty. No rolling green pastures and stone houses. Glaring heat, willy-willies and dust storms and a little convent made of brick and iron, if they were lucky, or asbestos and iron if they were not. They froze in winter and cooked in summer. Only the language was half-way the same.

Later in life I would meet one of those Irish nuns in an ashram in India. She told me the story of her departure from Ireland as a seventeen year old, with a small group of fellow postulants. The train taking them to the coast was to stop in a village where the parents of one of the girls lived. It was arranged that her parents would come to the train station to say goodbye. At the last minute the young women were told they were to take an earlier train. The girl begged her superior to inform her parents of the change. She did not. The train went through her home town while her parents were still at home getting ready to go to the station. She was not able to see them and be held by them one last time. She cried all the way to Australia. It was women like this who were our teachers. Today I have more understanding of what may have happened to their dreams. But as a child I found many of them angry, bitter women to be feared. By and large I fared pretty well under them, no doubt because I was an obedient student, and my father was a well-known and respected public figure and a practising Catholic. It was the girls of working-class parents, mostly miners, who were the targets of their meanness.

Religion was on the list of subjects for study every day. It took the form of a catechism class first thing after morning prayers. It was unthinkable that religious instruction include the discussion of other religious beliefs, or even the history of the Church itself after it ceased to be a source of heroic martyrs and became the Church of the ruling class. We recited our catechism like parrots and felt safe in God's hands. Questioning or criticism was not an issue. It just didn't happen. The same attitude permeated all other classes too. It was not a climate that encouraged enquiry or critical thinking.

At home Mum and Dad did not preach to us or call on God to augment their parenting skills, but nor did they ever expose us to any other religions or to any literature that might broaden our horizons in that regard. I suppose they did not want to raise doubts in our young minds about the one true Church. I had vaguely heard that the Vatican had a vast library of blacklisted books, which led to my conviction that to read other religious texts or critical literature was a sin. Any curiosity I may have had was fettered by the spectre of drawing guilt upon myself.

Home from boarding school for the holidays, Sue told me that she was going to be a nun. I felt a tremendous sense of relief. If Sue was going to be a nun then I didn't have to be one! While she was still at school Sue applied to join a missionary order. They wrote back to say she was too young and suggested she wait a year after finishing school. Missionary work was unusually demanding, they wrote, and recommended she learn to drive a car, and to type, and to learn to do simple mechanical repairs during her period of waiting. If she still felt she wanted to join them at the end of a year, she should write again. So when the school year ended Sue came home to wait and to do the things expected of her. But we had no car. We had never had a car. We walked or rode our bikes everywhere.

In his youth Dad had learned to drive a Model T, though he never owned a car of his own. Then he married, the war came and he had children, and with one thing and another he had never felt the need of a car. But now Sue needed to learn to drive, so he bought a Volkswagen Beetle. He had not driven for twenty-five years. He went down to the police station to see about a licence. He was headmaster of the high school and everybody knew him, including the policeman.

'I've bought a car and need a licence to drive it,' Dad said.

'You can drive can't you, Jack?' said the policeman.

'Yes,' said Dad. 'I thought so,' said the policeman, and wrote him out a licence.

Kalgoorlie streets were built for turning bullock drays so there was plenty of room for Dad to brush up his driving skills. Then he taught Sue to drive and, later, each of us younger children. With typical single-mindedness Sue also learned the other skills asked of her and at the end of the year again applied to join her chosen order. This time she was accepted and the following year she went to Melbourne to enter the novitiate. She was given a new name, Sister Pius, which I thought suited her very well, though I still called her Sue. She was only allowed to write one two-page letter home each month. She learned to write small and tight so she could fit as much as possible onto those two pages. She still writes that way.

On weekends we often drove into the bush for picnics and while we waited for the campfire to burn down enough to grill the sausages for lunch, Dad taught us to shoot with his .22 rifle. It was a single shot rifle and our targets were the rusty tin cans lying around the bush which Dad set before a tree stump. The golden rule was: 'Never, never let your gun point at me or anyone'. He impressed on us the importance of always having the safety catch on when the gun was loaded, of not walking with a loaded gun, and of always being aware of where the barrel of the gun was pointing. My brother and I became very proficient tin-can shooters.

The year I turned fifteen Dad took six months long service leave. Add to that the Christmas and August holidays and his leave added up to almost nine months. By now Dad had swapped the Beetle for a Kombi which, in preparation for the trip, was fitted out with a table and seats that folded down to make a double bed, a double-burner gas cooker, a small fridge, cupboards, a water tank and an extra fuel tank. Kombis didn't yet have high tops, so adults couldn't stand up straight inside, but it meant a large rack could be fitted on top. Duckboards were secured on the Porta-rack, as it was called, and a second, larger water tank went up there, along with mattresses for John and me and the canvas annex that completed the unit. Mary Lou had finished school and was going on to teachers' college in Perth so she couldn't come, but Mum and Dad and John and I were driving across the Nullarbor Plain to visit Sue in Melbourne. John and I were excused from school for almost a year. It was not considered unusual that we should miss school. Correspondence school and school of the air were well-established institutions for children who lived in the outback, and we were, after all, going travelling with our very own teacher! We set off after Christmas.

The road crossing the Nullarbor Plain was a dirt road in those days, with very limited opportunities for buying fuel or food. One needed to be pretty much self-sufficient until getting to Ceduna in South Australia. Open sheds were erected at irregular intervals along the track, with a rain-water tank to catch the run-off from the tin roof. We often pulled up under one of these sheds to spend the night. There was usually water in the tank and we would use it for cooking and washing in order to conserve our own water supply. I took to sleeping up on the Porta-rack and John would sleep on the front seat. It was a bench seat and as he was only ten years old he fitted there perfectly, even if it was a bit narrow.

We were not in a hurry, in fact it took us two weeks to get from Kalgoorlie to Ceduna. It was in the days before the introduction of myxomatosis when rabbits were everywhere and still considered good food. Out there on the Nullarbor Plain we came across an enormous rabbit warren the size of a football field. It was riddled with burrows, most of which were in use. Dad had brought traps with him. We stayed near the rabbit warren for a few days while Dad taught John and me to recognise a burrow that was in use, to set the traps, and to skin and clean a rabbit. Pretty soon rabbit stew was on the menu every day. Mum browned the rabbit pieces with some onions and salt bacon in the frying pan on the gas cooker, added a packet of chicken noodle soup and hot water, and brought it to the boil. The boiling brew was poured into a large wide-mouthed thermos flask, which was then tightly closed. Three hours later, lunch was ready!

Dad fulfilled his duties as a teacher by organising visits to steel mills, chocolate factories, museums and other places of cultural and historical interest. From time to time we made a detour to take in these educational activities. By the time we arrived in Melbourne it was winter. Although we stayed at the Sunshine Camping Grounds we never saw the sun. It was cold, and it rained every day.

We went to see Sue. I hardly recognised her. She looked like a real nun. She was wearing a white habit and a veil that covered her hair so only her face and hands were showing. Afternoon tea had been prepared for us but Sue was not allowed to have tea and biscuits with us. Oh, she could be in the room with us, but she sat away from the table and did not eat or drink anything. We had come all the way from Kalgoorlie to visit her and she couldn't even drink a cup of tea with us. I was very unhappy. It seemed to me that my second eldest sister had become a stranger too. The rest of our visit was no better. She was not permitted to come out with us at all. We could only visit her in the convent and then only for limited periods of time and under completely unnatural conditions. It seemed her days were filled with domestic duties, prayer and silence.

We went across on the ferry to Tasmania to visit Dad's brother Bob, and his family, returning to the mainland to see Sue one more time before heading north to Canberra. As part of our ongoing education, Dad took us to the War Museum and to Parliament House to show us government in action. Dad's family were traditionally a Labor family and Dad was at the time active in the Democratic Labor Party (DLP), which broke away from the Australian Labor Party at the time of the troubles on the wharves. The DLP was the Catholic labor party. It took the view that the strikes on the wharves and elsewhere were instigated by communists, and communism was an anathema to all devout Catholics like my Dad. The DLP had succeeded in getting two candidates into the senate. Dad knew both men personally and took the family to meet them and to watch them in action during a debate.

Our travels continued northwards. We camped and fished our way along the east coast, stopping whenever we felt like it. In Queensland we drove by banana and pineapple plantations and through rainforests to the glasshouse mountains. All too soon it was time to turn for home. We arrived back in time for the last school term of the year. It went by fast enough and then I said goodbye to the convent school for the last time. The following year I began school at Eastern Goldfields High School.

What a shock! First, second and third year high school at the convent had all taken place in one room with one nun to teach all subjects. Discussion was discouraged and lessons followed the textbooks exactly. At the high school there was a different teacher for each subject and, although we had a classroom, some classes took place at other venues. It was a co-ed school and students were encouraged to actively participate in classes. Needless to say the standard was much higher and I was struggling to keep up, but as was my habit I said nothing to my parents.

In the end my report card said it all. I finished first term with bare passes in all subjects. I was used to 95s and 100s at the convent. Now my marks were in the 50s and low 60s. I was crushed and became convinced that I lacked intelligence and was a disappointment to my parents, especially to my father, who was, after all, the headmaster. After that, Dad took me under his wing and we began sitting down every evening to do maths together. Although I had done three years of maths at the convent I didn't understand it at all. If the three sides of a triangle were called AB&C I was fine, but if it was suddenly called XY&Z I had no idea what was going on. With infinite patience Dad opened my eyes to the mysteries of mathematics. Mathematics was his speciality. Even when he was the headmaster of a very large school, he continued to teach at least one leaving maths class until he retired. He did it because he loved maths, but also because he said it was important to keep in touch with the students and teaching was the only real way to do it. Under his tuition I succeeded in passing both maths A & B at matriculation level.

There were other problems for me at the high school. A social was held once a month in the school hall for upper school students and staff. A social is a dancing affair, but I couldn't dance. In an all-girl convent there was no need to learn to dance. Dancing was something both my parents enjoyed greatly, so they understood that dancing was a desirable social skill to have. Mum and Dad reasoned that if I couldn't dance then neither could all the other Catholic kids who had been at convents or brothers' schools. In an extraordinary feat of persuasion Dad succeeded in getting Father Healy to agree to my parents holding dancing classes for the Catholic youth in the church hall. If it had been anybody else but Dad Father Healy would never have allowed it. Every Friday evening Mum and Dad loaded the record player and records into the Kombi and drove down to the church hall. They would demonstrate the steps together first, then each would take a partner from among the kids. In no time at all we could all dance up a storm and dancing classes became the Catholic youth social. Father Healy put in an appearance every Friday, standing in the doorway with his arms folded across his chest and a look of supreme mistrust on his face as he watched young men with young women in their arms fox-trotting and waltzing around the floor.

There was a quiet young man called Pat with whom I particularly liked to dance. One day he asked me out to the movies. Such a thing had never happened before to any of us Paul girls living at home. I knew he would have to ask Dad's permission so he said he would pop around on his moped the next day. When he arrived Dad was working out in the garden. As we approached him he stood up and greeted Pat. They exchanged pleasantries and then Pat said,

'I would like to take Jane to the movies this evening, Mr Paul.'

Dad, who was always so good with words and so considerate of people's feelings, stood there and said,

'She's too young.'

Too young! I was so mortified I wanted to disappear into the ground. And I was furious at such humiliation, though I never dared show it. My father was the head of our family. His word was law and it was unthinkable that I would challenge his authority in this, or any, matter.

Despite Hanni's best efforts, Dad's stomach ulcer returned, and in my final year of school Dad was often pale and silent around the house. He never complained but everything about him spoke of his suffering. School had finished and I was working a pre-Christmas job in a stationery shop, when his ulcer haemorrhaged. He was taken to hospital in a critical condition.

    A few days and many blood transfusions later, his condition had stabilised enough to send him to Perth for an operation. He was taken by ambulance to the train station and settled into a compartment with John as his companion. It was an overnight journey and next morning an ambulance was at the station to take him to the hospital. Mum and I drove through the night in the Kombi. We arrived early in the morning to find that Dad had already been operated on. Most of his stomach had been removed. He made a slow and painful recovery. At first a teaspoon of food was all it took to fill the little stomach left to him. Always of wiry build, he became frighteningly thin and frail. But he had a robust constitution and a very determined nature and with Mum's devoted care he slowly gained strength. We spent the summer holidays at the cottage in Busselton, with Mum preparing fish soup and sheep brains in parsley sauce for Dad to eat at regular intervals. His doctors predicted that he probably had another five years to live as he would likely die of malnutrition. Mum took that as a challenge, and as the thought that Dad might die was impossible for me to entertain, I never doubted that she would bring him through. He defied them all by living to the ripe old age of ninety-two, but for the rest of his life Mum provided him with a nourishing snack every couple of hours in order to maintain his weight, which would have qualified him as a lightweight jockey on any race track in the country.

    When the academic year began I enrolled at the University of Western Australia. I had no passion for any particular subject, it was simply something one did after successfully completing high school. Having had no exposure to the sciences throughout my school life, my options were limited and I enrolled in an arts degree. Aunty Bess, now widowed and living in Perth, offered me a room in her home and I began a new life as a student.

    I was the epitome of the naive country girl who goes to the big city. It was all I could do to navigate my way around the university campus. I attended lectures and sat in the library reading recommended texts, but I spent far more time in the coffee shop with my two new girlfriends. Adrian was studying Ancient Greek. She had missed the first lecture when the alphabet was explained. Never having quite grasped what was going on, she preferred to hang out in the coffee shop instead. She was a little older and was married. Completing the trio was a girl whose name I no longer remember. She had a boyfriend who drank a lot. He once knocked her policeman father down in a fight over her. I found her very daring, and Adrian very domestic. They represented for me two opposite poles. I liked both and swung back and forth, wanting to be first like one, and then the other.

During the year I met a young man who was studying geology. His name was Roger. He was from Esperance, which was practically a neighbouring town for a goldfielder like myself. We hit it off immediately and quickly established that we both liked dancing and fishing and camping. We began to meet regularly and were always to be seen at the weekly social at uni where we sang and danced to the latest Buddy Holly, Bill Haley and the Comets or Beatles releases. It was a time when there was a new Beatles song almost every week. Roger played football for the university and most Saturday afternoons found me cheering him on at the oval. At the end of a year of coffee drinking, dancing my feet off every weekend and attending football matches, I searched in vain for my name among the list of examinees published in the *Western Australian* at the start of the new year. I was in Kalgoorlie when the results came out. Dad came into the back garden with the newspaper and we sat on the edge of the lawn together to find my name. It was not there. I felt deeply humiliated and embarrassed and was ashamed to have let Dad down, although he himself showed no signs of disappointment in me.

I repeated the year successfully and then transferred to Claremont teachers' college, where after one year of additional study I would qualify as a primary school teacher. My parents had left Kalgoorlie and were now living in Perth. With their help I renovated an unused double garage in their back yard and moved back home. Mum was still making my clothes. Now, in addition to blouses and skirts and dresses for everyday wear, her skilled hands and the old treadle turned out rope skirts for dancing, an elegant suit, a swinging woollen overcoat and a long chiffon ball gown. The latter was shades of blue and I wore it to the university ball. Roger brought a magnolia corsage when he came to pick me up. I felt like a princess that night, and he was my prince.

When he finished his degree Roger began work with a consulting geologist. While I was still at teachers' college he gave me a diamond ring and asked me to marry him. It seemed to me the most natural thing in the world and I didn't hesitate to say yes. That was how it worked, wasn't it? One grew up and fell in love and married and raised a family and lived happily ever after. When he asked my parents for their permission they agreed but said we must wait until I was twenty-one.

A year later, on 6 September 1966, Roger and I married. Mum made my wedding gown and veil, the bridesmaids' dresses, the wedding cake and posies of white everlastings for me and pink everlastings for the bridesmaids. She also made a long royal blue satin cape to wrap around myself when, at the end of the festivities, I would leave with Roger to begin our life together. The day before my wedding day I was feverish and ill. I went to the local doctor in desperation, but when he heard I was to be wed the next day, he laughed and said he thought my symptoms were due to nervousness rather than infection. I was irritated by his flippancy, but he turned out to be right. That same day Mum suggested I try on my wedding dress one last time. Thank goodness she did, for I had lost so much weight in the weeks of excited preparations, my dress hung on me like a beautiful lacy sack. Unperturbed as always, Mum set about unpicking it and taking it in, so that when I walked down the aisle on my father's arm the next day, it was a perfect fit.

We were married in the chapel of Thomas More College where Roger had stayed while studying at university. Afterwards we celebrated with family and friends at a hotel in Cottesloe until, in the early hours of the morning, I donned my royal blue cape and left on the arm of my husband. I was twenty-one years old and he was twenty-four.

Roger had spent the year of waiting building a boat. He bought a kit for a wooden dinghy and assembled it in my double-garage room. Building that dinghy was a labour of love. It was a twelve-foot-long solid wood structure, a kind of Noah's ark. He completed it just before we married and we took it on its maiden voyage on our honeymoon. Happy and excited, we sailed off into our new life, the sun on our faces and the wind in our hair, with never a thought for the deep dark waters beneath us.

4

When Roger and I married I was teaching a class of third graders. While I taught, Roger pursued his work as a geologist. It meant that he was often away for weeks at a time and at the end of my second year of teaching I resigned in order to go with him into the field. Our first trip together was out east of Kalgoorlie where building of the standard gauge railway line was in progress and Roger had the job of locating water and blue metal for the project. To help him in his work he had at his disposal a drilling rig, with crew. For the first time I made the acquaintance of that particular breed of homo sapiens known as the 'Queensland drilling crew'. They were a heavy-drinking, foul-mouthed lot but once they got going they worked like Trojans.

From there we moved further north to Whim Creek, to map and take samples at a copper mine a Canadian company had taken an interest in. Mining had stopped when ground water flooded the shafts. Whim Creek was south of Port Hedland and consisted of a hotel with a petrol pump out front, serving the truckers and odd traveller that happened onto the series of dust-filled potholes that constituted the northwest highway at the time. The abandoned mining camp consisted of a row of well-constructed rooms for single men, an ablutions block, a large fully equipped kitchen and cafeteria and a number of small self-contained cabins for the married men. Although dusty and neglected, everything was in very good condition. Roger and I settled into one of the cabins. We were the only ones there. Roger went about his work and I assisted him in surveying, and drawing and colouring the resultant maps. On weekends we went to town or fished in the tidal creeks. I felt perfectly at home and enjoyed our easy, uncomplicated life. Following the example of my mother, I understood my role in life to be that of supporting my husband, and it seemed to me to be the greatest good fortune to have found a man who shared my love of the bush, and the ocean. I happily imagined us spending our lives in the outback, with intermittent trips home to visit family and friends.

Then two Canadians joined us. The tall thin one drank a bottle of red label Johnny Walker every day, the other was a friendly man of Inuit origins. He was built like a wrestler and looked like a man who was used to hard physical work. They stayed at the hotel until telephone and electricity services were restored at the mine, and the friendly wrestler had seduced the cook into coming up to the mine to live with him and bring the cafeteria back to life. It was a great scandal for it left the hotel without its cook. She was a large hard-working woman whose body had seen better days. She told me in happy confidence that her beau was going to take her back to Canada and make an honest woman of her. I was still very unworldly but even I could see that she would likely be disappointed. Even so, her wrestler was affectionate, gave her presents and treated her kindly and I dare say they were some of the happiest days of her life. Something she could look back on with fond memories, after the two Canadians returned home without her, and she resumed cooking responsibilities at the hotel.

Roger's next assignment was at Port Keats, west of Daly River, in the Northern Territory. He was to map and drill grid lines, taking core samples and sending promising ones off for analysis. The search was for coal and oil. We flew to Darwin where we picked up the caravan and Toyota Landcruiser readied for us and, after spending a couple of days buying supplies, headed south-west to Daly River, where we were to meet up with an Aboriginal guide. We arrived there in the late afternoon. The river flowed over the crossing we would traverse the next day, cascading over the down-river side like a waterfall. We camped under the trees on the wide river bank, laying our mattress on the sand and breaking sticks from the trees to erect the mosquito net. After a meal of barbecued chops on bread and butter, we settled down for the night, lulled to sleep by the sound of the water flowing over the crossing.

I woke in the night with a fright. There was no sound of falling water. All around was absolute silence. It was eerie and I didn't know what to make of it. After a while I detected a faint sound like a babbling brook. Slowly the babbling became louder until it became more the sound of perhaps little rapids, until finally it took on the sound of a waterfall again. Far as we were from the coast, the oceanic tidal movement reached all the way upriver, pushing the river up over the crossing. As the tide on the coast receded, so did the level of water in the river, until the crossing was once again exposed. We rookies were lucky to have made camp where we did. Any closer to the river and we might have found ourselves floating upriver on our mattress, and perish the thought of crocodiles!

Early next morning our Aboriginal guide arrived to take us into Port Keats. We drove over the crossing and were quickly grateful for Waragul's presence, for there was no road as such, only a track that wound through the bush and often disappeared altogether in the scrub or in a large waterhole. It was late in the year and building up to the wet season and there had clearly been a few downpours already. Giant termite nests dotted the red earth like so many giant temples pointing to the heavens. The vegetation was sparse. In places Waragul indicated we should simply drive through the bush to avoid a wash-out, or another buffalo hole, or sometimes the buffalo itself. It was a rough ride. When we arrived, we found a pipe had broken in the refrigerator and the cooling fluid had been lost.

Traditionally known as Wadeye, and home to the Kadu Diminin people, Port Keats was at that time a Catholic mission staffed by a priest, a couple of nuns and a handful of lay missionaries. There was a presbytery, a convent, a school, a small church, housing for the laypeople, and various administrative buildings. All the buildings were made of tin. A number of different Aboriginal clans lived at the mission in a collection of tiny 'houses' which were no more than one-room tin sheds. We were given the use of a tin carport as an annex for the caravan, and set up camp. I had never lived in the tropics before and while the muggy heat and sandflies were unpleasant, I loved the wide open spaces, the rich earthy smells and the spectacular skies associated with the approach of the wet season.

The tribal men took a great liking to Roger, and he to them. They took him fishing with them, invited him to corroborees, and gave him gifts of mangrove crabs and turtle eggs. They cut down termite-hollowed young trees to make him didgeridoos and then showed him how to coax sound from them. The artists among them peeled the bark from trees to paint him bark paintings depicting the Dreamtime stories. At high tide, the children clamoured around him, begging him to go swimming with them in the tidal creek adjoining the mission. There was a landing there which was a great place from which to spring into the murky waters when the tide was in. Roger never tired of jumping into the water with two or three ebony figures clinging to his back. It was as though he was a Kadu Dimini himself and these were his people.

That first visit Roger drew up geological maps of the entire region. We were out on the plains almost every day, until the wet set in, turning the land into an impassable bog. Leaving our camp where it was, we flew out with the mail run and were back in Perth for Christmas.

Five months later, when the rains had stopped and the land had dried out enough to be driven over again, we returned to Port Keats. The Queensland drilling crew arrived and we left the mission and set up camp on the edge of the plain where core samples were to be taken in a giant grid pattern. We returned to the mission every week to coincide with the arrival of the DC-3 bringing the mail and groceries from Darwin.

Living away from the mission in that hot humid climate, without refrigeration, challenged my domestic skills. I took to hunting our meat and fish. By far the easiest game were the masses of wild geese that inhabited the area. I became very skilled at shooting geese with Roger's .22. But wild geese have double-shafted feathers and dunking them in hot water did nothing to loosen them. After unsuccessfully trying various plucking methods, I finally skinned the birds. A skinned goose lacks a certain aesthetic beauty, but I made up for it by producing tasty goose stews in the camp oven. Of course an Aborigine would laugh and say the way to cook a wild goose is to throw it on the coals, feathers and all, but such a simple solution did not occur to me with my Golden Wattle upbringing. And even if it had I would probably have dismissed it as 'primitive', for I had been taught to pluck and truss a bird before cooking it.

Wak, an older man who spoke English, approached Roger one day to ask if he would take him and two tribal elders crocodile hunting. Wak explained that two large crocodiles had been marooned in a billabong at the end of the wet season. The billabong was far away, which would not have been a problem except that they would need a dinghy for the hunt and the means to bring home their catch. Roger had the Landcruiser, and the mission a dinghy. Would he carry the hunters to their objective, with the dinghy on the roof? They would have no objection to me accompanying them.

And so we set off, Roger and me in the front and three laughing and excited Aboriginal men in the back. They seemed not the least concerned that there were no back seats. One carried a smouldering firestick and that seemed to be the extent of their baggage, unlike Roger and I who had our mattress and mosquito net, changes of clothes, plates and cutlery and pots and pans, not to mention a box of tinned food. We travelled through densely wooded areas where, in patches, many trees had been shattered by lightning. Once we hit the open plain, Wak started throwing lighted matches out the window. The long dry grass immediately took fire, the wind fanning it into a ferocious blaze that roared across the plain behind us, and was spent before we reached the other side, where we promptly sank down in mud.

Nobody realised the ground was swampy until the Landcruiser literally sank into it. Wak and the old men sprang out, talking excitedly. Steam rose up from under the vehicle. For a moment we were afraid the hot exhaust had set fire to the grass, but luckily the ground was wet enough to extinguish any potential fire. The men put their shoulders to the vehicle and pushed with all their might while Roger engaged the four-wheel drive and attempted to drive forward. The wheels spun and the Landcruiser sank deeper and deeper into the mud. The men held a conference. Evening was coming on and Wak suggested we make camp and reassess the problem in the morning. He took his gun and disappeared. One of the elders began digging a hole with his hands and soon had a pool of water, from which he and his companion drank deeply. Then he used the firestick to start a fire. By the time Wak reappeared with a couple of wild geese the fire was blazing brightly. A respectable distance away Roger and I lit a fire, laid out our mattress and hung the mosquito net. The air was thick with the smell of burning feathers. Roger opened a tin of baked beans for supper and we ate them in silence to the sound of happy laughter around the neighbouring fire as the three men partook of their barbecued geese with audible delight.

Early next morning Wak and the two elders took an axe and walked to the edge of the plain, a distance of at least a mile. They returned some time later carrying a long thin tree trunk, which they then proceeded to chop into shorter lengths, long enough to span across the ground in front of the front wheels. Again and again they strode across the plain, each time bringing back with them the next instalment of the duckboard they were laboriously constructing. It was very hot out there, particularly as there was no shade, but those men walked back and forth with unmitigated enthusiasm, laughing and chatting the whole time, as though they were out gathering flowers rather than heavy tree trunks. By evening they had constructed a road of logs out of the quagmire. Now when Roger drove and they pushed, the Landcruiser moved forward onto the duckboard and out of the treacherous mud. Wak sprang ahead indicating firm ground. A cheer went up.

'Now we rest. Tomorrow we go hunting,' he said, and strode over to his companions who were already lighting the fire.

At dawn we rolled up camp and moved on. Wak went ahead on foot and we followed him in the Landcruiser. Slowly a large billabong came into view. We drove as close as Wak deemed safe, then stopped. Not a word was spoken. The dinghy was quietly lifted down and with it a long pole and a heavy rope coil attached to a harpoon. Wak took his rifle and indicated to me to bring two buckets. The men picked up the dinghy and moved forward silently. I followed close behind. We were soon wading through ankle-deep water, which quickly became knee-deep water. Wak climbed into the front of the boat, the two elders in the middle, and Roger and I at the back. The dinghy sat very low in the water. The two elders lowered their paddles over the edge and the boat moved forward out of the reeds. I looked down to find five leeches on my legs. I must have made a sound because one of the elders looked around and, seeing my predicament, adroitly plucked them off, gave me a big smile and returned to his soundless paddling.

Wak stood in the bow, scanning the billabong. He pointed to something in the water ahead. The paddlers eased the boat nearer and positioned it next to a stream of bubbles rising to the surface. Wak had tied the free end of the coil of rope to the bow of the boat. He now fitted the harpoon to the end of the long pole and lowered it down into the water by the stream of bubbles. With careful restraint he probed the murky waters. We hardly dared to breathe. Apparently satisfied that he had found his mark, Wak rose up to his full height and drove the harpoon home with all his might.

In an instant the entire coil of rope snaked out into the water and went taut. Pandemonium broke out as the boat suddenly took off across the water at breakneck speed, sending up a wake that spilled over into the boat. Now I knew what the buckets were for! Roger and I baled for all we were worth. The hunters broke their silence, babbling and gesticulating excitedly. The boat was dragged all over the billabong. Gradually, ever so gradually, the speed with which we raced across the water began to diminish and we could slow our frantic baling.

Wak began to pull on the rope. At first any slack he gained would fly out of his hands as the crocodile made another dash for freedom, dragging us over the water yet again. But the dashes slowly lost their power and little by little Wak won back more and more rope until the crocodile rose to the surface and we saw it for the first time. It was a monster.

Face to face with its adversaries the great animal thrashed its tail to and fro, sending great waves of water crashing over us. We were all drenched and, despite our desperate baling, the boat was half full of water. Wak continued to shorten the rope. Just when I was sure we would all perish, Wak raised his rifle and shot the crocodile between the eyes. Then, with powerful deliberate movements, he hauled in the rope until the crocodile's snout was touching the boat.

To my horror all three men made as if to lift the massive head right into the boat. I thought they meant to drag the whole huge creature in with us, although it was clear that it was much bigger than the boat itself and was still thrashing around, albeit rather weakly. Thoughts of leeches and of the other crocodile in the billabong raced through my head. But when the great head was almost over the side of the boat, Wak took a tomahawk and chopped through the massive neck, severing the spinal cord, and all movement ceased. The animal was secured to the boat and the elders paddled slowly back to shore. Roger and I were still baling when we slid to a halt in the tall reeds.

It took all four men to drag the crocodile out of the water and onto dry ground. It was a massive four metres long. The Aboriginal men immediately set about skinning it. Wak happily showed Roger where his harpoon had struck home at the base of the skull. It was the preferred place, he explained, because a crocodile skin had more value when it was one big skin without damage. In order to locate the right place it was necessary to 'feel' along the ridges on the crocodile's back with the harpoon, taking care, of course, not to disturb the crocodile. Our admiration was genuine. We were beginning to understand why Wak had the reputation of being a skilled hunter. When the skin was spread out on the grass and the tail separated from the rest of the animal, the men rose to go in search of the second crocodile. I stayed behind. They returned an hour or so later with their prey in tow. It was smaller than the first, perhaps three metres long, but still a massive animal. It too was skinned right there where it lay, and the tail cut off.

As dusk approached, the men lit a very smoky fire. They sat in the smoke talking and laughing together. Roger and I sat at a distance and wondered to each other why they did not make a proper fire. We got our answer when the sun sank below the horizon. A dense cloud of mosquitoes rose out of the grass and engulfed us. In the time it took to scramble under the mosquito net, the whining horde had bitten every inch of available skin. We sat there miserable and itchy, watching our friends sitting unperturbed in the smoke of their fire.

At dawn we broke camp. With the help of the winch, and considerable effort by the men, the two great masses of white muscle were lifted up onto the Landcruiser and secured firmly to the rack. The dinghy was placed over them and secured too, and we began the journey back. It was a slow trip. Wak directed Roger to various billabongs where the men shot and gathered small Johnston crocodiles, wild geese, and handfuls of long-necked tortoise, all of which were loaded into the vehicle.

Our homecoming evoked great excitement. It seemed the whole camp came out to greet us. That night the sounds of festivities drifted over the mission. The sharp click of the singing sticks, the drone of the didgeridoo and the chanting of corroboree songs continued until dawn.

They were good times and we were sad to leave. The dingo pup that Roger had befriended ran behind the caravan for a long time, before realising it could not follow us to where we were now going. At Daly River the mango trees were hanging full of fragrant ripe fruit and we stopped to fill our bellies and a box. The rainy season was building up again but we were unwilling to leave the Territory right away. When we hit the main road we headed down to Katherine, where we explored accessible parts of the imposing gorge and steadily ate our way through the box of luscious mangoes. Then we stocked up on supplies and headed to Jim Jim Falls. There was not a soul around and we made camp at the edge of the water. It was a tranquil magical place.

As the days passed I began to get a rash around my mouth. It got progressively worse, spreading out over my entire face until it was one great puffy red balloon, at which point I looked such a fright it was decided it was time to do something about it. Roger drove me to the hospital at Katherine. The doctor took one look at me, laughed and said,

'You have mango rash.'

I was crestfallen at the thought of no more mangoes, but he told me I just needed to peel them, instead of eating them off the skin. There was sap in the skin, he said, that could be very irritating. Happy as I was to hear mangoes were still on the menu, it was a long time before I actually ate one again.

Hardly had the swelling gone from my face than Roger developed a carbuncle on his derrière. It was very painful and again we found ourselves driving to the hospital at Katherine. The doctor said Roger needed a penicillin injection every day for a week.

'You can give them to him,' he said to me, and proceeded to show me how it was done. When he had demonstrated how to fill the syringe, he drew a vague cross with his hand on Roger's buttock and said,

'Don't get him here, or here (indicating towards the centre), or you will paralyse him.'

I had a restless night, worrying incessantly about paralysing my mate. Next morning I prepared the syringe and a nervous Roger bared his bottom. Slap! My hand came down as the doctor had shown me, slapping down on Roger's rump and driving the needle in with one movement.

'That was fine,' said Roger, not realising that in my nervousness I had put the needle in and straightaway pulled it out again! I did better after that.

In Katherine we were shocked to find that recent heavy rain had swelled the river dramatically. The demure clear water of our last visit was now a mighty mass of muddy water, filling the gorge in a swirling, raging torrent. Uprooted trees and debris collided and bobbed along the troubled surface of the river as it raced along. There was still one more thing we wanted to do before leaving the Territory and we knew we had to hurry if we were going to make it before the wet season set in in earnest. Ever since coming north people had been telling us tales of the fabled barramundi and we wanted to catch one before returning home.

We left the caravan behind and headed northwards into Arnhem Land. We felt a sense of urgency and were up at first light to continue our quest. Mid-afternoon we crossed a small creek, only to find a much larger creek blocking our way a couple of hundred metres further on. We drove along it a little way before realising it was a dead end, at which point Roger pulled up and got out the fishing lines. It was he who caught the barramundi. It put up quite a fight and he had to work hard to get it to shore. It was a good-sized fish, and solid. We admired it greatly before lighting a fire right there and grilling it whole. It was really too big for two people to eat but it was mouth-wateringly delicious and we didn't want to waste any, so we ate slowly, savouring every last mouthful. Perhaps it was the big meal or the euphoria of having finally caught a barramundi that dulled our common sense. With no thought for the time of year, we rolled out our bed by the fire and went to sleep.

In the middle of the night we were woken by thunder and lightning and heavy raindrops. By the time we had bundled our bedding into the Landcruiser, the rain was coming down in torrents. It was pitch black save for the flashes of lightning illuminating the sky. The rain was so heavy it swallowed the beam of the headlights, leaving us with only a pool of feeble light directly in front of the vehicle. We were in the middle of two creeks and knew we had to get out of there before we got bogged or the two creeks joined up. Again and again we ran up against flowing water until, by some miracle, Roger found a way through. He drove slowly along the track that opened up before us, until it eventually joined up with a road that took us to higher ground. Up ahead we could just make out a house under construction. It was a typical Queenslander, a large hardwood dwelling built on high stilts to keep it safe from flooding. Roger drove in under it and the pounding of the rain on the roof ceased. We sat there for a moment, exhausted and shaky. Then we dragged our damp mattress out of the Landcruiser, hung the mosquito net as best we could, and slept.

The sound of hammering and sawing woke us out of deep sleep. We opened our eyes to find it was broad daylight. Up above us the building crew was on the job. The sun shone and the only evidence of the tempest in the night was the steam rising from the puddles all around. Sobered by our adventure, we hastened back to Jim Jim where, after one last night of noisy flying foxes, and a breakfast of smoky tea and toast, it was time to hook up the caravan and head for Darwin. There we returned the caravan and Landcruiser before boarding a DC-3 for the flight back to Perth.

5

We were back home in time to spend Christmas with Roger's family in Esperance. I learned to water ski that summer and we spent hours on the water every day. We had been married now for two years. Roger was easygoing and fun to be with and I enjoyed his company a lot. The fact that we never discussed anything more profound than whether we would listen to dance or folk music did not strike me as a problem. I was happiest when we were in the bush together. It was my understanding that husband and wife should find complete fulfilment in each other and I found it easier to maintain this myth in the bush, where I did not have to vie with others for his attention, or be visited by insecurity and pangs of jealousy when, in the company of others, he sometimes appeared to forget me altogether.

Shortly before my twenty-fourth birthday I was pregnant with our first child. It seemed the next natural progression in our relationship. Many of our friends had babies or were pregnant and I was thrilled to join their ranks. It was an easy pregnancy. I continued to go bush with Roger and was surprised and rather offended when a station owner's wife chastised me for driving the Landrover over rough terrain in my 'condition'. I thought pregnancy to be a natural state and was oblivious to any need for caution. Nevertheless this admonition gave me a nudge and I realised it was time to settle down and make a nest for our child. Roger and I had a rented apartment in Nedlands as our Perth base. It was there that I now began making preparations. I read books on natural childbirth, attended antenatal classes and bought in baby clothes and a crib.

After completing her three-year novitiate in Melbourne, Sue had moved on to the order's hospital in Sydney to train as a nurse in preparation for the missions. There she came into conflict with her supervisor and before the year was out she abandoned her dream of so many years and returned home. Some time later she married and started a family. Following Sue's example, I took her gynaecologist as my doctor. At the end of November, when I was not quite full-term, he said he was going on holiday and wanted to induce the baby rather than have it come in his absence. I agreed, anxious as always not to inconvenience anybody. Arrangements were made with St John's in Subiaco, a Catholic hospital staffed by nuns. And so it was that on 3 December 1968, our not-quite-baked skinny little son came into the world. At his birth, the gynaecologist revealed himself as the kind of doctor who takes control, relegating the mother to the sidelines, with the help of a spinal block. Suddenly and unexpectedly robbed of all sensation, I could not participate in pushing my son into the world. Instead he was seized by the head with forceps and dragged out. He was whisked off for resuscitation, while I was stitched up and taken back to my room.

Roger and I were in shock. We had been together all day. Apart from the odd nurse coming in to check progress, we were alone. Roger had rubbed my back when the contractions came and in between times we had talked quietly and rested. Although nervous for lack of experience, I was not unduly distressed by the contractions. My mother had told me, 'Labour means work. It is your work.' Although Roger almost rubbed the skin off my lower back with his ministrations, we had successfully completed the first stage of labour. Then the contractions changed and we knew we were getting close. The arrival of the doctor with his entourage of nurses was like a surprise attack.

'Roll over,' the jab in the back, the loss of sensation, the confusion as I struggled to understand what was happening, stirrups, instruments, bright lights, being completely ignored as though what was happening had nothing to do with me.

Years later when I confronted the doctor about his methods and his blanket use of the spinal block, he sat back in his seat and said,

'You don't get a tooth pulled without an anaesthetic, do you?' apparently completely unaware of the difference between the birth of a child and the death of a tooth.

Now Roger and I were again alone. I felt as though I had been violated and I was bereft of my child. The doctor said we had a son but I had caught only a glimpse of him. Roger and I had not had an opportunity to hold him, to let him know that we were his parents and were happy to have him as our son. Where was he? The thought of him spending his first moments in the world in some strange place not knowing where his parents were made us weep. Roger went to ask what was happening. He was told his son was fine but that he could first see him in the morning. He came back to tell me and then went to smoke a cigar with my father.

Today the importance of newborn babies being with their mothers is well documented. In those days newborn babies were kept in the nursery and only brought to their mothers at 'feeding time'. At six o'clock the next morning my baby was brought to me. He slept in my arms until he was taken away again half an hour later. Four hours later he was again placed in my arms. The two of us did our best to adjust to our roles and get this feeding thing together. And so it went on, until on the tenth day an older nurse came in, poked me in the breast my child was nursing on and said,

'Dry as a bone. This child has to go on the bottle.'

I was devastated. A mother breastfed her baby. That's what mothers did. But the nurse was adamant.

'You cannot leave the hospital until this child is on the bottle,' she said.

When Roger came in the evening we talked and I cried about it. Finally we decided we would agree to the baby going on the bottle, and then when we got home I would go ahead and breastfeed. It is indicative of our awe of authority that it did not occur to either of us to just take our baby and go home.

Two weeks after his birth we finally brought our son home. Only then did I realise that a newborn wakes every three or four hours for a feed, round the clock. The nuns had kept the babies in the nursery throughout the night and bottle-fed them. What I did not know then was that bottle-feeding requires a completely different sucking technique to breastfeeding. Bottle-feeding undermines the baby's ability to successfully draw milk from the breast. Home at last, my best attempts to coax my baby back on the breast to stimulate my milk flow were unsuccessful. I did not think to seek help but struggled on alone until I had to accept that I was a failure and resigned myself to bottle-feeding my child.

Roger named our son Peter Xavier. Peter because every Lalor wants to claim Peter Lalor, the passionate leader of the Eureka Stockade, in their ancestral line, and Xavier because he was born on the feast of St Francis Xavier.

When Peter was three months old our little family flew to New Zealand where Roger had the task of searching for a mineable base metal deposit. It was the end of summer and as we flew over the Australian continent we looked down on a brown sunburned land. The difference when we landed in New Zealand was stunning. The country was a myriad shades of green. Everywhere we looked it was green. The pastures looked like green carpets. The forests were thick and lush.

We flew into Wellington where an apartment had been arranged for us in a house on Ellis Street. It had been a long day and we were grateful to get Peter settled and fall into bed. In the middle of the night we woke to a howling gale in the room. Closer inspection revealed that the window we had left ajar was missing. It had been torn from its hinges and frame and all had disappeared in the darkness. We secured what we could and slept in another room. In the morning Roger found the window three doors down in a neighbour's garden. 'Welcome to Windy Wellington!' he said cheerfully when Roger went down to reclaim it. Windy Wellington was to be our home for the next three years, as holes in the corners of Peter's nappies would attest. The wind wrapped the washing round the line so tightly that the pegs protruded right through it. Everything of any size had holes in all its corners.

Using Wellington as a base, Roger began scouring the country from the Coromandel Peninsula in the north, to Dunedin in the south. We were on the road again, nomads of a sort, only this time with a baby. I venture to say we went just about everywhere in New Zealand. We drove most places, but occasionally flew in small single-engine planes, the pilots landing on beaches at low tide, or coming in very low to chase the sheep from grassy runways before banking steeply to swoop down and land before they returned to graze. Peter was of sunny disposition and a good traveller, and life was good.

My mother's father and all eleven of his siblings had been born in Gisborne, on the north island. On 28 February 1971 another family member was born in New Zealand. Our daughter Kylie was born in Wellington. Birds were singing and the sunlight shining through the open window kissed her cheek as she came into the world. Her birth was the opposite of Peter's. Instead of seeking out a gynaecologist, this time I had stayed with our GP. I was encouraged by the large poster hanging on his waiting room wall, an excerpt from *The Prophet* by Kahlil Gibran:

Your children are not your children.
They are the sons and daughters of Life's longing for itself.
They come through you but not from you,
And though they are with you yet they belong not to you.
You may give them your love but not your thoughts,

For they have their own thoughts.
You may house their bodies but not their souls,
For their souls dwell in the house of tomorrow,
Which you cannot visit, not even in your dreams.
You may strive to be like them,
   but seek not to make them like you.
For life goes not backward nor tarries with yesterday.
You are the bows from which your children
As living arrows are sent forth.
The Archer sees the mark upon the path of the infinite,
And He bends you with His might
That His arrows may go swift and far.
Let your bending in the Archer's hand be for gladness;
For even as He loves the arrow that flies,
So He loves also the bow that is stable.

Throughout the pregnancy our GP simply reassured me and encouraged me to trust my body to do its job. He saw his role as an attendant. In the tiny twelve-bed hospital he directed me to, there were no stirrups. When, in birthing my baby, I told him I felt most comfortable on my side, he directed the nurse to support my leg, while he waited patiently to receive my bonny nine-pound daughter as she slid out. When the staff heard I had not succeeded in breastfeeding my firstborn, they offered me every advice and support so that things went as nature intended. I am deeply grateful to that GP for supporting me in my role as birthing mother. Had he been of the controlling, impatient kind I should never have known the indescribable joy and power that fills a woman when she brings new life into the world.

6

We returned to Australia at the end of 1971. Peter was just three years old and Kylie was taking her first wobbly steps. Australia was in mining boom fever. Roger's dad, an inveterate and passionate prospector with a number of promising finds, was anxious to take advantage of the prevailing atmosphere. Money was flowing into mining ventures, why not into one of his? He asked Roger to join him in testing the extent of a talc deposit he had found east of Marble Bar in the Pilbara, in Western Australia. They travelled north to look at it and when they returned Roger resigned his position as a consulting geologist and went to work for his dad. Extensive drilling and excavation yielded promising results, so a public company was floated to raise money for the full-scale development of a mine. The company was called Westside Mines.

A camp was set up near the talc deposit. It consisted of a row of sleeping accommodation set down opposite a canteen and ablution block. Roger and I and the children spent a lot of time on site in those early days. Peter made elaborate roadways in the dusty courtyard and drove his trucks and loaders over them. Kylie was always close by, never letting him out of her sight. We went for bush walks and dug holes in the dry creek beds looking for water to fill the moats around the sandcastles we made. Mum and Dad showed up in their Kombi and began planting a garden between the two rows of trailers. They planted lippia as a ground cover to contain the dust and spent hours on the banks of the creek finding and transplanting native plants up to the camp. Down below the trailers they planted a predominantly pumpkin vegetable garden to take advantage of the water from the showers.

They were easy days. We were perpetually dusty and dirty but we felt at home in the bush and were busy and happy. We had two good-natured, high-spirited children and I was revelling in motherhood. Roger was a loving, affectionate father who always had a lot of time for his children. Then the day came when we had to return to Perth to the serious business of managing a company. Roger took off his boots and put away his geology pick. He donned a suit and became a businessman. It was his father's wish that he be on the board of directors of the new company, and the board members elected him chairman. He was thirty years old. For the next two years he made trips to Japan to sell the talc and began fretting over spreadsheets and the stock exchange.

Shares in the company were fifty cents each. They were sold at ten cents and calls could be made up to fifty cents as and when the company needed more money to develop the mine. Roger's dad was a major shareholder, and both our families and many friends had also bought in. When the first ten-cent call was needed, Roger worried about the cost to his dad and the family. As time went by he lost his light-hearted manner and became more and more serious and withdrawn. I was busy with the children and didn't really pay attention to what was happening. I noted that he no longer slept well, that he would get out of bed in the middle of the night and wander around the house, but I put it down to the mine and didn't think any more of it.

Besides, I had my own problems. I was having trouble adjusting to the change in our lives. In the bush we had had lots of adventures and had been together all the time. I was now a housewife and mother in the more traditional sense. My husband left the house in the morning and came home again in the evening. I felt left out and was struggling to deal with the increasing resentment I couldn't quite put a name to. When he did not take me and the children to Japan with him I felt abandoned and was angry. A part of me knew well enough that it was his work, but another part of me wanted to be included in everything he did.

Here I must mention what was perhaps the distinctive feature of our marriage, a feature I became aware of only many, many years later: Roger and I did not talk to each other about what was really important to us. We talked about all kinds of things – the weather, what wallpaper to put up in the kids' room, inviting friends over for dinner, what we would eat, what movie to see, what we thought of it after seeing it . . . But we never talked about the things that really mattered. Neither of us. We did not talk about what was going on inside us. We did not relate to each other. We lived together, we slept together every night, we made love together, but we were completely unable to communicate our feelings to each other. We were considered a good match and a lovely couple and in our lack of consciousness we thought we were those things. Apart from the odd outburst of anger on my part, we were harmonious together. We had two beautiful children, a block of land that we would build on near the beach at Cottesloe, a European car and a boat, and

Roger had a well-paid job. We were happy with each other, like two playmates playing a particularly good game of mothers and fathers.

Roger and I had both grown up in families that were probably normal for the times in as much as children were considered innocent beings with no notion of what was going on in the adult world. It was therefore considered unnecessary, even undesirable, to inform children of anything to do with the real, adult world. So it was that in my family the implications of what had happened to Rosemary were never explained to us children. Mum and Dad considered it their problem. There were no discussions about what was going on and how we, as a family, might deal with the changes. Instead our parents did their best to give us the impression that nothing had changed and that we were a happy, intact family. I am sure they acted out of the best of intentions. They did the best they could to protect us from a harsh reality, not realising that children feel everything. Children may not understand what is happening, but they are very attuned to the emotional climate in their family, and particularly to the emotional state of their parents.

In our case the result was that we children never probed or questioned. Out of love of our parents, aware that they were troubled, we tried with all our childish might not to add to their troubles. I never, for example, thought to talk to my parents about what was happening to me at school. I pretended to be okay and if they asked I said everything was fine. They never came to know of my insecurities and fears, or of the ill treatment the nuns meted out.

In Roger's family it was the same, beginning with the fact that his father was so silent. By the time we married we had both come to associate loving someone with not disturbing them, a situation of which neither of us was the least bit aware. We were simply behaving in a normal way. Normal, that is, for us. We grew up and married and had children, and whenever an 'adult problem' arose we kept quiet. I carried a blueprint of the perfect husband and father inside myself. That perfect man was always on top of things and knew what to do in any situation. He took care of his family and was brave and fearless and certainly never lost sleep worrying about things. If he did, then his perfection must be flawed, an unpleasant fact which would have constituted an 'adult problem'.

When Roger stopped sleeping at night, it would have been easy to ask him what was troubling him, but instead I pretended not to notice. In retrospect there were many times when I registered his distress but seemed to be inside a bubble, unable to take action. And the more the incidents accumulated and the more overwhelming the situation became, the more I seemed to turn to a pillar of stone. It was a bit like in a dream when you are trying to call out to warn someone or to run away from danger but no sound comes out or your legs won't move.

About this time, Roger made an effort to communicate something to me. He told me a story from when he was thirteen years old. There was an older boy in town who one day asked Roger to join him for some boy stuff. They rode off on their bikes and the older boy led Roger to an abandoned house. The sergeant of police noticed the two of them heading off. He knew the older boy and put two and two together. He followed them and walked in to find both boys naked on the floor. He told them to get their clothes on and come over to the police station. There they were separated. After a while the sergeant came and took Roger into his office.

'I've called your father about this,' he said. 'Nothing is going to happen to you this time, but you are to keep away from that fellow. We know all about him. Now you go home and apologise to your father.'

Apologise to his father? What had he done to his father? Roger was terrified. He didn't know why he was in trouble with the police. He just knew that something terrible had happened but he didn't know what. He went home and found his father sitting in the living room. He went in, eyes cast down. His knees and his voice were shaking as he said,

'Sorry Dad.'

'We won't bother the women about this,' was all his father said.

Roger's dad was a big silent Irishman. If you knew him you would not have been surprised at this minimal use of words. When Roger first took me to Esperance to meet his family I cried most of the weekend because I thought his dad didn't like me. Only as I came to know him did I realise that, unlike my own father who was good with words, Roger's father used words very sparingly. Roger and I used to laughingly say his dad only talked about mining and the weather and otherwise he kept silent.

It took Roger the longest time to tell me the story. His voice kept failing him and he was shaking all over. He was quiet when he finished, and so was I. After a while he added,

'I used to think I must be homosexual but now I have you and the kids I don't think so any more,' and we laughed nervously.

That was it. I was unable to grasp the significance of the story he had told me. It never occurred to me that he had a deeply ingrained pattern 'not to bother the women' that squeezed his larynx shut whenever he wanted to tell me something important. How could I see what was happening to him when I was completely oblivious to my own unconscious drives? I had my own ingrained pattern of 'I don't need anyone' that prevented me opening to another and being able to empathise with them. His pattern 'not to bother the women' was the perfect negative complement to my 'no need to bother anybody because I don't need them anyway'. It was, however, a crippling combination for a relationship. Happy though we thought ourselves to be, our marriage was constantly eroded by our ignorance of the undercurrents ebbing and flowing in the darkness of our unconscious.

Another ten-cent call was made. Roger did all he could to prevent it, but what could he do? A mine was being developed, money was needed, and the way the agreement worked the money must come from the shareholders. Meantime we had designed a house for our land at Cottesloe. It was a new development and a couple of Roger's friends were also building there. We put the plans out for tender and the quotes came in. It was time to make a decision. Whereas the decision initially was to be for a builder, it quickly turned into 'do we want to do this?'. Signing off on the building contract would have committed us to repayment of a large debt over many years. Roger was the only wage earner and he was by now desperately unhappy in his job. He was out of his depth and treading water for all he was worth. Had it not been for his deep love of his dad, he would probably have gotten out much sooner, or never have gotten involved in the first place, but the ties between father and son kept him bound to a job that had taken him far away from his area of expertise into a foreign world of movers and shakers and high finance in which he felt completely lost. Roger was a good geologist. He knew his stuff and he was at home in the bush. He was not a businessman, not then or ever.

Instead of building the house, we decided to sell the block, and Roger resigned his position with Westside Mines. Although it should have been a relief, it was not. A house of our own fit snugly into my view of the way things should be and this unexpected turn of events troubled me, particularly as I didn't really understand what was happening. Twenty-five years later Roger would travel halfway around the world to Germany to tell me what he had not been able to tell me when we lived together every day as man and wife. He told me that he had been elected chairman of the board because his father had forced his will on the other board members, most of whom were old buddies of his dad's from other adventures. They were tough wily types with a lifetime of wheeling and dealing behind them. Roger was the young heir apparent, still green behind the ears. Those cronies of his father's began surreptitiously undermining Roger's authority and confidence. They did it with the cunning of experience and with such adroitness that their manoeuvres remained hidden from his father, until the day came when they succeeded in shoving him from his position. Another chairman was elected and Roger had to take his place next to his father as a regular board member. Roger was unable to speak to his father about what was happening to him. Father and son spoke only of the mine. They found no words to speak of personal feelings and fears. This loss of face was the last straw. Roger was convinced he was a failure and had betrayed the trust his father had put in him. Unable to tolerate the daily humiliation, he resigned, a broken man.

When Roger was born his father was in a TB sanatorium over east. Mick did not see his son until Roger was a year old, and then only briefly because he had been posted to Darwin as part of an army defence corps, the recent TB precluding him from active service overseas. Perhaps it was that lack of early bonding between father and son, or Mick's silent awkward way, or both, but deep down Roger thought his father did not love him. It was never something he could put into words. Mick was a bearlike, goodhearted man but he was unable to show affection. Roger's inability to bring the maturity needed to the chairmanship dashed what must have been the desperate bid of a small child to win his father's love.

It was not until after his father died many years later that Roger, sorting through his papers, found his dad had kept every report card from school, every award and sport trophy Roger had ever won. When he came across them Roger knew that his father had always loved him and was proud of him. But until that day, so late in his own life, he was to suffer agonies of rejection and self-doubt, never able to feel the strength of manhood that was his father's true gift to him.

His family were confused and upset at his resignation, particularly as Roger did not want to take another job as a geologist, not then or, as it would turn out, ever again.

I forgot my misgivings in the excitement of preparing for what promised to be a grand camping trip. We bought a trailer and an aluminium dinghy and a large army surplus tent, packed the kids in the car and drove north. We didn't have a goal, we were just 'going camping'. When we came to Coral Bay, sixteen hundred kilometres north of Perth, we knew we had arrived. In the early 1970s Coral Bay was a virtually untouched oasis. The long offshore reef broke the swells from the Indian Ocean, creating a long sweeping bay of tranquil blue-green water where flying fish skimmed across the surface and great tortoises swam in the clear depths. The shores were home to cowries and other magnificent shells. Oysters clung to the rocks and octopuses sunbathed in the rock pools. It was paradise.

We made camp in the dunes. Our tent was a large square with a tall centre pole and an attached fly-screened annex. The tent itself was the bedroom/play room/living room, and the annex became the kitchen. There was no fresh water at Coral Bay. The nearest source was at Exmouth, a hundred and fifty kilometres away. We drove there once a week to get fresh water and fresh fruit and vegetables, and to take a shower at the caravan park. The fresh water was only used for drinking; all other activities requiring water were carried out with salt water from the ocean. We used salt water to cook the vegetables, to wash the dishes, ourselves and the clothes and bedding.

We went out in the dinghy every day to catch our food. Usually one fish would provide us with enough for a good meal, so once a fish was caught we rolled up the lines and explored the semi-exposed reef. The children ate oysters for as long as Roger and I cracked them from the rocks, and henceforth they would always associate eating oysters with those tranquil days in Coral Bay. Occasionally we would catch an unsuspecting octopus from a rock pool and I would pound it on the rocks to tenderise it, the way it was described in my Greek cookbook, before cooking it in wine and olive oil with tomatoes and garlic over the camp fire. Roger found some old kerosene tins and cut them down into bread tins for me and I made bread of sorts, and bread rolls in the camp oven. In Exmouth I bought books about the local flora and fauna and we would spend hours wandering the shores studying the information in them. We sometimes dug up shells as big as our hands decorated by nature with breathtaking patterns and colours. We admired them, identified them and then returned them to the shallow waters.

Apart from us, the only other sign of human habitation was a small motel tucked into one end of the bay. It was so far from our camp that we hardly noticed it. Everything was perfect, except for one thing. Roger was still not sleeping at night. He would get up and leave the tent and come back cold and sandy sometime later. I would register his going and his returning but we never talked about his insomnia or possible reasons for it. And so it went on. We spent our days fishing and playing, never talking about the future, or the past, as though they did not exist. Until the sky fell in.

7

Roger had been out walking as usual during the night. The next morning we got up and had breakfast and went out in the boat. We were together in our dinghy out on the water all morning. We hardly spoke as Roger was not very talkative that morning and the kids were doing enough talking for all of us. When we returned around noon there was a police car parked down below the dunes. I didn't think anything of it. A police patrol would drive through from time to time and it was not unusual for it to stop and enquire about the fishing, or just to say hello. Roger went down there while I cleaned the fish and fed the children. We were all done and Roger was still down there talking to the two policemen. I began to worry that his father might be ill. I left the kids playing and went down to join them. Roger looked terrible. His face had lost all colour and he looked as though he might collapse at any moment. I was sure his father must be ill, or maybe dead.

'What's happening?' I asked.

'We are arresting your husband and taking him to Exmouth,' said the taller of the two policemen.

I felt the ground move under my feet. It had to be a joke, but the way Roger was looking I knew it wasn't. Here we were out in the middle of nowhere, what on earth was he supposed to have done? A sleeping tiger began to stir in my belly. It didn't matter what he was accused of, this intrusion on our idyll was a violence against me and my family.

'You are not taking him anywhere,' I said firmly, surprised at my own clarity and the strength that filled me as the tiger stretched and gave a low growl. 'You are not leaving me alone out here in the middle of nowhere with two small children.'

Roger began to cry.

'He was trying to break into the motel last night. He has to come with us,' the policeman said.

Breaking and entering the motel? Preposterous! The tiger in my belly stood full height and roared. In my outrage I had never felt so much strength and determination. The whole thing was clearly absurd. It had reached our ears that the owner of the motel wanted to know where we had the money to camp there for months on end without working. He was clearly jealous, but he must be deranged to make such charges. I was furious. I stood my ground and demanded that they leave Roger with me. They were to tell me where and when he was to appear in court and we would be there, but they could not take him away like that, leaving the children and me alone in such an isolated place. The policemen put up a bit of resistance but they seemed to be reasonable men and they finally agreed. They said Roger was to appear in court in Exmouth at nine o'clock the next morning, and got into their car and drove away.

As the car disappeared into the distance I was aware only of the laughter of the children in the tent, and of Roger cowering next to me, crying softly. I asked him what had happened, but he could not speak. He just cried and cried, the tears coursing down his pale cheeks and soaking into his shirt. The tiger in my belly growled again. I began gathering the things we would need to take with us. We would have to drive up to Exmouth and spend the night there in order to be in court in time. I drove with the kids in the back and Roger crying quietly next to me all the way. I drove to the camping ground where we had stayed before and knew the owners. They agreed to look after the children in the morning while Roger and I went to the courthouse. Roger never said a word. It was as though he had been struck dumb.

At the courthouse he was fingerprinted before going into court. I never left his side, and in the courtroom I spoke for him. I said he was not guilty and asked the judge to hold proceedings over so we could return to Perth and engage a lawyer. He agreed, giving us a new date for a hearing a month later. We left the courtroom, picked up the children from the camping ground and returned to Coral Bay. My eyes could no longer see its beauty. A menacing dark cloud hung over us now, blurring my vision and dulling my senses. Silently we packed up our camp. Even the children were silent. It was unthinkable to me that this should be happening. We had lived in paradise for five months and now we were being driven out, forced to return to the world we had left behind.

When Roger was able to speak again he told me he had been walking along the beach sometime after midnight. He walked right down to the corner of the bay where the motel lay. Returning back he walked across the sand dunes quite close to the motel. Suddenly the motel owner and another equally big man, both smelling of beer, rushed out and grabbed him, angrily accusing him of trying to break into the motel. Unlike his dad who was a big man, Roger took after his mum, a tiny vivacious woman of Italian descent. The two big beery men pulled and pushed him, shouting angrily and threateningly. Then they must have thought better of it and called the police. The police said they were not coming down at such a late hour, that Roger would not be going anywhere in the dark. They would come down in the morning. Having relayed that to Roger, the men shoved him out into the darkness. He returned to camp and crawled back into bed next to me. He didn't say anything. Next morning we had breakfast and went out fishing. We sat out in the boat all morning and he didn't say a word about what had happened. When we returned at noon and he saw the police car he knew why they were there, but he didn't, or couldn't, say a word.

We returned to Perth and Roger went to see a lawyer friend from university days. And that was the end of it. We did not have to return to Exmouth. The incident disappeared like a bad dream, as though it had never happened. As was our custom, we did not talk about it or address the implications. The months at Coral Bay retreated to a misty, surreal place, along with the bad dream that ended them. What Roger couldn't tell me then, or ever, though he would one day travel to Germany with the intention of doing so, was that he had approached the motel to look through the window at a young woman taking a shower. After Roger died, his best friend told me that he had wanted me to know but was never able to tell me.

Today it is clear that Roger had suffered a nervous breakdown, the incident at Coral Bay being the last straw to months, if not years, of self-doubt and fear of failure. I have to say that in my own way I broke down along with him. Strange as it may seem, my world fell apart on that day I touched on the slumbering strength within me for the first time. The destruction of my childhood dream overshadowed the significance of everything else. The bubble had finally burst. My fairytale world of falling in love and getting married and living happily ever after was shattered. My knight in shining armour had turned out to be no more than an ordinary man. He was not my protector and hero at all. To me he was a weak and broken thing, and I began slowly to pity him and, as time went on, to despise him. It seemed to me that I had no man at all, but three children instead. Only the last of these opinions was slowly penetrating my consciousness. All the other annihilating judgements were going on in the shadowy recesses of my mind where I was unaware of them. They certainly did not fit with my image of the good and loving wife I believed myself to be, so I kept them well hidden from myself, and everyone else.

Woe to the man who married a Paul girl! Whatever other issues were at work in me, first and foremost was my childish attachment to the greatest knight in shining armour of all, my father. He was a formidable role model for any poor unsuspecting man to follow. Add to that my overlay of 'I don't need anybody' and you can begin to see what was happening. Roger had, of course, miserably failed the knight-in-shining-armour test. Now unacknowledged unconscious forces behind the scenes were set in motion to push him off the stage altogether.

Back in the conscious world it was business as usual. Locked into patterns of behaviour we could not see through, Roger and I were unable to grasp that something was wrong and we needed help to remedy it. We went along as though the world was in order, slavishly following the equation 'no problem = nothing to solve'. My father had retired and he and Mum had moved to the cottage in Busselton, leaving their house in Hollywood at our disposal. We were not paying rent but it was a situation that could not go on indefinitely. Roger made an effort to busy himself with the house and the children but his spark was gone. He had completely lost confidence in himself, a situation that was no doubt compounded by my inner rejection of him as a man, hidden though it remained from us both. He made no effort to look for work, saying he did not feel up to it. There was so much I didn't understand. At times I longed to return to the simplicity of childhood where I knew what was right and what was wrong, and Mum and Dad took care of everything.

Peter had started at the local primary school. The sight of him walking across the tarred playground in his steel-grey uniform had made me uneasy, and when he began coming home with stories of the teacher shouting and smacking the children, my not-so-distant memories of the unhappy nuns of my own school days surfaced. I began reading books about education; Ivan Illich's *Deschooling Society*, books about experimental schools in England, and Maria Montessori's work. I wanted my children to be treated kindly and I wanted their natural intelligence, which manifested in their creativity and inquisitiveness, to be recognised and encouraged. I had made the observation that normal, healthy children are fascinated by the world they live in. Most recently I had seen Peter and Kylie's passionate interest in the flora and fauna of Coral Bay, their natural respect and appreciation of the many life forms there, their imaginative building of castles and villages, sailing ships and highways out of sand, their ability to take pleasure in the smallest things – a seed carried through the air by the wind or the rainbow in a soap bubble. Roger and I sought out the nearest Montessori school and found that they would take not only Peter but Kylie too. So at the start of the new school year the children began bussing north of Perth to the Montessori school there.

One day a friend showed us an advertisement in the paper for a health food shop in Midland. He thought it might be something Roger and I could do together. We had become friendly with neighbours who ran a co-op from their back veranda. Their house always smelled of patchouli oil and incense. Maureen wore long flowing dresses and her mate a long flowing beard. Sitar music issued from the tape recorder, and they were vegetarians. We had begun buying grains and dried fruits from their co-op and our friend must have thought our new familiarity with brown rice and lentils qualified us to run a health food shop. He was not to know that that was the extent of our 'alternative' food culture and that Roger thought currant and sultana were two names for the same thing.

We still had a good deal of money left from the sale of the Cottesloe block and, as it turned out, it was just enough to buy *Mother Nature* outright, for that was the name of the shop. The owner was moving to Singapore and was in a hurry to sell. In fact he was in such a hurry that the sale, stocktaking, money transfer and handover all happened within a week. He flew out on the Saturday evening and the following Monday we opened for business. In the rush, things like customer bread orders were forgotten and the first few days were spent reinstating standing orders and becoming familiar with the stock, and our customers. One of the first things we did was to read all the books for sale on the shelves. There were books on organic gardening, compost making, 'perfect' diets, vegetarianism, bread baking, the environment, and the less concrete world of esoterics. These books opened our eyes to a whole new world of whole foods, grains and stone flour mills, sourdough bread, sundried fruits and nuts, raw honey and maple syrup, goat's milk, yoghurt and virgin cold-pressed olive oil, and to the existence of things not seen in everyday life, things we had never dreamed existed. We read, for example, about the aura or astral body, a strange luminescence radiating from all living things, which the Russian, Semyon Kirlian, had succeeded in making visible on film. We would laughingly talk about grumpy people needing to take their aura to the cleaner to brighten it up.

We began eating muesli and fruit and wholemeal toast, instead of puffed wheat or Weet-Bix for breakfast. We drank kefir instead of sweet fizzy drinks, and instead of coffee we had Caro and herbal teas. When we thought we needed a boost to get us through the day we took a couple of drops of ginseng extract. Brown rice and lentils became a standard item on our dinner table. And we began to enlarge our stock. We drove down south to buy forty-four gallon drums of honey that had been extracted from the honeycomb without heat. We found a Swiss woman growing herbs in a small nursery in her back yard and began to sell fresh herbs in pots. When the fig tree at Busselton was breaking under the weight of the figs, Mum made large batches of fig, ginger and almond jam for us to sell. Later she would take boxes of dried apricots and dried peaches from the cool room and return them as apricot and peach jams. People brought empty jars when they came shopping and we weighed out honey and jam and goat's milk into them.

On Wednesdays our friend and neighbour, Sue, came to help in the shop while Roger did a shopping run. Sue and her husband lived in a house across the back lane. They had two boys who were a bit younger than Peter and Kylie and the children spent most of their free time together. When Sue couldn't give us a hand, my brother jumped in to help. John had recently returned from extended backpacking travels through Europe and Asia and was living with us in our parents' house. Rosemary came to the shop for a chat every Wednesday morning. Despite her deafness she drove herself all over town to visit with friends and family. The two of us would withdraw to the little office to talk so she could sit across from me and read my lips. She drank black coffee and smoked and laughed good-humouredly at my pale chamomile tea.

Every day I would leave the shop mid-afternoon to pick up the children from the bus stop, and then go on home with them to make dinner. On Saturdays they came to the shop with us. Midland was on the other side of Perth, so the whole family was now travelling long distances every day. We worked hard and business was good and soon we had found a routine and were settling into our new way of life. Roger began to sleep better. We had no time to dwell on the past, even if we had wanted to. But we were not yet ready and would learn the hard way that ignoring things does not make them go away.

It was a pattern of our relationship that things would go along fine for weeks or even months, but then I would get angry about something and make a scene and then sulk for a couple of days lest my anger be taken too lightly. I was angry when Roger went out fishing with his mates and a crate of beer and left me at home with the kids. I was angry when he didn't come home after a football match and I found him the next day at a house in Cottesloe with his football mates, finishing off the keg, and his equally drunk mates called out derisively,

'Aw, leave him alone. Can't a bloke have a drink with his mates without his missus giving him a bad time?'

I was angry when he left the house in the morning and forgot to kiss me goodbye. Often something trivial, even ridiculous, acted as a trigger and my anger would erupt like a volcano.

My attitude to anger almost certainly began with the example of my father and was compounded and cemented by my Catholic upbringing. The bottom line was that anger was bad. It was wrong to be angry. Dad was a good man. More than any other person I know, he lived what he believed. And he believed the biblical admonition to 'Love one another as I have loved you'. That pretty much ruled out being angry with people. When he felt angry he would go quiet. In retrospect it would probably have been better, for me at least, if he had yelled. But he didn't. As much as was childishly possible, I tried to follow his example.

Of course you cannot prevent anger arising, but as a child that was my goal. I could not allow myself to even think an angry thought, let alone express it, or I would be consumed with guilt. At the age of seven I made my first communion. This mysterious event was preceded by my first confession. From then on I would accompany my family to the church every Saturday to confess my sins to the priest. Anger showed up regularly on my list of sins for confession. 'I was angry with my sister' was pretty much top of the list every week. And every week I would be very sorry and sincerely promise not to sin again. I dreaded having to admit week after week that my determination to be good had not protected me from my anger. There were even times when I was angry with God. I was very angry with God, for example, when Sister Lucy said that only Catholics would go to heaven. Those who were not baptised Catholic would, if they were very good people, go to limbo when they died. Limbo seemed to be a kind of no-man's-land between heaven and hell, though closer to heaven than hell. My Nan was not a Catholic, and it made me very angry to think that she would be denied access to heaven. I asked myself what kind of a God would make rules like that. I was angry with Him for a long time about it, though I never told the priest.

As a young wife and mother I continued my battle with anger, never stopping to ask myself how I could become so angry over such ordinary things. I would feel justified in my anger when it boiled over. It clearly had nothing to do with me but was due to some shortcoming in the object of my wrath, usually Roger. But when I was done with being angry, I always felt awful. I felt drained and flat and almost dirty and would already begin dreading the next outburst. Anger was like a shadowy monster at my shoulder, following me around, just waiting for an excuse to pounce again, and it was becoming an increasingly frequent visitor. Since Coral Bay unspoken thoughts and feelings were becoming more and more difficult to contain, building up to a sinister dark cloud of ever increasing proportions.

It was while we had the shop that, after another bout with anger, I suddenly found myself saying, 'I don't want to feel like this again.' I was thirty years old and experience had long since taught me that good intentions were not enough. If I really didn't want to feel like that again I had to do something. But what? Maureen had once mentioned a psychologist at the public health offices in West Perth who was 'good with young people'. I asked her for his name and called his office. The receptionist told me he was on long service leave but gave me his home number saying he was taking calls at home. I called him there and we arranged to meet the following Saturday at a place in Jandakot, on the outskirts of Perth.

Roger drove me there. I was having second thoughts about the whole thing. What on earth was I doing? I was going to meet a professional counsellor to talk to him about my life. What would I say? That I didn't want to be angry any more? That would mean explaining to him about my anger and the things that made me angry. I was very nervous. I never talked about my inner world with anyone, let alone a stranger. The directions led us off the main road and down a track through the bush to a small shed-like structure with a covered patio on one side. Roger parked the car and we got out and walked towards the building. My mind was racing and my emotions seemed to be running wild. I had a lump in my throat the size of a fist. I was so worked up I didn't even notice that the man who walked towards us was wearing a long orange robe and had a string of beads around his neck. He smiled in greeting and introduced himself as the man I had spoken to on the phone. He did not ask what was wrong or why I was there. He talked about the building and the covered patio and said it was early days yet but it would become a meditation centre.

I don't think I had ever heard the word 'meditation' before. I was hardly listening, I was so occupied with the lump in my throat and the fear of the moment when we would sit down to talk and I would burst into tears. But we didn't sit down to talk. Instead the man said we would do a dynamic meditation. We stood on the patio and he explained how it worked, then he gave Roger and me masks to cover our eyes, and turned on the music. It was strange wild music. He had told us first to take short sharp breaths through the nose and when the music changed to move in whatever way we felt. I was rooted to the spot and stayed there, hardly breathing or moving, until it was over. Then while Roger chatted with the psychologist I walked off into the bush and cried my eyes out. As we were leaving the psychologist told us there would be meditations there every Saturday and invited us to come again. We drove away and I relaxed. I had got out of that pretty lightly. I had cried, but alone where no one could see me, and I hadn't had to talk about myself at all.

I never did talk to the psychologist about my anger, but Roger and I found ourselves driving out to Jandakot every weekend to see him and join in the meditation. Roger enjoyed the crazy chaotic exercise, and I enjoyed listening to the taped discourses that were played beforehand. They were the talks of someone called Bhagwan Shree Rajneesh. Large photos of him hung around the meditation centre. His liquid eyes gazing out at me and the words he spoke soon convinced me that he was a sage.

He knew so much about so many things. The timbre of his voice was warm and he spoke in an unhurried, deliberate way. Everything he said made sense to me. It was like a breath of fresh air after the narrow confinement of the Catholic doctrine. He had an eclectic style that borrowed from great religious leaders and mystics throughout history, bringing them to life in a colourful, provocative presentation peppered with jokes and new words like 'enlightenment', 'chakra' and 'nirvana'. It was exciting and magical. Religion had always been a very serious thing for me and I found the addition of laughter very appealing. I was enthralled to hear anecdotes about Buddha and Socrates and Zarathustra and so many others I had never heard of before. I began to understand that there is not one narrow path to heaven but many different paths. When he spoke it was as though I had stepped through a door into another world. It was like in *The Wizard of Oz* when Judy Garland steps out of the insipid sepia world of her everyday life into the vibrant colourful land of Oz. I was fascinated by it and hungry to know more. I looked forward to the weekends in the same way I had looked forward to the Saturday matinee when I was a kid.

Although I was shocked when Rajneesh condemned established religions, saying they were dead things of empty rituals and crippling guilt, it struck a chord with me. My religion had been a religion of guilt. Even when I ceased to make the weekly pilgrimage to the confessional, I was still deeply influenced by those voices that said, 'Thou shalt not . . .' and the unseen God that watched and judged my every move. I felt understood by this wise man I had never met, who exhorted his listeners to be themselves and enjoy life, and not to feel guilty about anything. He was not preaching rules and regulations and eternal damnation. He was not preaching at all. He was telling stories and jokes and at the same time drawing attention to what a mess our lives were in. I could relate to that! It was as though he knew me and was talking to me personally.

Before long I forgot what it was that had brought me there. The psychologist became my mentor and I began to feel a sense of belonging in the group that quickly gathered around him. In the beginning there were only a handful of people, but soon the numbers grew so that sometimes there was hardly space for everyone on the patio. They were mostly young people like ourselves, marrieds and singles and couples from all walks of life. Many of them brought their children along with them, as did we, and the children played together while their parents snorted and shook and shouted their way through the hour-long dynamic meditation.

Later I learned that the psychologist had just spent his long service leave in India in an ashram, where he had become a disciple of Rajneesh, and that the picture in the locket around his neck was of his master. Master and disciple were concepts beyond my comprehension then. All I knew was that Jesus had twelve disciples who followed Him and did His bidding. But Jesus was God's son and I was not aware that regular people could be masters with disciples. Even when, a few months later, I filled out a form applying for sannyas, I did not really grasp that I was entering into a master–disciple relationship. Sannyas is Sanskrit and means simply 'seeker'.

When, a few weeks after our first meeting, the psychologist invited me to participate in a weekend therapy group at the meditation centre, I agreed. I was nervous as I didn't really know what to expect, but I trusted him and wanted to be a part of what was happening. The group did dynamic and other meditations every day, listened to Rajneesh's tapes, engaged in structured relaxation exercises, ate light vegetarian food and walked silently in the bush. It was my first experience of anything like that and by the end of the weekend I felt very light-headed and happy, almost euphoric, and was hell bent on becoming a sannyasin, a bona fide seeker. I had never met Bhagwan, as everyone called him, but that didn't matter. I would be a mail-order sannyasin! I sent off the form and waited in nervous anticipation for the response, dying some of my clothes orange in the interim. Back came a sheet of Bhagwan's letter head with my new name handwritten on it: *Ma Shanti Bhadra.* Underneath was Bhagwan's signature. On the back of the paper he had written the meaning of my new name: shanti : peace, bhadra : grace. The envelope also held instructions of what was required of me now that I was a sannyasin. Henceforth I was to:

1. Use the new name.
2. Wear the mala.
3. Wear only orange coloured clothes.
4. Do a meditation every day.

I set to dying the rest of my clothes. Wearing orange and getting up early every morning to do dynamic meditation was no problem.

Nor was wearing the mala, which I received in a ceremony at the meditation centre. It was the name that I baulked at. Every time I had to use it, my stomach turned over, my tongue tied itself in knots and I had to force myself to say it. But just as I had been a devout Catholic, so I now became a devout sannyasin, faithfully following the rules.

Roger didn't take sannyas but he stuck close to me, following my lead, afraid to be left behind. He called me by my new name and always came to the meditation centre with me. One day during a dynamic meditation he broke through the mass of people to pull desperately at my clothes, crying

'Come back! Come back!' I tried to shake him off but he held on, sobbing pitifully and begging, 'Come back. Come back.'

My family had mixed reactions to my new appearance. The children seemed not to notice. To my parents I was still their Janie. Rosemary thought it was all good fun, though she did not consider for a moment calling me anything other than the name she had always called me. Sue and Mary Lou kept at a safe distance and stopped calling and coming to visit. Mary Lou would eventually feel compelled to write to the police asking them to save me, displaying a typical Paul girl tendency to call on a higher authority rather than confront the situation herself. John watched my antics with a bemused smile. Our young neighbourhood friends used my new name and customers who knew no other, but old friends from earlier days, and family on both sides, wanted nothing to do with it. Many old friends disappeared out of our life. We had new friends now; some of them were sannyasins, some were not, but they all came to do the meditations and afterwards we chatted about Bhagwan and going to India to see him.

As a young teenager at high school and then at university, I had been painfully aware that I could not defend my Catholic faith, despite reciting the catechism daily throughout nine years of convent school. I carefully avoided any mention of Catholicism lest I be asked a question I did not know the answer to. Today I see that I was in no way convinced of the truth of the Catholic teachings. There was always the question of Nan, and my cousins and aunts and uncles on Mum's side of the family who, being Christians but not Catholics, were supposedly not to be allowed into heaven. I just couldn't accept that. And I would ask myself what was in store for the millions of people in the world who had never heard of the

Catholic Church. The whole thing seemed to me to be completely arbitrary. I also had the example of the nuns in my life, the majority of whom did not live the teachings they sought to convince us of.

Now here I was a sannyasin, just as insecure in my new beliefs as I had been in the old. Everything had happened so fast and I didn't really know what I actually believed, other than that Bhagwan was a great master. Suddenly I was walking around in bright orange clothes with a mala around my neck telling people my name was Shanti Bhadra. I was no longer inconspicuous and people asked questions. An old lady who frequented the shop took a close look at Bhagwan's picture in the locket hanging around my neck and asked,

'Is that your grandfather, dear?'

I found I had an unexpected need to convince people of what I was doing, as though their approval was necessary in order for me not to doubt myself.

I was in a hurry to get to Pune. I needed to get to where the master was, perhaps sensing that without his implicit support I would falter and fall by the wayside. I was driven at that time. I was determined to push through all obstacles to my goal, and my goal was to sit at Bhagwan's feet. I believed I had the great good fortune to have found a living buddha. I was one of the chosen ones. The idea was not new to me, for had not I been one of the chosen ones as a Catholic? But this was different. This was real. This great master, this god, did not sit on a throne somewhere in an invisible heaven, he sat on a chair in India, where you could go and talk to him and he would tell you what to do.

It is easy to see what was going on when you read this, but I was completely blind. I was not aware of what was really happening. I did not ask myself why I needed someone to tell me what to do. I did not give it a moment's thought. I plunged headlong into sannyas with a drive that should have set bells ringing and red lights flashing. If it did, I didn't see or hear them. I was fast asleep and dreaming, driven by unconscious forces I knew nothing about. For in truth my goal was to get as far away as possible from the disappointment and confusion of my life.

A new unexpected factor had entered my disintegrating world. I don't remember how it came up in the first place, perhaps in the general discussion that was taking place at the time about new sexual freedoms, but there began to be talk of 'wife swapping'. The terminology alone suggests that the initiative came from the men. Apart from a couple of schoolgirl crushes, Roger was my first love and my only sexual experience. I had never felt attracted to another man. What seemed like silly, risqué talk suddenly became reality when I popped over to see our neighbour Sue one day and found she and Roger making out on the living-room floor. Although it somehow came as no great surprise, I was in turmoil. My marriage was deviating badly from the course I had expected of it. I felt terribly insecure and didn't know whether to laugh or cry, but I put on a brave face, pretending I was a worldly woman in step with the times.

I did not feel attracted to Sue's husband, but with things having come so far, I was suddenly seized with a certain recklessness at the idea of doing something forbidden, something so completely against all I had been taught. I would show everyone what a good sport I was! I agreed to spend the night with Sue's husband while Roger and Sue spent the night together. What a night! I was completely ill at ease, doing something not because I wanted to but because I thought I should. I was repulsed by Sue's husband's odour and his demands. I just wanted to run away. Of course I was nowhere near honest enough to do that and held up my part of the bargain, but I was desperate knowing that Roger and Sue were happy with their combination and there was no way I was going to be able to continue my part of the arrangement. I would rather be alone, even knowing that Roger and Sue were together. I felt obliged to maintain an air of generous understanding for their attraction to each other, but my lack of enthusiasm for further participation in the arrangement put a damper on the whole incident and it died a natural death. In retrospect, although I was married and had two children, I was still a virgin, and would remain a virgin for a long time to come. Years later a French boyfriend would express it perfectly when he derisively described me as 'a nun'.

It wasn't until I met Roger that I had found out one did not get pregnant from kissing. Beginning before we married, our sex life was accompanied by shame and guilt and fear of pregnancy. A priest one day refused me absolution because I would not promise to end the 'sinful' relationship, and I left the confessional in tears. Even when we married, the Church forbad all birth control other than abstinence. Sex was not seen as a normal healthy drive but a necessary, somewhat repugnant reproductive act. Husband and wife were not supposed to enjoy sex, in fact they were expected to refrain from it except for the purpose of begetting children. Only loose, frivolous women sullied the sanctity of sex by enjoying themselves. Those kind of women were branded whores. The teachings of the Church, the example of celibate nuns, the stories I grew up with of virginal martyrs, the impression gained from society in general that a woman was there to serve the needs of her husband, together with any number of unknown psychic factors, combined to keep my sexuality in a Sleeping Beauty state of suspended animation.

As a child growing up I dreamed of going to France to see Paris, to Italy to see the ruins of the Roman Empire, and to Egypt to see the pyramids. Whenever I dreamed of travelling abroad, I would always add, 'But I never want to go to India or America.' Years later, now a young wife and mother, I forgot those childhood musings and the only place I wanted to go was to India. I talked about it incessantly. Roger, afraid of me going too far away, said if I was going to India, he was coming too. We began making arrangements for our trip. Plans were made to leave the children with my parents, and John and our neighbour Sue agreed to manage the shop in our absence. By April we were finally ready. When we dropped the children off with my parents in Busselton, Mum presented me with a long orange seersucker skirt she had made for me. It was completely in keeping with the easy hippie style to be seen everywhere at the time.

As we were leaving the house, Dad took Roger aside.

'Take care of her,' he said, little dreaming that my husband could barely take care of himself, let alone me.

India

8

It was the first time either of us had been outside Australia and New Zealand, apart from a short holiday in Fiji, on our way home from New Zealand six years earlier. Our plane landed in Bombay, later to go by its earlier name of Mumbai. The moment we left the terminal we were surrounded by a seething mass of dark-skinned humanity with outstretched hands. Men, women and children of all ages clambered around us. *Blessed are the poor* popped into my mind, although they did not seem blessed at all with their meagre clothing and thin, gaunt limbs. *When you give unto the least of My brethren, you give unto Me.* I felt I must empty out my purse to them and felt guilty that I didn't, but I needed my money for my quest. On the way to the domestic airport we passed cardboard and tin dwellings pretending to be houses, and everywhere there were people asleep on the ground. The air was a strange combination of decay and pungent spices, with a whiff of fragrant frangipani and jasmine now and again. I was completely overwhelmed. Naïve as I was I had no concept of other countries and ways of being. Arrogant as I was it never occurred to me to read about the history and culture of India or even to enquire into their language. I just assumed everyone would speak English for me. In my complete ignorance I brought my typically British colonial judgements along with me, looking down at the sleeping figures as we drove by in our taxi and feeling that tell-tale combination of pity and superiority.

From Mumbai we flew the short hop to Pune. Pune was a teeming metropolis. It had been a hill station during the British occupancy where officers took their families in summer to escape from the oppressive heat. Our hotel was close to the ashram in Koregon Park, a less populated suburb with many gracious old houses and tree-lined streets. We showered and fell into bed. The next morning we took a rickshaw to the ashram.

The ashram was in the middle of Pune suburbia. A high fence ran around the boundary. The rickshaw driver took us to the front gate. After Mumbai and the trip through Pune, walking into the ashram was like walking into a church. There was no clamouring and pushing and haste. Men and women in long orange robes moved around quietly. They were almost all Europeans. Some sat in small groups on the stone wall, chatting and laughing. There was lush green growth everywhere you looked. I asked where Bhagwan lived and the guard pointed down the promenade. 'There,' he said. Right there! Roger and I walked down to where the guard had pointed. Within the grounds, Bhagwan's house and garden were fenced off again. Guards stood on duty at his gate. We stood outside the gate for the longest time, gazing into the green oasis that all but screened his house. We had arrived.

Having paid our silent respects at Bhagwan's house, Roger and I made our way to the office to make an appointment to attend darshan. Darshan is a meeting with the master. Every evening Bhagwan held darshan on a covered patio attached to his house. It was the opportunity to sit in his presence, to meet him personally and to talk with him. He would give sannyas to those who indicated their wish for it, and he might say a few words or assign therapy groups and individual sessions to the person at his feet.

We were shown into a long room with large glass windows overlooking the front gate and the promenade. There was a long desk along one wall with three women sitting side by side behind it. In the middle was an Indian woman wearing a headscarf; she was so tiny she was practically swallowed by the chair she sat on. On either side of her sat more substantial European women, one with long wavy blonde hair, the other with somewhat darker straight hair. The Indian woman and the blonde-haired woman were engaged in animated conversation with the people sitting in front of them. We were ushered before the other woman. She spoke English with an accent and we would later learn that she came from Holland. She was pleasant and friendly and asked us about ourselves. Roger surprised me by telling her he wanted to take sannyas. We were given appointments to attend darshan a few days later. She emphasised the importance of avoiding all perfumes and soaps and shampoos with fragrance. We were to sit at Bhagwan's feet free of all smells of the West. She encouraged us to participate in the meditations, and we left to make way for those waiting their turn.

That done we went exploring. Most of the ashram was closed to visitors so it did not take us long to get our bearings. When we first entered we had seen what was to become the big open meeting place. It was a huge oval concrete pad which would later be covered by a tin roof hung with white cloth on the inside to screen the bare tin. It would later be known as *Buddha Hall*, and Bhagwan would give his daily discourse there. We found the cafeteria, called *Vrindavan*, and learned that it served only vegetarian food. We would come to know that Bhagwan had been raised a Jain, and was a strict vegetarian. While we were eating a bowl of rice and vegetables an acquaintance from Jandakot came over to greet us. A friend! Someone to show us the ropes. There were more people from Perth, and from other parts of Australia, and they gathered around us new arrivals. They explained about discourse and 'sniffing' and the times of the different meditations. In short, all we needed to know. We were set.

Early next morning we stood in line to be sniffed before being allowed through the gate into Bhagwan's enclave. As each person walked through the gates they were sniffed by two women standing face to face to form a narrow arch through which everyone passed. Should perfume, smoke and other smells be detected, you would be turned away. Alas, we were sniffed out, apparently still too fresh from the west. I almost cried. The next morning was the same, and I did cry.

On the third morning we were allowed through. We had bought little flat cushions to sit on to guard against the cold concrete, a tip from our new Australian friends. The patio was full of people, almost all in long orange robes, settling themselves on the floor, all facing in the direction of a chair which sat against the wall, next to a door. We followed their lead.

After a while all activity ceased. The door opened and the tiny Indian woman from the office came through. Her appearance was the signal for everyone to join their hands and raise them in greeting, for as she sank to her place on the floor Bhagwan stepped through the door. His hands were joined and raised in greeting. He wore the same simple style of white cotton gown I had seen in photos of him. It was an austerely cut, long-sleeved white robe that reached to his ankles. The long sleeves had perfectly ironed creases from wrist to shoulder. On his feet were wide-strapped thongs. He walked slowly, almost floating, as though his feet did not touch the ground. His long grey beard wafted in the gentle breeze created by his forward movement. His liquid eyes shone and he smiled faintly. He approached the chair and sat down, an apparition in white. I was light-headed and overcome with emotion. I pressed my hands, still joined in greeting, to my lips and cried silent tears of joy. I no longer remember what he said, or whether he spoke Hindi or English. It didn't matter. I was there, sitting at his feet.

    I didn't want to waste a moment. I pushed Roger out of bed at the crack of dawn every morning and we took a rickshaw to the ashram, getting there in time to participate in the dynamic meditation at six o'clock. Then we would shower and drink a quick chai before lining up to attend Bhagwan's daily discourse. Later in the day I would join in the humming meditation, and watch with fascination the small group of people moving slowly through Tai Chi exercises. Roger and I spent the whole day in the ashram. We spent a lot of time in Vrindavan drinking chai and long cool drinks and talking with our friends. One advantage of being in the ashram was that I did not have to do the work of convincing people of the rightness of what I was doing. Everyone was already convinced. This brought with it a welcome feeling of security, of belonging. The last meditation of the day was another dynamic body-shaking exercise called kundalini. Then it was evening, and all outside activities stopped. It was time for darshan.

    For some reason Roger and I were not called to Bhagwan as a couple, we were called up independently. I was called first. I was terribly nervous and excited when my name was called out. I stood up and made my way to the front and sat down on the floor at Bhagwan's feet. I practically swooned to be so close to him. He smiled. There was some small exchange: when had I arrived, how long would I be staying? I could hardly speak. He took a card from the little Indian woman seated on the floor at his side, studied it for a moment and then said I should do Primal group beginning in the next couple of days, followed by Tantra group. Then he sat back in his chair and began speaking about how everything had to go, the whole edifice had to go, and made a sweeping movement with his arm. In my mind's eye I saw him wave his magic wand, only to be called back in the same instant to hear him say he would crucify me. Had not Christ been crucified? In my complete lack of understanding I felt very proud to be destined for such exalted treatment and drifted back to my place on cloud nine, clutching a piece of paper someone had pressed into my hand. On it were written the groups Bhagwan had given me and the dates on which they would take place.

When it was Roger's turn to sit at Bhagwan's feet, he was given the name *Swami Prem Riten* and received his mala from the master's hands. Then Bhagwan told him to do Primal group, followed by Encounter group. After darshan we emerged through the gate to find our new friends waiting for us. When they heard which groups we had been given they said there must be a mistake, as couples did not do groups together, especially not Primal group. They suggested one of us do the Primal group that was about to begin, and the other do the one after that. But I would not listen. The master had given me Primal group to do, and if he had given Roger the same one then he must have his reasons. For me Bhagwan was God and I knew that God could see everything. He knew Roger and I were a couple, and if he had given us the same Primal group then that's what we must do.

A couple of years later I would work in the booking office where people registered and paid to attend groups and individual sessions. Most people came to make their bookings with the small slips of paper they had been handed at darshan the night before. When the shutters were lowered at the end of the day, we went through all the group cards and filled in a pristine white card with the number of places still empty in each therapy group, and whether women or men were needed to balance and fill the group. The white card was for Bhagwan, and had to be ready for him before darshan each evening.

Primal group lasted ten days. Participants were required to eat light vegetarian food and to live in silence and isolation from each other and the world for the duration of the group. They only spoke and related within the group sessions. Outside the group room they walked with eyes cast down, avoiding contact with everyone. Food could be chosen and paid for at Vrindavan without talking. The rickshaw driver had to be told the name of your hotel when it was time to return there in the evening, and that you wanted to return to the ashram in the morning, but that was about the extent of contact with the outside world. Before the group began I took a room in another hotel. Primal group was to be our initiation into sannyas.

There were many group rooms scattered in ashram-owned houses throughout Koregon Park. The Primal group met in one of a complex of underground rooms inside the ashram itself. The bathroom for these underground rooms was one large white-tiled room without partitions. There were showers along one wall and toilets on the opposite wall for the use of both sexes. I had grown up in a family where parents covered themselves, and the children too. Even taking a pee in the bush required finding a bush or tree to pee behind. It was a matter of the deepest shame for me to sit on the toilet to urinate or, worse still, defecate, in full view of other peeing and pooing strangers, while other naked men and women took showers opposite me. Although I got used to showering with other people, I never got used to using the toilet so publicly.

The group room had padded walls and the floor was covered with mattresses. There were small windows high up under the ceiling on one wall. I don't remember exactly how many participants we were, perhaps twelve. The sexes were matched, and there were three group leaders, two men and a woman. The group activities were highly structured. They often involved a lot of movement which almost always ended in shouting and screaming and crying; in short, catharsis. Catharsis, a word I had never heard before, soon became part of my vocabulary, and my life. I had only ever done the one weekend group at the meditation centre in Jandakot and it had been very low-key and nonconfronting. Primal group was something else altogether.

By far the most powerful and disturbing exercise for me was when we were lined up opposite each other and told to express anger to the person in front of us. It was a few days into the group and I was beginning to lose my control over things I would normally have kept hidden. Some might say I was beginning to let go. Everybody started shouting. Every so often the group leaders would move people in the rows so they stood opposite a different person. Suddenly Roger was standing in front of me. A torrent of unexpressed anger and resentment exploded out of me with a force that nearly knocked us both off our feet. I screamed abuse at him for the things he had done and for the things he had not done, raging at his shortcomings and weaknesses, and pouring venom on his manhood. Once he recovered from the first onslaught, he screamed back. We hardly listened to what the other said. We screamed insults at each other with a passion that threatened to demolish us both on the spot. The group leaders moved us opposite different partners but I saw only Roger before me now and continued in my fury until I was hoarse and spent. Later the group sat in a ring and talked about their experiences during the exercise. Roger sat on the opposite side of the ring to me. I was in shock at what had happened and exhausted by the intensity of it. Something in me wanted to get up and walk away from the group, and from Roger, and never come back. Instead, I crawled across the circle to him on my hands and knees and burst into tears in his lap.

After the group had ended I moved back into the hotel with Roger. We did not talk about it. The silence kept outside the group bonded to the silence we had kept all our lives together and wrapped everything that had come up within the group in its shroud. We had a couple of days before we were to go into our next groups and so we spent them taking a holiday. We slept in, then went out to eat chicken korma, before taking a rickshaw to Mahatma Gandhi Road to window-shop at the gold jewellery and saris. Those shops reminded me of Aladdin's cave, exotic and sparkling and brilliantly colourful. But all around it was dirty and crowded and beggars appeared wherever we went. It was only inside the ashram that I felt safe. Outside I was truly on the outside, a white-skinned interloper with not the slightest understanding of Indian culture, local customs or language. Excursions outside the ashram involved fending off beggars, arguing with rickshaw drivers and being completely overwhelmed by the unfamiliar smells, noise and sheer numbers of people and traffic. In all the years I lived in India my European arrogance never left me. It was not until much later that I began to realise what I had missed, because I had been more blind than the beggars who sat by the roadside with scarred, unseeing eyes.

Then our holiday was over and it was back to the serious business of sannyas and groups. Our friends were impressed that Roger was to do Encounter group.

'Everything is allowed,' they said, 'People break bones in that group!' He became a kind of hero among them. 'Tantra is all about sex,' was all they said to me.

I will not pretend to explain the ancient teachings of Tantra that speak of transforming sexual energy into something sacred.

When I did the Tantra group I had no inkling of such things, and I dare say neither did the group leaders. I was still light-years away from understanding my own dormant sexuality, let alone that of the opposite sex. The group was again very structured but this time there was a lot of nudity and intimacy, which often led to sexual coupling. Very quickly I wished I was anywhere but there, but Bhagwan had given me the group to do so I must do it. From the first day I clung to one man in the group, always seeking him out when it seemed as though things were about to get too intimate. I no longer remember anything about him except that he did not speak English and was missing a front tooth, but he saved me from having to get too close to the other men. We also had sex together. A month before such a thing would have been unthinkable. Having sex with a virtual stranger in a room with a bunch of other people engaged in the same activity! I was getting further and further away from my Catholic origins and from the loyal wife I had thought myself to be. I comforted myself that it was just one man, whose smell I liked, and not a lot of different men, as though that somehow made it okay. After the group we never saw each other again, or if we did I did not recognise him.

By the time his Encounter group was over Roger had bonded with the group leader. This man was like the high priest of Bhagwan's temple. He lived in Bhagwan's house on the first floor in a room above Bhagwan's bedroom. He placed his bed so that it was exactly over Bhagwan's bed, no doubt the better to receive the energy transfer from the master as he slept. The high priest was well known for his charms. Women fell in love with him all the time and he had his pick of the loveliest of them. I too fell in love with him and was nervous and proud when he obtained permission for me to enter Bhagwan's house so I could accompany him to his room. I experienced a strange mixture of chagrin and relief when it became clear that he needed someone to run messages for him, not to share his bed. Bhagwan once said of his high priest that he was enlightened in his first chakra.

Roger said he wanted to stay longer than the month we had planned. He extended his ticket and I booked a leaving darshan. When I was called up to Bhagwan to sit at his feet, he asked me why I was leaving. I said I had two children and a business back home in Australia. He told me to go home and get the children, and 'leave everything and come and be with me'. I almost fainted. A personal invitation from the master to come and live in his ashram! From that moment on I had only one goal in life – to leave everything behind and come back to India to live close to Bhagwan. When Roger returned home a few weeks later he had genital herpes and was sick with amoebic dysentery, but he too was entertaining the idea of moving to India.

Whatever had happened in the therapy groups at the ashram was slipped into the *do not disturb* compartment of our lives. We picked up where we had left off as though nothing had happened and quickly became involved in everyday life again. When it came to taking steps to leave everything, Roger's enthusiasm waned. Of course we would move to India, but later. We continued running the shop and going to Jandakot on the weekend. Surrounded by so many people in orange, Peter and Kylie asked to become sannyasins. Peter was given the name *Swami Prem Santosh*, and Kylie, *Ma Prem Aruna*. They began wearing orange clothes and malas too. The whole family had a new identity. From now on we were a sannyasin family.

Then a letter came from the high priest telling Roger that he should come back now. Bhagwan was speaking on the Diamond Sutra, he wrote. This sutra emphasises how rare it is to be born at all; how rare it is to be born in the form of a man; how rare it is to be born in the time of a buddha; how rare it is to see the buddha, and how (by this point impossibly) rare it is to become a disciple of the buddha. We were indeed the chosen few! He should hesitate no longer.

The letter was the catalyst I had been waiting for. I began energetically pushing to leave. Roger still held back a little but allowed himself to be drawn into making lists and tentative plans. It was at this time that the police came knocking on the door in response to Mary Lou's letter. They were polite and friendly and, after satisfying themselves that nothing sinister was going on, took their leave. Although I was angry with Mary Lou, I didn't worry too much because I was leaving town.

John said he would be interested in buying the shop but that he and his girlfriend (who later became his wife) only had a bicycle and a hundred dollars between them. We were not short of money, so we worked out a payment plan that would allow them to buy the shop as they worked it. We began selling and giving away all our considerable belongings. Almost everything we owned, even

'Noah's ark' was disposed of. We kept only our orange clothes and Peter's Lego, and just a few things we could not bring ourselves to part with. The latter we packed into two tea-chests which we stored in a friend's basement. On my one and only visit home three years later, I went to get those tea-chests. When I opened them I was struck by the things we had considered too precious to throw away: fishing lines, a squid jag, Roger's geological hammer, a cast-iron pan we had used over innumerable camp fires, the camp oven, bark paintings and the stiff salt-preserved crocodile feet from our time at Port Keats. Everything in those boxes represented carefree days of long ago, days spent together in the bush or on the ocean.

Others, sannyasins among them, may wonder at our totality. I believe our extreme degree of commitment at the time was indicative of and in direct proportion to our inability to cope with our problems. Rather than acknowledge them and face them, we ran away, as children often do, in the mistaken belief that if we were to run far enough and destroy the bridges behind us, we could escape them, and they would not be able to follow us. For in truth, we were children, not coping with the realities of life, running back to the safety of Big Daddy, who appeared to our hopeful, trusting eyes to be God himself. He would take care of us. He would tell us what to do. We would no longer have to struggle with the problems of everyday life.

What a relief it was for me. It felt good to hand over responsibility to someone who knew better. In those days of upheaval I could not conceive of myself as being insecure and frightened and vulnerable. I saw myself as a true spiritual adventurer, unafraid to step over the boundaries of convention, ready to give up everything I knew to surrender to the master, and to serve him with all the fervour I could muster.

In January 1978 I flew to India alone. Roger and the children would follow two weeks later. In Mumbai I found that my suitcases had flown on to London. The airline assured me that when the cases returned they would be sent on to Pune. I was distrustful and took a hotel near the airport to wait. It took two days for them to return and in those two days everything in me was screaming at me to go back home to Australia. India seemed more dirty and foreign and frightening than I remembered. Rats ran across the dining room in the hotel and ate the soap in the bathroom at night. I was afraid of what I was doing. But the bridges were in ruins. I would have been too ashamed and humiliated to return to the family and friends I had just said goodbye to. What would I say? I had changed my mind? I had made a mistake? No, I had to go forward. There was no turning back.

9

With my well-travelled suitcases in hand, I flew on to Pune where I took an apartment near the ashram and prepared for the arrival of Roger and the children. It was a very basic dwelling in a concrete apartment block. The floors were decked with concrete mosaic tiles. The toilet was a white enamelled squat toilet set into the floor in the bathroom, and the shower was a shower head fixed to the wall. There was no shower stall or partition. Experience quickly taught me that water on walls and floor dried up very quickly in the tropical climate. For the same reason I opted for no floor coverings. Bare floors were cool and easy to sweep and mop.

I bought a double mattress for Roger and me, two single mattresses for the children, a number of free-standing bamboo shelves, and a minimum of kitchen utensils, cutlery and crockery. Friends pointed out that I would need someone to take care of things while I was at the ashram every day, and so I arranged for a local woman, known as an ayah, to clean the apartment and wash and cook for us.

The kitchen consisted of a cement work bench with a two-burner gas cooker on top and two simple shelves underneath. Our ayah was a wonderful cook. She would whip up delicious food in no time at all, in what seemed to me to be very rudimentary conditions. She had a twinkle in her eye and was incorrigibly cheerful. She was ayah to a number of westerners orbiting around the ashram, from which one can deduce that she worked long hours.

Bhagwan always spoke affectionately of children and I was glad that Peter and Kylie were coming to live near him. I felt very lucky that my children would grow up in the presence of such a wise and loving man. I imagined them developing as creative individuals, free from the torment of guilt and the insecurity that had overshadowed so much of my own childhood. And indeed, once they arrived it didn't take them long to realise that our new lifestyle in Pune afforded them a degree of freedom they had not had before. Although there was an unofficial ashram school they could attend in the mornings, I wasn't too concerned about enforcing regular attendance. They could already read and write and I was inclined to agree with the thinking of alternative educators who thought children learn best from their environment. Formal education could come later. In no time at all they made friends among the ashram kids and began exploring Koregon Park. They discarded their shoes and with time developed thick leathery soles on their feet. They discovered the best lassi stands, where they could get sugar cane juice, and who of the street vendors made the best pakoras. They didn't wait for Roger or me but walked or took rickshaws wherever they wanted to go, always coming back to the apartment when they knew our ayah would be there to make them chapatis and dhal. They viewed it all as a great adventure and it made me happy to see them enjoying themselves and growing up in such a carefree way.

The beginning of my new life in India was marked by chronic bronchitis. It began as a raging sore throat and a wet heavy cough. I went to the doctor. He diagnosed bronchitis and prescribed antibiotics. The sore throat went away but the cough didn't. It persisted over days, and weeks, and then months. I felt terrible. I was weak and my chest hurt with each cough and I stayed in bed a lot of the time. I took antibiotics of one kind or another for weeks on end. In the language of the ashram, sickness of any kind was considered 'resistance' and I began to feel guilty.

Still coughing, but desperate to get on with my chosen life, I went to the ashram one day to ask that I be given a job. The receptionist indicated to a young Indian woman sitting at one end of the long table in the big office. She would give me work, she said. When my turn came, I approached the young woman and asked for work. She looked at me and said,

'Oh yes, we need a responsible person in cleaning.'

Cleaning? Responsible? I registered where I was to report for work and mumbled my thanks, but my mind was racing. A cleaner! Cleaning was a menial task. I was surely destined for greater, holier things. Had I come all this way to clean toilets? For toilets it was that I cleaned. For more than a year I cleaned the toilets in the ashram, comforting myself all the while that I would one day be chosen to clean Bhagwan's toilet. The work, as it was known, was my meditation now and so, despite my misgivings, I carried it out with all the awareness and care I could muster. My duties also included joining a team of cleaners to mop the great assembly area of Buddha Hall every day. Since our first visit the hall had been finished and it was there that Bhagwan now gave his discourse every morning. It was for me a holy place. Dissatisfied with the cleaning mops provided, I bought great lengths of towelling and made double-thickness cleaning cloths with a reinforced hole in the middle for the broom handle. I also had occasion to clean the private bathrooms of certain ashramites.

As with most organisations, there was a hierarchy around Bhagwan. Many 'old' sannyasins, those who lived in his house, or who served him in some way, perhaps as group leaders or accountants or cafeteria manager or benefactors, enjoyed privileges, others did not. Perhaps the most prized privilege, next to being close to the master, was to have a room to oneself. And who could ask for anything more when that room also had its own bathroom. Such a room was a supreme luxury enjoyed by very few.

The ashram was on six acres, part of which was fenced off to create the master's compound. Accommodation within the ashram itself was at a premium. People who worked were not paid. Working for Bhagwan and his cause was considered a privilege. Once someone began working they received a food pass, enabling them to eat their meals at the ashram cafeteria. Later, if things went well, they would also be accommodated by the ashram. The ashram owned or rented many buildings in Koregon Park to house its workers. Roger and I had been working for almost a year when we were given accommodation in ashram quarters. It consisted of a room in a house that had been renovated to house samadhi tanks, one of the many individual therapies offered by the ashram.

A samadhi tank is another name for a sensory-deprivation tank, which is a large submarine-like structure filled with warm salt water. The salt water is deep enough and salty enough to fully support a person floating in it. You entered through a door at one end of the tank and lay down in the water. The door was closed and you found yourself in absolute darkness, to all intents and purposes floating in nothingness. No sound penetrated the tank. The only sound was of your own breathing. A session normally lasted an hour and a half. I did three such sessions. As I remember I slept through them all, waking only once to enjoy the sounds of a full symphony orchestra playing in my head.

We were the only people living in the house, which was an easy walk from the ashram. Roger and I brought our and the children's beds from the apartment, along with the sets of bamboo shelves for our clothes and a rack to hang our robes from. There was no need of a kitchen, or an ayah, as we now ate all our meals at the ashram and gave our laundry to an Indian laundryman who picked it up from the door and returned it the next day cleaned and ironed.

Roger continued to have digestive troubles from the amoebas he had picked up on his first visit. Amoebas were to be a constant factor in our lives for the years we lived in India, and for many years afterwards. In Pune no foreign sannyasin escaped infection, and once infected it was virtually impossible to get rid of the minute single-celled organisms. Not only were they reproducing themselves at an alarming rate, but reinfection was happening all the time. Our European constitutions were not accustomed to the climate, the water or the foods of India. We were not familiar with the chillies and many spices in Indian cuisine, nor Indian medicine that provides protection from such infections. We would quickly learn that when the bloating and cramping in our guts got too much, a handful of Flagyl did the trick. It was a strong antibiotic that made you feel terrible for a couple of days, but afterwards one had relief from the amoeba symptoms, until the next time. It was typical of the general impatience and disregard of physical maladies among sannyasins at the ashram that we did not take the time to follow a proper treatment with Flagyl, which would have entailed taking one or two of the large tablets every day for a week. Instead we carelessly took one overdose. Amoebas, giardia and lice were some of the constant irritations that challenged us Europeans living in Pune. With time I became very adept with a lice comb. Both Peter and Kylie had long hair and were never completely free of lice, despite constant vigilance and countless hours of combing.

Our little family left the house every morning at seven o'clock, stopping on our way to the ashram at the chai wallah on the corner for a couple of vegetable pakoras and a cup of chai. Half an hour later I was standing in line to be sniffed before going into Buddha Hall for discourse; the children had disappeared somewhere with their friends, and Roger may or may not have been standing by my side. He was not as pious as I. Although raised Catholic, there was no Catholic school in Esperance and the priest only came once a month to say mass, so he had missed out on the indoctrination aspect of his religion. It was nothing for Roger to skip Hindi discourse and occasionally English discourse to take the children to the Blue Diamond hotel for a lavish breakfast.

Bhagwan had been a lecturer in philosophy. In the early 1960s he began developing unusually dynamic meditations and holding meditation camps. By the end of the sixties he had quit his job as a university lecturer and was speaking publicly on a regular basis. He already had a reputation for being irreverent when it came to society's institutions and more than once incurred the wrath of his countrymen. At first it was Indian nationals who gravitated to him. India has a long tradition of spiritual masters and discipleship. It would not have appeared strange to an Indian that a professor of philosophy should hold public gatherings to talk of spiritual matters.

Meanwhile, in Europe and elsewhere, a wave of what became known as 'new-age' consciousness was sweeping the western world. A new generation of youth rose up in protest against the schizophrenic morality of the wealthy societies in which they lived. America's involvement in Vietnam led to unprecedented outcry and rebellion at home and abroad. The young in particular were at the forefront of an ever-increasing wave of protest. They marched in the streets. They wrote songs and poetry and novels of protest, hope and fear. In America, young men burned their draft cards and went to prison for refusing to be a part of something they considered immoral. The outrage of the young found its voice on campuses across Europe and America. When the National Guard opened fire and killed demonstrating students at Kent State University it simply underlined what young people were rejecting about the society in which they lived – a society that called itself democratic, and in the name of freedom waged official and unofficial wars against peoples of other beliefs and cultures, in many cases financing and supporting the very thing it purported to be defending against; a society that was all too eager to use institutions set up to defend and protect the rights of its citizens to silence those same citizens, and when that did not have the desired result to unhesitatingly turn to brute force and violence.

Many young people left their own countries in search of a better world where people cared for each other and their planet, and nations no longer warred against each other for transparently materialistic reasons. Others went where it was easy to experiment with drugs, in those days mostly marijuana, although LSD, cocaine and morphine were moving out of the moneyed class and the entertainment industry into mainstream society. Sex, drugs and rock and roll were shaking the foundations of western society. Inner growth and therapy groups sprang up to cater to the needs of predominantly young people seeking to understand themselves and their fellow man. Many travelled to Asia, to Nepal and India, seeking out wise ones who would show them the way out of the perpetual misery of this worldly existence. Even the Beatles went to India to consult a guru. Bob Dylan's song *The Times They Are A-Changin'* said it all.

It was in this climate of rebellion against the old ways and seeking for new ones that young Europeans began showing up in Mumbai. Perhaps they were just stopping over on their way from Goa to the Himalayas. I don't know how they came to be there or how they came to hear of the provocative professor of philosophy. But soon word spread and young Europeans and Americans began travelling directly to Mumbai to hear him speak and to take part in his unusual meditations. By the beginning of the seventies Bhagwan had started giving sannyas. He had lockets made with his image and hung from a beaded necklace which he put over the head of the initiate as part of the ceremony of bestowing sannyas. The disciple was given a new Sanskrit name and instructed to henceforth wear the orange colour of the traditional sannyasin. Bhagwan was doing what many had done before him. What was different was that he was giving sannyas to seekers of both sexes, from a foreign culture. We have in our culture, monks and nuns who are also given new names, a cross to wear around their necks and required to wear a particular distinguishing dress, usually a long black or brown or white robe. But here the similarity ends, both to traditional sannyas in India and Asia, and to men and women entering a monastery in Europe.

Free love was now finding expression all over the western world as young people took advantage of the new pill that removed the fear of pregnancy from casual sex. Casting off the restraints of the parental home, they began living together in loose relationships, and a whole generation threw themselves into sexual experimentation. 'Make love, not war', was the catchphrase of the day. Perhaps Bhagwan was quick to recognise this new trend. Whatever his reasons, he did not ban sex from the lives of his new disciples, as one might expect. Instead he encouraged them to fully explore their sexuality, free of the expectations of society. Only in this way, he said, could one transcend sex. Over the years he refined his permissive attitude to such a degree that he was known throughout the world as 'the sex guru'. 'Free sex' became his trump card.

I think it is fair to say that most sannyasins understood this sexual freedom to mean that they were free to change partners at will. If their wife or girlfriend, or husband or boyfriend, was nagging or jealous or too demanding or in any way unsatisfactory, they could simply leave them, without feeling guilty, and take another who was more fun to be with. Or even if they felt committed and happy with their partner, if they were attracted to another person they would not be inhibited in approaching that person for sex. Their partner was supposed not to feel jealous or insecure if that happened. The downside to this seductive arrangement was that people did not learn to cultivate and maintain lasting relationships.

Particularly in India, it became customary for Bhagwan's sannyasins to wear long orange robes. The tropical climate lent itself to loose flowing clothes, and western sannyasins adapted easily, discarding their tight-fitting jeans and tops in favour of the unrestrictive robes. In Pune, where Bhagwan eventually established his ashram, there were any number of tailors on Mahatma Gandhi Road available to cut the cloth brought to them to any desired pattern. Light cottons were the preferred material and were to be had cheaply in every hue of orange from any cloth merchant. The women had their tailors make them more shapely, feminine dresses, whereas the men wore a simple long kurta-type robe, with or without sleeves according to the season. Underwear was discarded by both sexes, in keeping with the general consensus that one should not restrict the flow of energy in one's body. Men and women alike let their hair grow long, and men, their beards. This too was a hallmark of Bhagwan's liberal style of sannyas, for in most traditional schools, sannyasins of both sexes shave or cover their heads. As time went by the orange colour began to be transcended by shades of red, until it all but disappeared and red became the predominant colour worn by Bhagwan's new breed of sannyasin.

Bhagwan's daily discourse was always recorded on tape, and would later be videotaped too. He alternated between one month of delivering his discourse in Hindi and one month of delivering it in English. Devout as I was, I always attended discourse, regardless of the fact that I did not understand a word of Hindi. Each month was devoted to a particular topic or theme. The recordings of Bhagwan's discourses for each month were transcribed and prepared for publication. Every aspect of the production was carried out by sannyasins. Bhagwan attracted a large following of well-educated people from all walks of life, among them many skilled craftsmen and women. A steady stream of titles flowed from the ashram workshops to the printer, and back. The hundreds of titles published under Bhagwan's name were all spoken by him. He never wrote a book as such. It was part of the mystique surrounding him that he spoke for two hours or more a day, day after day, year after year, without notes or prompting, except for the jokes his sannyasins sent him, the notepaper they were written on lying on his lap ready for use.

Within each month itself, Bhagwan alternated between delivering a discourse one morning, and answering questions the next. Questions were written down and sent to him via the main office. Questions covered the whole palette of human desires from everyday relationship problems to reaching the coveted heights of spiritual fulfilment, known as enlightenment. Bhagwan chose the questions he would answer publicly. Invariably he would answer just one or two questions, and the answers would become discourses in themselves. The greater majority went unanswered, though in some cases a verbal message would be transmitted from Bhagwan to an individual via his secretary. He never committed himself to paper. I only ever asked one question, and he answered it.

It was sometime in the second year of being there and I had moved on from cleaning toilets to the group booking office. Despite my determination to be a good sannyasin and a devoted disciple, I was visited again and again by doubts about Bhagwan, just as I had doubted elements of my Catholic faith. In those days doubts were the work of the devil. Now they were a test of my worthiness as a disciple. Once when he spoke familiarly about Jesus I felt offended and found myself thinking, 'What does he know about Jesus? He's not even a Christian.' When he ridiculed a popular group leader who had left him I thought he was being nasty and didn't like it. I laughed along with everyone else when he made fun of relationship problems, but felt uncomfortable when he ridiculed marriage and encouraged people to move on and try another partner. That might be all right for other people, but not for me.

It was with considerable effort that I put pen to paper, and bared my soul. I wrote: Bhagwan, all my life I have said 'yes' and now that I am here with you and the 'yes' seems really right, there comes only 'no'. What is this 'no'?

He answered my question at great length, pointing out that 'yes' and 'no' are two wings of the bird and that he was helping my 'no' come to the surface so I could fly. He said beautiful things – that man was a question mark, that sincerity was more valuable than dogma, that belief was a trick of the mind, that we must learn to lean not on certainties but on possibilities. He said my parents, religion and society had done great mischief to me, and finished with two jokes about parents and their children. I hardly heard what he said. I went into a kind of trance from the moment he spoke my name, though when he said he would help me heal the wounds that had been inflicted on me, I cried in gratitude.

Today I recognise his words to me as basic philosophy on the phenomenon of opposites, or as he so poetically expressed it, 'the intrinsic polarity of life', with the customary blaming of the parents for my one-winged condition thrown in for good measure. On that point I was only too ready to concur. Had I not turned my back on my parents? And had I not the words of Jesus ringing in my ears to justify it: 'Unless you leave your father and mother and follow Me, you shall not enter the kingdom of Heaven'? That Bhagwan should speak derisively of parents, and mine in particular, was fine with me. At thirty-four years of age I was catching up for the rebellious teenage years I had missed. In the way of a teenager trying to make sense of her world in a jumble of confusing feelings and conflicting emotions, I was happy for any support I could get in distancing myself from my parents and from all that had been my life before, desperately trying to convince myself that I was grown-up and knew what I was doing.

My question presented Bhagwan with a perfect opportunity to set yet another wedge between his sannyasins and their pasts. The answer was, of course, not just for me, it was for everyone listening. Painting the parents as the bad guys is a useful ploy to isolate disciples from previous attachments and old support systems. At other times Bhagwan might use a question to encourage the discarding of attachments to a spouse or long-term partner. Relationships of commitment, to husbands and wives, to children, and to family were made fun of and laughed at as old patterns of unenlightened behaviour. It is a subtle process leading almost unnoticeably to ever-increasing isolation. Ultimately, the isolation from parents and family and a committed relationship creates a vacuum, and it is the master who steps in to fill it. He becomes the primary emotional bond. One attaches quite naturally to him. It seems perfect, for he is wiser and more loving than any mere human. In the eyes of the disciple he is a superhuman.

Bhagwan liked to say he was just an ordinary man, but who of his disciples really believed that? It was clearly another of his cosmic jokes. Who is going to follow an ordinary man? A disciple of three decades said to me recently, 'I believe Bhagwan was a great master.'

Of course he was, for who wants to admit to following a mediocre master for half his life? Or worse still, an ordinary man? No, we were all sure we were disciples of a great master. Bhagwan was not an ordinary man. What ordinary man do you know would live such a reclusive life, unmarried and without children or friends? His house was in a small fenced and guarded compound, within a larger fenced and guarded compound. He only ever came out of his enclosure to be driven the one hundred metres to Buddha Hall for discourse every morning. He never left the greater compound. He was virtually a prisoner in his own house.

Why do people choose to imprison themselves behind guarded walls? Generally it is to keep out the madding crowd, who may want something from them that they are not willing to give. But in this case the greater compound was peopled by Bhagwan's devoted disciples. Could he not have felt comfortable mixing with them? Well, at least in my case, and I think one can safely say that of most disciples, I was busy projecting every sort of perfection and majesty onto him. To some, like me, he was God himself, all-seeing, all-knowing, the saviour of the world. At the sight of him hands were joined in prayerful greeting and many sank to their knees in humble adoration. It must be hard to have a conversation when you are not seen for yourself but as the projection of someone or something else. And how can a man who cultivates exclusivity and mystery around himself come out and mix with the people? He can't. It blows the whole thing – for everyone concerned. Such a man has no friends – he cannot afford friends. He cannot pop down to the pub for a drink, or call up a friend and invite them over for dinner and a game of cards, or to play a game of golf on the weekend. He needs to remain an enigma to the world, and especially to his disciples, for his sake and theirs. It is an unspoken agreement between them.

10

By early 1979 I was working in the group booking office and it would remain my place of work until Bhagwan escaped from us and the ashram dissolved. When I began working there it was a small room tucked into a back corner, but it grew considerably and eventually occupied a key position on the main thoroughfare, between the main gate and Bhagwan's house. A kind of bank was incorporated into the office which allowed people to deposit their rupees for safekeeping, and then draw on them as needed. As with all ashram businesses, it was open seven days a week. All sales were in cash, in rupee, the Indian currency. Every sale was recorded in a register. Each salesperson had a cash box and two sets of books. Sales of most groups and sessions were recorded in the one register, but certain specific sales were recorded in the second one. I never thought to ask why, but then it was of no interest to me. I mindlessly did what I was told. In the evening we counted the cash and balanced our books, before filling out Bhagwan's group 'vacancies' card in time for darshan.

Groups and sessions were a very lucrative source of income for the ashram. They were also places where people 'fell in love' with Bhagwan. Large photos of him were prominently displayed in all the rooms. He was always the focus. It was usual to give Bhagwan the credit for insights or successful emotional release or a particularly enjoyable experience. Long after I had graduated from doing groups, I continued to give Bhagwan the credit for all the good and desirable things in my life. I, the seemingly eternal child, was of course to blame when things went wrong. It was the same childish phenomenon my Catholic upbringing had imprinted on me. God was great and mighty and the source of all good, while I was just a poor weak sinner.

Within two years of moving to India Roger and I and the children no longer lived as a family. There was no such thing as family life in the ashram; in fact, everything spoke against it, beginning with the tacit understanding that marriage was an archaic institution with no place in the life of a true seeker. As ashramites we no longer cooked or cleaned or took care of a home together, and both Roger and I worked all day. The children were pretty much left to their own devices. They were not alone in as much as there were other children in the same situation, with parents too busy to attend to them, what with being present at discourse every morning, working in the ashram and seeking enlightenment. The children attended the ashram school as they liked, or spent their days playing together in one of the ashram properties or roaming the streets of Koregon Park, playing and scrapping with beggar kids. At times Peter and Kylie ran past the booking office, waving as they went, or stopping for a moment to breathlessly inform me of their latest adventure. They took their meals in the ashram cafeteria, and in the evening we found each other for supper together and talk of the day, and I would comb their hair for lice before they showered and Roger and I tucked them into bed.

The groups and catharsis Roger and I had done seemed to have had little to do with everyday life and we still remained deeply unaware of the unconscious forces that produced the dysfunctional dynamic in our relationship. Nothing had changed and we maintained our pattern of keeping silent about our hopes and fears and the things that really mattered to us. We slept together in the same bed every night, and apart from the wife-swapping escapade and the sexual encounters in groups, which we never mentioned, we were monogamous. But the thousand things that hold families together had eroded away and in the end it was relatively easy to slip out of the marriage bond and the responsibilities I had once so joyfully embraced. It was all a thing of the past. The ashram community now constituted the family and it was to the main office I went to ask for separate accommodation. Disguised as the act of a devoted disciple, it was in fact the final shove to push the man who had not lived up to my expectations out of my life. On that day I gave my diamond engagement ring and my gold wedding ring to Bhagwan. I handed them over to be given to Bhagwan's jewellers to be melted down and made into jewellery for him. In that act I denied my real-life husband to become a bride of God, in much the same way as a nun considers herself a bride of Christ. Roger had panned the gold for my wedding ring from Australian rivers to surprise me on our wedding day. Inside it was engraved Leave no stone unturned.

I did not allow myself to consider that my actions might have a profound impact on the children. On the contrary, I told myself that the commune was one big family, like a tribe. Our little family was pretty much already absorbed into it. Other people watched out for the children too. It was not like the world outside where separations were traumatic affairs and there were arguments about who the children would live with. We were all in the same commune and nothing would be very different.

Within a few days Roger, Peter, Kylie and I were all assigned different living quarters on a large ashram property in Koregon Park. The large house on the compound was partly used for groups and individual sessions, so accommodation for ashramites was augmented with bamboo huts erected on the perimeter of the grounds, a common enough measure at the time. Our family was each assigned accommodation in one of the many huts. I shared my bamboo hut with an older man I did not know. He had his bed and belongings in one corner of the hut, and I set up mine in another corner. It was indicative of my state of mind that I found nothing unduly distressing in this new arrangement.

The move, however, was devastating for the children. Years later they would tell me that as long as Roger and I were together and we were still a family and hung out together in the evening and slept together in the same living space, they were happy, but when the family broke up, their world fell apart. With no home base anymore, their security was shattered and they felt cast adrift. The freedom they had so enjoyed became a threatening burden.

They had never been separated from us, except for the month spent with their grandparents when Roger and I made our first trip to India. Up until then they had always slept in one room together. Not only were they now separated from their parents, but they were also separated from each other, and found themselves in shared accommodation with people they hardly knew. Peter showed his distress by getting very ill, first with a painful swollen testicle, and then with hepatitis. Roger also came down with hepatitis. He was so angry that I had left him and given away my rings that he refused my visits at the clinic. Kylie came by the booking office every day, but I was generally too busy to give her more than a perfunctory hello and a few minutes of my time. Lost in my own distorted world of pious devotion, I did not see that I was creating the selfsame situation for her that I had experienced in my childhood. I had given her over to another 'family', telling myself it was a wonderful family and she would be better off there. In my blindness I did not see her anxiety and suffering.

Shortly after Roger and Peter recovered from hepatitis, a very large circular bamboo hut was built on an ashram property to house the ashram children. It was called 'the kids' hut' and hailed as the ultimate solution to the accommodation problem posed by the children of parents who worked in the ashram. Henceforth all children of ashramites would live in the kids' hut. Double-decker bunks with two small storage shelves were built-in all around the walls, leaving a large open space in the middle for play. The kids' hut was a nightmare for Peter. He read a lot and was a child in need of privacy and periods of quiet. He also had a lot of Lego and took great delight in building very complex structures with it. Kylie seemed to have been born with a natural respect for his Lego constructions, for although she sat and watched him build, she never interfered or broke anything he made. In the kids' hut there was no privacy and nothing was sacred. Not only would the structures he so painstakingly made and kept on the end of his bunk be destroyed by other kids, but, worse still, he would return from the ashram to find his Lego gone. Peter did not cry easily, but he cried many bitter tears in the kids' hut.

Peter and Kylie continued to run wild with the other kids. They sometimes came to see me in the booking office and I attended to their hair and clothes in the evenings, but there were days when we did not see each other at all. I had become close friends with a nursing nun who had cared for my dad on the night his ulcer haemorrhaged. Maria had left the convent after eighteen years of service and when I met her again she was a sannyasin. Once, Kylie came by to announce her intention of travelling to Ireland with Maria and, as I had no objections, she persuaded Roger to buy her a ticket and take her to Mumbai to catch the plane. She spent three months in Ireland with Maria and her family on their farm. Another time, Kylie came to show me her newly pierced ears. She had gone to Mahatma Gandhi Road by herself and for a couple of rupees had had her ears pierced with the pieces of wire that now hung from her earlobes, the ends twisted together to form rings. Afraid of infection, I insisted we change them for gold hoops which I bought that same day, unaware that every Indian girl has her ears pierced as Kylie's were. Changing the wires was well nigh impossible, and horribly painful.

To my knowledge, no children were born in the ashram to ashram residents, a situation that would one day lead to a letter in an Oregon newspaper, charging that sannyasins ate their babies. The truth is much simpler, and less gory. Although in public

Bhagwan spoke eloquently about the innocence and beauty of children, he wanted no new additions to the number of children in the ashram. Children were a nuisance and a distraction to their parents. They were not, could not, be committed as their parents were, and Bhagwan wanted only committed disciples. He gave children sannyas, but only to humour their parents. If a woman became pregnant and asked Bhagwan what she should do, she was told to abort and sterilise. It was never said publicly. It was a discreet message delivered to the pregnant woman via the main office.

In Pune hundreds of men and women were sterilised. Sterilisations became so popular they were carried out en masse on ashram property. I myself, ever devout and ever ready to prove my devotion, was sterilised as one of a group of eight women. I already had children but most of the other women did not. Young men who worked in construction and in the cafeteria, under the command of Mussolini's granddaughter, were systematically ordered off the job to go for a vasectomy.

Even had I not been sterilised, there was little chance of me becoming pregnant, as once I had moved away from Roger I led a reclusive life, as befitted a vestal virgin. Only rarely did I show interest in a man, and when I did, a night spent with him was usually enough to cool the ardour of both parties. It was usual to share a room with another person, or perhaps two or three other people. It is hard to give expression to romantic or erotic stirrings in the close proximity of uninvolved room-mates, who may be trying to sleep, or are themselves wrestling with the same problem with their bed companion. Not everyone was troubled by such niceties. When I subsequently moved to accommodation within the ashram itself, I was regularly woken by a young woman giving unfettered expression to her orgasmic ecstasy. Her abode was on the flat roof of a building so that her cries carried easily all over the ashram and became the stuff of many a bawdy joke. She had separated from her long-term lover, with whom she had enjoyed a comfortable private room, and may have been wanting to let him know that she was fine up there on the roof without him. I remained far, far removed from such antics and kept mostly to myself. It had one practical advantage: at a time when eighty-seven percent of the ashram population had venereal disease of one kind or another, I was one of the thirteen percent who did not.

When I moved within the confines of the ashram itself, it was to Vege Villas, a row of small rooms built in the former vegetable garden that backed onto Bhagwan's compound. It was at a time when the darshan of old had expanded into a spectacle known as 'energy darshan'. Although it was still possible to speak with Bhagwan, most people now opted for an energy darshan instead, which, as the name implies, was an exchange of energy rather than an exchange of words. Bhagwan had chosen a number of attractive young women (including the young lady on the roof) to act as mediums for him. At darshan they were uniformly dressed in long burgundy gowns gathered onto a sleeveless bodice. A number were present at darshan every night and sat together on the floor to the side of Bhagwan's chair. The recipient's name was called and the person came forward to sit at Bhagwan's feet. Bhagwan indicated to his mediums where they were to position themselves around the beneficiary. One or two might stand or kneel behind the person with their hands on the person's shoulders or head, others might be placed sitting or kneeling beside them. Once the fine details were in place Bhagwan might indicate to the remainder of his mediums to come and position themselves around the tableau. A small group of musicians were also a part of the new energy darshan. When everybody was in place, they began playing, and Bhagwan placed the fingers of his right hand on the person's forehead, on the third eye. Sometimes he would also reach over with his left hand to lay it on the forehead of one of his mediums. Then the lights went out and the music rapidly rose to a crescendo, all but drowning out the ecstatic cries of recipient and mediums. The people sitting on the patio were also expected to abandon themselves to the energy, which they happily did, resulting in a state that could be accurately described as general pandemonium. It was a far cry from earlier days of quiet respect and piety.

During energy darshan the lights were turned out throughout the ashram. It became popular for people to gather within the confines of the ashram for the period of darshan so they could also partake of the energy. Maria liked to come to my room in Vege Villas, where she would lie on my bed for the duration of the blackout. Sometimes she would fall asleep there, to wake again at dawn. She lived outside the ashram and it was not unusual for her to crawl into my bed to spend a night close to the master. Years later I learned that people thought we were a lesbian couple, but alas, we were just two chaste nuns basking in the glow of the master's aura.

Although we never talked about it, all three of us younger Paul girls apparently imagined one of us had to be a nun. It must have been a virtuous childish idea that formed during our years of attending mass and convent school, and listening to stories of saints and martyrs. And didn't we have a debt to pay to God for letting Rosemary live? Conscious or not, we no doubt carried the conviction that by becoming nuns we would be pleasing our father, who was a very devout Catholic. As neither our father nor our mother ever gave the slightest indication of wanting any of us to be nuns, it can safely be said that the idea was the product of our own imaginations. Mary Lou gave it a go after Sue's failed attempt, but opted out after a year. Then I took up the baton.

My life in my convent was lived to the ordered rhythm of discourse, work and occasional darshans. There might be the odd trip down Mahatma Gandhi Road to the tailor for a new dress for Kylie or myself, or a T-shirt for Peter, or to a restaurant with Maria for palak paneer or alu gobi, but by far the greater part of my life was spent within the ashram. I read a lot, but only Bhagwan's books. I never read a newspaper, so I knew nothing of what was happening in the outside world, nor did I want to know. The ashram was my world.

Other sannyasins were not like me. Many travelled throughout India and Nepal, paid no attention to being a vegetarian and regularly skipped discourse. They read all kinds of books, listened to the BBC and kept in touch with their friends back home. I all but ignored the letters my parents wrote, deigning to write once in a while to point out to them the error of their ways and to send Dad Bhagwan books, impressing on him the good fortune we had to have a true master in our midst.

11

So determinedly had I distanced myself from my parents, it came as a complete surprise when, in early 1981 I was suddenly and inexplicably seized by the desire to see them. After agonising for some time, I wrote to Bhagwan to ask if I could go home to visit my parents. The message came back: Go for one month and return. I did not think to take the children, convinced as I was that the commune was the perfect place for them.

When the high priest heard I was going to Australia he came to me with a small shopping list. Could I bring him a large feather pillow, a gold watch for his current girlfriend, and a couple of other small things? He did not offer me any money to cover the cost of his requests. Nor did the ashram when I was asked to bring back an electric typewriter and a number of medical supplies. I was, of course, happy to pay for everything myself, even if buying a gold watch for someone else's girlfriend did strike me as odd, particularly as I did not own one myself.

Arriving in Perth, I stayed with the sannyasin friend who was storing our tea-chests. I spent the first couple of days conscientiously buying all I had been asked to bring back, before calling my parents to let them know I was in Australia and would be coming down to Busselton on the bus the following morning. Perhaps it was seeing them never waiver in their love for Rosemary all those years when she ran away and was so wild and wilful that gave me the impression they would never turn their back on any of their children. Perhaps I was checking in to see if my sense of them was correct. I need not have worried.

It was as though I had never left. They treated me with the same loving kindness and affection they had always shown me, and made no comments about my long orange robes and mala and long hair. We went fishing and swimming as we had always done, and avoided any mention of India, except to talk about the children. I did not tell them that Roger and I had separated and that we were no longer living as a family. I pretended everything was normal, as did they. Many years later Mum told me she and Dad always believed I would eventually get Bhagwan out of my system, and they were giving me an unspoken message that they would be there for me when I did. Although I would never have admitted it, I loved being with them again and was sad to leave.

But Bhagwan had said I should return in a month and I did not consider staying longer. Mum and Dad drove me to Perth the day before I was to leave and we stayed overnight with Rosemary and Tony. Rosemary was very affectionate towards me and I was glad to see her again. In the middle of the night I woke with a feeling of foreboding. It was as though a dark threatening spirit were in the house. It was so tangible that for a time I wanted to climb out of the window and run away.

Not long after my return, Bhagwan stopped talking. That is, he stopped speaking publicly.

'Enough of you are ready now to commune with me in silence,' he told us, and stayed out of sight in his compound.

His empty chair was placed in its usual place in Buddha Hall every morning and we continued to sit on the floor before it, but he did not come. No white car drove slowly around to the back of the hall, crunching on the gravel and stopping behind the screen. No car door opened, and closed. And no Bhagwan appeared from behind the screen and wafted to his chair with his unmistakable ethereal gait. It was a terrible shock. Life revolved around listening to Bhagwan at discourse. That I might be ready to commune with him in silence was no comfort whatsoever. I was addicted to sitting in Buddha Hall every day listening to him speak. I was in mourning. I continued to sit in Buddha Hall every morning with others of my kind, supposedly communing in silence with the master, but it was not the same and life would never be the same again. My secure world was beginning to get cracks in it.

It was business as usual with other ashram activities. As there was no darshan, visitors were now assigned groups and individual sessions by people in the main office. Those wanting to take sannyas were accommodated by an unseen hand, their new name now coming to them typed on Bhagwan's letterhead. As time went by the number of visitors dwindled as word spread that Bhagwan, the heart of the whole operation, was no longer accessible.

I was sitting at my desk in the booking office one day, perhaps three months after Bhagwan had stopped speaking, when my boss called urgently for me and my colleagues to come outside. He was a quiet, retiring man not given to making speeches or raising his voice and we sprang to obey. As we approached him, he motioned discreetly towards Bhagwan's gate. The gate was open and the white armoured Rolls-Royce drove out. Unbelievably, it drove straight ahead, past our little group of four, down the promenade and out through the front gate. Was it a vision I saw of Bhagwan sitting in the back seat as the car rolled by? Where was he going? Instantly rumours began flying that Bhagwan had gone for medical treatment. Although nothing official was ever said, it was understood that he suffered from delicate health, which had probably contributed to his decision to stop speaking. It made sense that he should have gone to a clinic or something like that. I felt calmer and waited in happy expectation for his return. Little did I know that seven years were to pass before he would drive back through the front gate, and that by then I would be an outcast.

I waited patiently. He did not come back. There was no official word of his whereabouts. Soon an exodus began, at first a few people here and there, but then more and more began packing their bags and leaving. Roger decided to take the children to Australia for a holiday and asked me if I would like to come. No, I was holding vigil, unable and unwilling to grasp that Bhagwan had gone and would not be coming back. It was beyond my capacity to try to imagine what that might mean. I had left everything to come and live with him. He would not abandon me. I went to the kids' hut to help the children pack their cases. Peter's was already carefully packed with boxes of Lego. Lying on top were two pairs of red trousers and two red singlets. That was all he considered precious enough to take with him. I said goodbye to the children, convinced that they, and Bhagwan, would soon return.

At some point an announcement was made that Bhagwan had gone to another country and that sannyasins should return to their own countries to await further news. It was not said which country he was in, but rumour had it that he was in America. I could not entertain the idea of going back to Australia again. There was no going back. I stayed, half hoping that my devotion would work some magic and Bhagwan would reappear. The booking office closed for lack of group leaders to run groups and visitors to participate in them. The myriad temporary structures that had been erected throughout the ashram were dismantled and the timber and iron sheeting sold. Buddha Hall was dismantled, and returned to the great oval concrete slab it had been when I had seen it for the first time. The carpentry and jewellery shop where the malas were made, the shop that sold robes and shawls and flat cushions and Bhagwan's books, vanished as though carried off by an army of ants. My world was literally being dismantled before my eyes. It was the most uncanny feeling. It was as though my house were being taken apart piece by piece around me until I stood there, exposed to the elements. I was in shock, seemingly riveted to the holy ground the ashram represented for me. I simply could not find the impulse to move. I was mesmerised by the methodical destruction of all that had been familiar to me and constituted my world. Even the booking office was dismantled and disappeared, as though it had never existed.

In September 1981 I received a message to come to Bhagwan's house, where I was shown into the holy of holies. There a woman I had often seen in the main office asked me what my plans were. When I said I had none, she said I was to buy a plane ticket to New York for a flight leaving a few days later. She said the last of the westerners would be leaving the ashram on that flight, and just a small group of Indian sannyasins would remain as caretakers. I was to buy myself some pants and shirts that would be more appropriate garb in America than the robes we were used to. She asked if I had any money I could make available, as a lot of money would be needed for the new project. I didn't ask any questions. It never occurred to me to ask what the new project was, or where it was. I felt Bhagwan was sending me a message and I was galvanised into action. Hardly stopping to take another look at what remained of the ashram, I arranged the ticket, bought clothes, gave the ashram whatever money I had left over, cleared my departure with the tax office, packed my few belongings in a suitcase and, in the company of a mixed group of people from all over the world, flew to Mumbai to catch the flight to America.

Oregon

12

I was exhausted when the plane touched down in New York. We were met by smiling sannyasins and driven to a very grand estate in New Jersey.

'Bhagwan is here,' they whispered as we drove up to a building adjacent to a castle.

I hardly dared believe it. Bhagwan here! I was so tired I could barely register what was going on. Our hosts showed us to comfortable rooms with mattresses ready made up, and I showered and fell into the nearest one.

'Bhagwan here! This must be paradise,' I thought as I fell asleep.

I was shaken out of a deep sleep by someone telling me to wake up and get dressed. It was the last thing I wanted to do. I wanted to sleep for a week. But I was being told to get up and be ready for departure in a couple of hours. Departure? I had only just arrived, and I still hadn't seen Bhagwan. And I was very tired. But the voice was insistent. I was to get up and get dressed and have breakfast. I would be leaving for Oregon in two hours. Tickets would be handed out in the van taking us to the airport. Another plane trip was the last thing I wanted and it was with a degree of irritation that I climbed out of bed and headed for the bathroom.

'Oh well,' I thought, 'I'll catch up on my sleep in Oregon,' without really knowing what I would be doing there or why I was going there at all.

It was another long day and I began to lose track of time completely. The flight across the country was followed by a long drive. Our route took us along a great river before leaving it behind to continue uphill into dry stony country with sparse vegetation and very few inhabitants. Then the van left the paved road and drove downhill on a narrow gravel road. The hillsides were dotted with a kind of tree I had never seen before. 'Junipers,' said the driver when I asked what they were. It struck me as odd that there were no other varieties of tree, only juniper. In fact there was not much of anything else at all. It was rocky, inhospitable terrain with a certain rugged beauty.

'It is all ours,' said the driver, making a large sweeping motion with his hand. 'One hundred and twenty-six square miles.'

I was so tired I couldn't take in what he was saying. One hundred and twenty-six square miles of junipers? We were in the middle of nowhere with no sign of civilisation anywhere and all I wanted to do was sleep.

Finally the road levelled out and a couple of humble buildings came into view. We seemed to have arrived at a ranch. There were a couple of houses and a large barn, and a few tents pitched close by. Red-clad people emerged from the buildings as the vehicle came to a halt.

'Welcome to the Big Muddy!' said the smiling man who opened the door.

I and my fellow travelers stepped out into the dust. With some surprise I registered that many of the people standing around were familiar to me. They were wearing red clothes so they must be sannyasins. But they wore regular clothes and the men were clean-shaven and had short hair. Nobody was wearing a robe. That was it! I knew them from the ashram in Pune! A flood of recognition and a wave of relief. Smiles and nods and chuckles at the bewilderment of yet another van load of newcomers. Then a meal and a shower and bed. My night quarters were in the barn on one of a row of mattresses. It was bliss to get horizontal again, and to sleep.

Early next morning there was a buzz of activity in the barn. I ignored the movement all around me. I was not ready to get up and gave myself permission to sleep in, my weary brain reasoning that I had come a long way in the last two days and was in need of more sleep. But no. Someone shook me awake and insisted I get up and come to breakfast. I resisted, saying I was not hungry but tired.

'Bhagwan is coming tomorrow,' she said, 'you are needed to help clean his house.'

Any other time I would have been excited and honoured, but I was so exhausted it was with resentment that I complied. My bad temper accompanied me throughout the day. I was shocked at my own apathy and complete disinterest in the hygiene of Bhagwan's house, and sometime in the late afternoon I slipped away and went back to my mattress in the barn. I had no interest in eating or company. I just wanted to sleep.

Fourteen hours later I opened my eyes and was ready to take an interest in my surroundings. All around me people were stirring. A murmur of excitement filled the air. It was infectious. Gone was my hesitation and ill will of the previous day. Bhagwan was coming today! I was up and dressed in no time and skipped over to breakfast like a happy child. People ate down their food and hurried off to take care of the thousand last-minute things that needed to be done. My name was on the list to report to Bhagwan's house for cleaning. It was as though I had never been there before. I went to my work with vigour, washing and wiping, wiping and washing, and washing and wiping again.

His house was a prefabricated structure that had been transported to the site and put together there. A team of gardeners had done their best to create a mini oasis around it but time constraints prevented a garden of any size and the gully was dry and dusty. Bhagwan was said to be sensitive to dust, so it was the job of the cleaners to remove every last dust particle from his house. I was assigned an area outside which I washed over and over, like one possessed. Then our supervisor shooed us all away and we returned to the barn to clean ourselves, in readiness for the arrival of the master. I no longer remember what kind of car he arrived in, but he arrived. He was driven up to his spotless house and he walked in and took up residence.

There was a chill in the air that spoke of approaching winter. It would soon be too cold to be sleeping out in tents. Housing was needed, and fast. With breathtaking speed, roads were cut to new housing sites and pads leveled, and a veritable caravan of prefabricated houses began rolling into the valley. The telephone on the ranch was a party line, a clearly untenable situation for such a dynamic undertaking as was in progress. A trailer was set up in Antelope, the sleepy hollow that constituted the last frontier before the descent through the juniper-studded hills to the Big Muddy.

I had been helping in the cook house since my arrival. The young Indian woman who had given me my first job in the ashram dropped in one day to tell me I was needed to answer the telephone in Antelope. Her name was Sheela. She was to be seen all over the place and seemed to have her finger on the pulse of the entire operation. People said she was Bhagwan's new secretary, his former secretary, the tiny Indian woman, having apparently finally been swallowed by the chair in the main office.

So I moved out of the barn to the trailer in Antelope, along with two other people, one of whom was destined to become the mayor of the city that was beginning to take shape out on the Big Muddy. Although I was sad to be so far away from Bhagwan, the truth is that the ranch was so huge the master was even more inaccessible than he had been in Pune. His compound was built in a secluded gorge branching off the main valley. There was no more walking by his gate as I had done every day for years. There were no more darshans. There were no more discourses. Sheela sometimes took him on a little tour in the car to show him the progress that was taking place, and he might have her stop so he could greet the workers, but that was all.

Sheela came to the trailer almost every day to make phone calls and use the fax machine. She and the future mayor had long involved discussions with whoever she might have brought with her, about permits and buying machinery and more housing and getting phone lines down to the ranch, and where to find reliable suppliers. My job was to answer incoming calls and take messages. When Sheela came I made her cups of tea, shielded phone calls for her and ran errands. On her instruction I befriended an old couple who lived in a trailer on the edge of town. She would send me to visit with them to find out what people were saying about us, and about Bhagwan. I liked them. It was like visiting with old neighbours back home. Sheela talked a lot about Bhagwan and I began to understand that she met with him every day in his house.

One day Sheela was unusually agitated when she came down to use the phone. That day Bhagwan must have tired of being cooped up like a prize cock in a cage and decided to drive out and see the world. Together with his young English companion, Vivek, he took the white armoured Rolls-Royce which had been brought from India, and drove out along the county road towards Antelope. Now I am not sure that Bhagwan had ever driven a car in his life, but even if he had, an armoured Rolls-Royce is not a good choice of vehicle for a jaunt on a mountainous unpaved road in central Oregon. Not only is it unusually long, it is also extremely heavy. Just opening the door requires a feat of strength. It must have given him problems of control for hardly had he set off on his adventure than he collided head on with a loaded cement truck coming down to the ranch. He was lucky. Although the armour buckled, it withstood the impact without injury to the occupants of the car. But now Bhagwan had the taste of freedom. He wanted a more comfortable car, not so heavy, easy to get around in. He wanted a regular Rolls-Royce.

And so the Rolls-Royce saga began. Sheela procured catalogues for him and he made his choice. Soon afterwards a truck rolled into the ranch with a Rolls-Royce inside, or was it two? The second one may have come a week or two later. At the height of his collector's passion he liked to order them two and three at a time. He began driving out every day, leaving his disciples at home building their dreams. It caused a lot of trouble in the neighbourhood for a Rolls-Royce is a provocatively ostentatious vehicle in central Oregon where almost everyone drives a pick-up truck with a rifle or two mounted in the back.

Bhagwan was a terrible driver and he paid no heed to speed limits. That first winter on a cold snowy day the old man from the trailer at the edge of town pulled up in his pick-up and came in to announce,

'Your guru is off the road up the hill.'

There was just myself and one of the accountants, Savita, in the office that day. We were without a car so I asked the old man if he would be kind enough to take us to the scene of the accident. I called into the ranch to let Sheela know before we took off. The old man drove us through town and uphill towards the high desert country. Low cloud hung over everything and visibility was very poor. We were quite a way from Antelope when we came round a curve and our driver pointed off to the right.

'There he is,' he said.

The Rolls-Royce had failed to take the curve and must have literally flown straight ahead to where it now stood among the rocks fifteen metres from the road. We two women jumped out and ran down to the car. Bhagwan sat behind the wheel, clearly very annoyed that it would not obey its gearbox and get back on the road. Though he was wearing a long knitted robe, neither he nor his companion were dressed for the cold. Savita convinced him that the only thing to do was to leave the car there and to come back to the office in the pick-up and wait there for a second car to be brought from the ranch.

There were other similar incidents so that it was soon considered necessary to take an escort car along to pull him out of the ditches and scare off inquisitive, sometimes aggressive locals. The escort car was a large off-road vehicle and was equipped for all emergencies. A mechanic was always on board and, in time, an armed guard joined the crew. It drove far enough ahead of the Rolls-Royce to give Bhagwan the impression that he was the only one on the road. It was also equipped with a two-way radio and when a two-way was installed at the Antelope office, the escort would radio ahead to us so we had time to go out and stand by the roadside to wave to Bhagwan as he drove by. It was the highlight of my day and a bonus that more than compensated for having to live in Antelope.

One day I received a letter from Dad telling me Rosemary had cancer of the liver. I felt strangely removed from the implications of this news. I did not know anything about cancer of the liver but somewhere I understood that Rosemary was dying. It never occurred to me to go and see her. It seemed to be something happening far away that had nothing to do with me. Instead I sent her a picture of Bhagwan and told her to look into his eyes. The idea was that she would die happy if she did that. Using the same logic that if you were baptised a Catholic you would go to heaven, I thought to ensure a place for my dying sister in nirvana, the new paradise, with a picture of Bhagwan. It was the hopeless superstitious gesture of a desperate kid sister. Thirty years earlier I would have sent her medals and holy pictures.

Rosemary died on 16 December 1981. She was forty-four years old. I did not go to her funeral, nor did I write to her husband or her children expressing my sorrow for their loss. I didn't feel sorrow. I didn't feel anything. I pushed it as far away as possible. The physical distance from Australia and the emotional distance from my family helped me push it so far away I could pretend it had never happened. Roger was still in Australia with Peter and Kylie, but so successful was I in my denial that I did not even think to let them know that Rosemary had died.

In time telephones were installed at the ranch and Sheela did not come so often. Once I began living at the ranch and commuting to Antelope every day, I would often drop in at Sheela's house in the evening to be there when she returned from visiting Bhagwan. I was not the only one who was hungry for news of him. Others came, eager to know how he looked that day and to hear what he had said. We sat at Sheela's feet and listened in rapture to her recounting her visits with him. Bhagwan spoke of his vision of transforming the Big Muddy into a great 'Buddhafield', and gave her very specific instructions as to how she was to go about it. He took an interest in every detail of progress so that Sheela's meetings with him were a daily debriefing, during which he would give her directions for the next steps, which she would in turn pass on to those who were to carry them out. She was the master's voice. My devotion to the master overflowed onto her. For me she was an extension of him, and more – I could speak with her, travel in her car with her, drink a cup of tea with her. She was accessible to me in a way the master never was. I revered her and felt proud and privileged to serve her. In time she would become my substitute master.

Sitting at Sheela's feet I also heard things I did not want to hear. I was devastated when she reported Bhagwan was displeased that she was baulking at ordering the three new Rolls-Royces he wanted. When she tried to appease him with one, pointing out that the mortgage payments on the six-million-dollar property and daily expenses were astronomical, he had said that if it was too much trouble for his disciples to come up with the money, then he would just close his eyes and disappear. He did not need the cars, he said, but they helped him stay in his body, a difficult enough thing but something he was willing to do for us. We women wept and hugged each other and doubled our efforts to raise the money to fulfil his wishes.

In the beginning Sunday was a day of rest. However, when a young man died in a swimming accident in the river, Bhagwan cancelled the day off. From then on everyone worked seven days a week, ten hours a day, and more. But we were spending money, not making it. The enormous amount of money needed to finance the massive project of building the infrastructure and buildings that were to constitute the city of Rajneeshpuram came from sannyasins all over the world. Particularly in Europe, but also in Australia and America and elsewhere, sannyasins were exhorted to organise themselves into communes and run businesses for the support of Bhagwan's Buddhafield. They copied the Oregon model, providing food and board to their workers, who worked long hours without pay, running very successful discotheques and restaurants. The profits were channelled to Oregon.

There were also those very rich who contributed generously when informed that Bhagwan was threatening to close his eyes and disappear because money was not forthcoming. The implication was that the money was needed for the Buddhafield project. Mention of cars was generally avoided.

Bhagwan eventually extended his tastes to include diamond-studded watches and jewellery, designer sunglasses and wild clothes. He was very creative in getting what he wanted. He turned out to be a very expensive guru, but his people loved him and kept coming up with the money for as long as they could. When the traditional austere white robe he had worn in India no longer fitted his newly acquired flamboyant style, it was replaced, at first with knitted robes with matching caps and socks, and later with full flowing robes in velvet, silks and satins that would have been the envy of the French kings. In time his robes became like his cars in that he did not like to use the same one twice.

13

There was a downside to going as big as the Big Muddy. First, it was practically impossible to create clean living conditions with paved roads and walkways to keep the mud at bay. Every house had a mud room, where caked boots were deposited before entering the house. And second, people were scattered to the four winds and needed transport to get to the cafeteria, to work, to where they lived. People were moved around in vans and, more commonly, in the backs of utility trucks. Quite a few sannyasins from the early days could not make the transition from the intimacy and tranquillity of the Pune ashram to the vast open spaces of Oregon. Those spaces were rugged and unwieldy, and one was constantly exposed to the elements – icy winds and sleet and snow in winter, through the thaw mud of spring, to the heat and dust of summer. There was no place for nice clothes and gracious living, popping out to a restaurant for dinner, or down to the shops for a new dress. Add to that the fact that Bhagwan no longer gave darshan or discourse and lived in seclusion in the hills. And then there was the sheer magnitude of the undertaking that required prolonged hard work and dedication.

It was pioneer work and not everyone is cut out to be a pioneer. It is little wonder then that more than a few long-term followers chose to leave the burgeoning Buddhafield, never to return. Some left because of the raw conditions, some left because their work no longer brought them in contact with Bhagwan, and some because the passion of their devotion had burned itself out.

My devotion burned brighter than ever. Not long after arriving at the ranch, each of the workers was invited to a private audience. Bhagwan sat in a room and we were ushered one at a time into his presence. When it was my turn and I sat at his feet, he told me we would build a Buddhafield and that there was much work to be done, and he encouraged me to work hard. Then he gave me a small gold ring with a blue gemstone in it and placed it on my finger. And then he placed his hand on my forehead. I was afire with the belief that I was the follower of a great master destined to save mankind. Just as the Jesus of my childhood had come to save the world, so now Bhagwan had come to create a vast energy field in the wilderness that would impact on the whole world and raise mankind out of its misery. I was prepared to put up with a little discomfort to be at the vanguard of such noble work.

There were never enough people to do all that had to be done. All over the world sannyasins were waiting impatiently for an invitation to participate in the project. The moment a new trailer was in place, it would be filled with new arrivals. As in the ashram in Pune, each room had two or three people assigned to it. At first Americans had been given priority, but now foreigners began arriving. Among the first of them were Roger and the children. Convinced that the Big Muddy would be our home for the rest of our lives, I had asked many times for permission for them to join me. In spring it was finally granted. I was so relieved and happy to see them again. Peter was now thirteen years old and Kylie was eleven. Both had grown noticeably in the ten months since I had last seen them. They chattered about the places their father had taken them to in Western Australia and about their cousins, and fishing and prospecting for gold with their grandparents. Roger eyed off the rugged hills and remarked that they probably had gold in them too. After an excited reunion they were all, as before, assigned accommodation in different houses. I was by then living on the ranch, but continued to commute to Antelope.

It had quickly been recognised that the non-Americans posed a problem. One could perhaps argue that they were not really working because they were not being paid and therefore not taking away a paid job from an American citizen. But even so, the tourist visa on which most of us entered the country was for a limited time only. It was usual in India to solve visa problems with baksheesh, but that was not the way in America.

On legal advice, Roger and I and the children went to the immigration office in Portland and Roger applied for a business visa for the family. We were dressed in our orange and red clothes and Roger explained that he would be doing geological work out on the Big Muddy. Naïvely satisfied that the necessary steps had been taken to ensure that we could stay there for the rest of our lives, we returned to the ranch. On the way back I talked nonstop about the importance of our complete support for the establishment of the Buddhafield. With typical fervour I argued that it was going to be our home now. We were completely taken care of and wouldn't need any money of our own any more, and the project was desperately in need of money. By the time we got back I had talked Roger into donating all the money we had and was well pleased with myself. He was not enthusiastic about it, but he arranged for the transfer of the thirty thousand dollars that remained from the sale of the shop. Now we had nothing. At the time there was nothing to spend money on anyway. Shops had not yet been built. We had a place to live; basic necessities like food and clothing and transport were provided. We had no rent or utilities to pay. It never occurred to me that I might want to take a trip anywhere, let alone go home to see my parents. I didn't even think about birthday presents for Peter and Kylie. When my parents sent me a hundred dollars for my birthday I donated it. My whole security was the master and my belief that he would take care of us.

On Bhagwan's instructions, a school with accredited teachers was organised for the children. The fast-growing community was under observation from the outside world and it was considered necessary that state education guidelines be seen to be followed meticulously. I became involved in planning the school curriculum and class schedules. I was a firm believer in whatever new ways were being proposed by Bhagwan and genuinely keen that the children receive an education at this time of their lives. Bhagwan wanted the children to be productive workers from an early age. To that end they were to be given hands-on experience in as many areas of activity as possible. The children attended school in the morning, and in the afternoon they were assigned work in the different departments, under the supervision of a department employee. Subjects learned on the job, like mathematics in the accounts department, or domestic science in the cafeteria, were carefully listed and credits given. In fact the children did learn a wide range of skills. As teenagers, and later as young adults, many of them showed an enviable ability to tackle and solve problems with creativity and alacrity.

For the duration of his stay in Oregon, Peter worked in the electronics department. When he was sixteen he won a state-wide competition with an innovative lightshow he built for the kids' disco. Kylie did a number of different jobs. At various times she worked in the bakery, on the farm with the chickens, in the garage where vehicles were maintained and repaired, in photography, and later as an air hostess for the commune airline flying between Portland and the ranch.

After more than a year of answering phones in the Antelope office, I was assigned work on the ranch. A long two-storeyed building had been built in the downtown area of the emerging city. The ground floor was divided into shops and a restaurant, and above were the administrative offices. As could be expected, there was a large purchasing department, an accounts department, a secretariat where correspondence to Bhagwan and requests for sannyas were dealt with, a sales department for books and tapes, a planning department, the beginnings of city hall, and a rapidly growing legal department. It was to this legal office that I was recruited, as assistant to the manager, a job that would bring me in close contact with Sheela again. At the time the legal department's duties were expanding exponentially to deal with the obstacles being laid in the way by planning laws and people who did not recognise the vision of a Buddhafield but rather held that a rurally zoned area was a place where hundreds of cattle might live, not hundreds of people. Efforts to have the zoning changed were being fiercely opposed by citizens calling themselves the *Thousand Friends of Oregon.*

The speed with which the development on the Big Muddy took place unsettled local people. The constant caravan of trucks carrying prefabricated houses, building materials, cement and foodstuffs into central Oregon, and the sheer number of permit applications made to the local planning office in the Dalles, gave them the impression their territory was being invaded by a tribe of red-clad people. Rumours were rife. Initially good-humoured efforts were made to calm people's fears, but as opposition grew and solidified and organised itself, Bhagwan went on the offensive. In doing so he discovered a very effective way of keeping his followers together and working hard in the wide open spaces of the ranch.

He had Sheela call a meeting to deliver a message to us all.

'We are a minority,' he said. 'We have to be assertive and one hundred percent together to survive. We want to set a precedent. For the first time in world history we will not allow a Jesus to be persecuted!'

Taking a page from Hitler's propaganda minister Goebbels, Bhagwan created an outside enemy: *Them.* With time *Them* came to include the people of central Oregon, government agencies and planning boards, politicians and law-enforcement agencies, in fact anyone who dared to question anything that was being done at the ranch. *Them* were against *Us* and would stoop to any cunning tricks to stop the master's vision being realised. At first it was a sort of game, but as time went by it became more earnest, until eventually a paranoid siege mentality would prevail throughout the commune.

Sheela spent hours with Bhagwan every evening receiving detailed instructions, not only for every aspect of commune life, but also for her public appearances. As opposition increased, he instructed Sheela to continue to be charming where it paid off, but outrageous and impolite towards critics and those who sought to thwart his plans. He watched every TV interview she gave, and she read him newspaper articles and summarised radio reports of her appearances. Like the producer he was, he criticised her performances, telling her where she could have done better and giving her clear instructions for her next public appearance. He was always an instigator, never a mediator and was very pleased when a major TV network cut her microphone in the middle of an interview because she continued to swear after being warned not to. She would one day outrage Australians with a 'tough titties' response to a question as to what she thought of local opposition to a Rajneeshee project in Western Australia. Bhagwan was pleased with the furore it caused, his maxim being that all publicity was good, but bad publicity was very good.

Once the city had been incorporated and the mayor installed in office, Sheela's provocative, irreverent public appearances were a source of great anxiety to the mayor, who wished to foster a public image of a model city of law-abiding citizens. He pleaded with her to take a more conciliatory attitude in public. Finally Sheela took him to see Bhagwan. The mayor argued passionately for a more temperate approach. Bhagwan was very angry with him and told him in no uncertain terms that he, Bhagwan, knew what he was doing and that it was his wish that Sheela be as confronting and controversial as possible.

'Everything Sheela does she does because that is what I want her to do,' he said, 'You are not to question her.'

14

Bhagwan had entered America on a medical visa: it did not give him the right to stay indefinitely. Among possible alternatives was a visa category for religious leaders, but to be a religious leader there must be a religion to lead. Bhagwan had always spoken vehemently against organised religion, but necessity is the mother of invention and he now went to work inventing a religion.

Modelling his religion on long-established organisations, he called it Rajneeshism. He dictated his bible to Sheela over a series of evenings, calling it the Book of Rajneeshism. He decreed that it be printed and bound in red binding, perhaps a joke on Mao's little red book. He created a priesthood and named dozens of sannyasins to it. There were different categories, the names of which I no longer remember. I was named to the category of priests who could perform the ceremonies of marriage and death. He named Sheela to a priestly race and appointed her the temporal head of the Church. Whenever she appeared in public in her religious capacity, she was to wear red satin robes and a red satin scarf on her head.

With the religion in place, the next thing was to solicit letters from people proclaiming Bhagwan to be the head of his religion. An intensive effort to contact hundreds of university lecturers, businessmen, artists, authors, musicians, lords and ladies, and famous people all over the world, resulted in a formidable number of letters, some on very impressive letterheads, pouring into the office. When the day came to take these proofs of Bhagwan's authenticity as a religious leader to the Immigration and Naturalisation Services (INS) in Portland, there were metre-high piles of filed letters. The press was alerted and I was present when, in the glare of news cameras, we stacked the letters on the steps of the INS and Sheela stood there and demanded that Bhagwan be granted the visa to which he was so clearly entitled.

An additional advantage of the new religion was that those of priestly castes permitted to conduct marriage ceremonies could register themselves as ministers of religion with the county, and the marriages performed by them were then recognised as being legal. I myself was married by one of our new priests.

Roger's application for a business visa was never processed. It was apparently put into a wait-and-see file, while the authorities tried to get a handle on what was happening down there in central

Oregon. In 1983 I was advised that Roger and I should divorce and find American partners to marry. With a cunning that was beginning to permeate all our dealings with authority, I applied for a divorce in Perth. When it came through, Roger borrowed some blue jeans from someone and went to Los Angeles with his American girlfriend to get married and apply for residency as a regular member of society. They were a genuine couple so they were not being deceptive, other than keeping silent about their affiliation with the ranch.

A young man was suggested to me as a good candidate for a husband. After spending a few hours with him I decided to take things into my own hands. I sought out an old acquaintance from my days as a cleaner in Pune. He and I had mopped Buddha Hall together and we had always got on well. I knew he had a steady girlfriend and that he had up until that point managed to resist all attempts to marry him off to a foreigner. We discussed my problem at length and he agreed to marry me. We were both clear that it was to help me out and neither of us was in any way interested in a relationship.

It was decided by others that we should make our application to the INS in Portland, as sannyasins living on the ranch. To add weight to our application, it was suggested my new husband adopt my children. As far as I was concerned it was all part of the charade and did not change anything at all, and that's what I told Roger and the children. My whole focus was on securing visas that would allow us all to stay in the Buddhafield. I was deeply committed to Bhagwan's vision being realised and by that point I had all my eggs in his basket. Roger, on the other hand, was very upset and only agreed to the adoption because he felt obliged to support me as a fellow sannyasin. The very first thing he did when I left Bhagwan was to ask me to sign papers allowing him to reverse it.

15

Tax laws in America made it necessary to set up a host of independent corporations, each covering a specific aspect of activities on the ranch. The overview was held by Savita, who answered to Sheela, who answered to Bhagwan. Money coming in from abroad was channelled to where it was needed through the appropriate corporation. At some point Sheela appointed me treasurer of the Church corporation, Rajneesh Foundation International (RFI), and I began attending court proceedings as the representative of the Church, which was a party in most of the legal cases making their way through the courts. It was a purely paper appointment. I had not the slightest idea about the workings of RFI and was not encouraged to find out. From time to time I would be asked to sign a letter, and at festival times I would be asked to sign cheques for large sums of money, but no other demands were made of me in my capacity as treasurer.

Money was a limited resource, although the impression given by the massive investments in infrastructure and buildings may have veiled that fact, and some may have forgotten it altogether. After the initial explosion of building activity, more careful planning was needed to continue and maintain development. Priorities needed to be set. It was here that the rift between Bhagwan and Sheela began and continued to grow. Bhagwan wanted his personal desires fulfilled immediately. He was not interested in postponing the purchase of another two or three Rolls-Royces so the mortgage could be paid. While he siphoned off the cream, Sheela and Savita juggled to feed the child of his making from the increasingly thin milk that remained.

Sheela's real office was her bedroom. The only furniture in it was a double bed and one chair. Sheela would sit on her bed or on the chair to receive visitors, who sat on the carpeted floor. One evening I went down to her house to deliver a document to her. I found her in her bedroom with Savita and the personnel manager. She looked up and nodded as I opened the door but continued talking to the other two. I stood there hesitantly. I seemed to have walked in on a very intense discussion. Sheela was talking about a watch of some sort that Bhagwan wanted. She was very angry about it. Savita was clearly upset too. I slipped out and closed the door behind me. I did not want to hear. I did not want anything to intrude on my image of Bhagwan as perfect.

In the days that followed, Sheela continued to be upset about the watch and spoke about it so often that I could not avoid hearing. It seemed that a woman of considerable means had approached Bhagwan's companion Vivek and given her a brochure of a diamond-studded watch, with the request that she show it to Bhagwan. Of course the moment Bhagwan saw it he wanted it, which wouldn't have been so bad except that it cost a million dollars. Sheela refused to buy it for him. Now if there was one thing Bhagwan did not like it was to be told no. That refusal was Sheela's death knell. From that day on a new dynamic came into play.

It had always been that Bhagwan's secretary was the go-between between him and his people. She was not a secretary in the sense of taking shorthand and typing up memos and so on. Her function was more that of bringing him news and information and relaying his words back to the people. In addition, it was the secretary's task to set things in motion in order that his wishes be fulfilled and his instructions carried out. If someone wanted Bhagwan to know something, or to ask him a question or give him something, they would contact Sheela and she would relay the information to Bhagwan and bring back the response. It should perhaps be mentioned that Bhagwan kept a strict separation between work and play. His secretary did not share his bed, however much she may have wished to.

In fact the lady with the watch brochure had brought it first to Sheela, who declined to take it to Bhagwan. Unperturbed, the lady cultivated channels of her own and it can be no surprise to hear that she ultimately replaced Sheela as Bhagwan's secretary. For not only did she get the watch brochure to Bhagwan, but with it she gained access to him. She soon became a regular independent visitor to his house, and eventually she married his doctor. If there was one thing Bhagwan liked, it was a millionairess and her friends. They had the price of a ticket to sit at his feet, talk with him and bask in his presence.

Bhagwan was a master at playing one person off against another. He played on the jealousy between Sheela and Vivek with such virtuosity that Sheela was ready to kill the girl to save Bhagwan from her supposed mistreatment of him. It would not be unreasonable to suggest that may have been his intention for he wanted to be free of Vivek. Their relationship had deteriorated into depression and sullen insults, interspersed with regular angry exchanges. Vivek was a city girl and she hated the Big Muddy with its inhospitable terrain and its isolation from any form of pleasant diversion. Her jealous rages against his inclination to shapely young women taxed Bhagwan's patience such that he one day hit her across the face with his sandal, leaving her with a black eye. When she became more and more depressed, Bhagwan advised her to end her life. He complained constantly to Sheela that she made his life a hell. Sheela and Vivek were both young and could just as well have been friends. Instead they became rivals and gave Bhagwan the opportunity to play them off against each other. The game expanded to include the two households, so that while Vivek had no friend in Sheela's house, Sheela had no friend among the inhabitants of Bhagwan's house.

It was Bhagwan's constant complaints about Vivek that gave Sheela the idea to tap his room. Bhagwan suffered from diabetes. Feigning concern for his health and arguing the necessity that someone trustworthy be available to him at all times, Sheela convinced Bhagwan that a beeper should be wired into his room in order that he be able to contact her at any time of the day or night. At the same time she took the opportunity to have the telephones in his house tapped and a listening device installed in his room. He was not aware of it and Sheela justified it to herself and others as necessary for his protection. She had a receiving centre set up in a small room in her house and appointed two trusted people to listen to the tapes. I first came to know of it when Sheela took me into the room to listen to a tape of Bhagwan and Vivek having a row, the day he hit her. She wanted me to know how much Bhagwan was suffering from the unhappiness of his companion. I was so dismayed that Bhagwan should be exposed to the temper tantrums of the person I thought to be closest to him, I never thought to question that he had hit her, or the way in which the incident came to light. I concluded, as I always did when the truth intruded on my idyll, that these must be devices he was using to test my faith and spiritual growth.

Continuing to make use of the survival skills I had learned as a child, I had developed my own ways of avoiding impositions on the well-ordered precepts of my inner world. There was the tried and true, 'See no evil; hear no evil', which simply involved (mentally) shutting my eyes tightly, and putting my hands over my ears – the proverbial ostrich with its head in the sand – a favourite trick of small children who imagine that by closing their eyes they make the world go away. A further refinement of this was that I did not ask questions. I simply did not want to know. Holding grimly to the underlying deceit that the master has no self-interest at all, I would withdraw physically and/or mentally to avoid exposure to an unpleasant reality that could threaten my 'perfect' world, so painstakingly constructed under the auspices of the 'perfect' master.

16

Bhagwan was still not speaking publicly, but he could not remain hidden indefinitely if he wanted people to remain motivated to support the dream. So he created Master's Day. It was a device to boost morale and to raise much-needed capital. Even before hotels were built, a rudimentary Buddha Hall rose out of the mud in time for the first festival in July 1982. In order to accommodate the visitors, wooden platforms were built and set out on every available flat piece of land. Tents were erected on the platforms. Those tents constituted the entire accommodation for the first festival. Thousands of sannyasins came from all over the world to sit in silence with Bhagwan in the Buddhafield they were helping to finance.

The following year there was some limited hotel accommodation, tents and A-frames to house the festival visitors, and a restaurant or two. By the third Master's Day celebration the city of Rajneeshpuram boasted a two-acre Buddha Hall, a lively downtown with shops and restaurants, a large dam where people could swim, an airport with daily flights to Portland, a fleet of buses to transport people within the city itself, hotels and A-frame cabins, a newspaper and a casino.

In India Bhagwan had been a controversial figure long before he had begun giving sannyas. Hindu leaders were scandalised by his public utterances on free sex and his verbal attacks on many of the things their society held dear, but otherwise nobody took him too seriously, except perhaps the angry man who once threw a knife at him and missed. He was a colourful character in an essentially colourful country.

The United States of America was a different kettle of fish altogether. By the time the infrastructure was in place to receive paying visitors, relations with the neighbours and the State of Oregon were very poor. *Better Dead Than Red* bumper stickers could be seen on cars in the area and T-shirts depicting Bhagwan caught in the crosshairs of a riflescope were worn openly. The sannyasin community received phone calls and mail on a daily basis with threats to kill Bhagwan and bomb the city; road signs to the city were shot full of holes, and there were incidents of ranchers telling sannyasins to their faces that they were going to blow their heads off. These were people who didn't mince their words and who were wont to take things into their own hands.

As far as they were concerned, here was this foreigner who flaunted his wealth by driving around the countryside in a different Rolls-Royce every day, who attracted a horde of red-clad followers and had a secretary with a loud mouth. As if that wasn't enough, the intruder was moving his people into one of their towns and building a city out on the Big Muddy where who knew how many more of the red pest would live. They joined forces to combat what they perceived as a threat to their way of life.

The day came when it was considered too dangerous for Bhagwan to drive off the ranch any more. He postponed the decision as long as possible, but when incidents of obstacles being placed on the road and gunshots fired became increasingly numerous, he decided to withdraw back to the ranch. He was loath to be restricted again and so a massive road-building project got under way on the property to build him a road of his own to drive on.

With the completion of the road, Drive-By came into being. Now when Bhagwan went for a drive, sannyasins would stop whatever they were doing and gather by the side of the road to wave as he drove by. He drove slowly and smiled and waved back. Then some people began bringing musical instruments and playing and singing as he drove by. He liked that and sometimes stopped to conduct the music from the driver's seat. Occasionally, though infrequently, he might stop and roll down the window to exchange a few words with someone. During festivals he sometimes passed a small present to a favoured sannyasin through the window. He never drove alone. Vivek was always next to him in the passenger seat, except on those rare occasions when he took Sheela with him instead, to point out to her the young women he would like her to bring to him in the evening.

These young maidens were given to understand that they had been chosen by Bhagwan to be vessels for his transformative energy in the world. In order to facilitate the transfer of this energy from the master to themselves, they were instructed to wear no underwear and to clothe themselves in a loose flowing gown. Sheela chauffeured the young woman in question up to Bhagwan's house, and waited outside in the car to drive her back again.

As time went by and Rajneeshpuram had its own police force and security service, armed guards walked behind the car to augment the security car travelling in front. Sheela, or a trusted other, began walking beside his car with a revolver on her hip, and during festivals the Rajneesh helicopter swept overhead with an armed guard leaning out over the crowd with an Uzi at the ready.

It was the INS who provided the impetus for Bhagwan to begin speaking again. Ever since they had been obliged to issue him a visa as a religious leader, they had kept a close eye on him. Observing that Bhagwan did not speak to his people, they threatened to cancel his visa. At first he began teaching privately to a select group in his house, but eventually he began speaking publicly again in Buddha Hall. It was at a time when public opinion and dozens of lawsuits were exerting enormous pressures on the community. Bhagwan had always believed in using the press as a deterrent to the authorities taking any overt action against himself or the community, so when he resumed public speaking he also began inviting members of the press to private audiences.

While there were certain journalists who were considered enemies of the commune, the public relations department worked hard to maintain friendly relations with many other newspaper and TV reporters. It was they who toured the city to report on progress and interviewed Sheela, and Rajneeshee lawyers, and later Bhagwan. It was always a balancing act between being outrageous and being seen to be intelligent, thoughtful citizens protecting their human rights.

That's what Rajneeshees were doing when they voted their representatives to a majority on the school board in Antelope, effectively taking over the only school in town. They were exercising their human rights and their rights as voters. They were also carrying out the wishes of their master. As opposition to the building of a city down on the Big Muddy grew and progress threatened to bog down in a plethora of lawsuits, Bhagwan ordered a larger Rajneeshee presence in Antelope. It was his way of creating a bargaining chip, along the lines of 'Give us our city and we will leave you to yours'. Half the buildings in town were empty and for sale, so the best of them were bought and Rajneeshees moved into them. These sannyasins then began attending city council and school board meetings.

Faced with a school staffed by Rajneeshee teachers, the local people bused their children to school in another town. With the school in Rajneeshee hands, Bhagwan decreed that all the school-age children on the ranch should move to Antelope and attend school there. Parents organised a roster to go to Antelope in the evenings to feed and care for the children. For the duration of this arrangement I went to Antelope once a week to eat dinner with the children, to read them bedtime stories and treat them for lice when necessary. In the morning I made breakfast and helped them get ready for school, before kissing my own two children goodbye and returning to the ranch until the next week. It was a dark period for parents and children. Parents who had a problem with the arrangement were called to order. It was Bhagwan's wish. If they didn't like it they could take their children and go, a dictate that at least one couple with two small children followed.

Although I felt disturbed by what was happening, I continued to be unable to seriously question anything Bhagwan said. Knowing Peter and Kylie were not on the ranch left me with a sense of bereavement, but I told myself it was another test of my devotion and said nothing. They themselves found the arrangement far from satisfactory and were very happy when, a few months later, all the children were moved back to the ranch.

17

Early in 1984 Bhagwan raised a number of his sannyasins to the rank of *bodhisattva*. In other words, he declared them to be enlightened. Such a thing had never happened before. My name was not on the list. Savita's was, and the high priest's, and Vivek's, and Bhagwan's doctors, and many others who were either useful, rich or both. It was like being made a knight, or awarded an MBE or a Medal of Honour.

At the same time Bhagwan called Sheela, Savita and the personnel manager to his room and asked them to take over the running of the commune. They were to take care of the people and their physical needs, and his needs were henceforth to be met by a completely separate legal entity. He separated the secular from the spiritual or, in plain terms, he separated the needs of commune residents for housing and food and clothing from his personal needs. It was an accounting problem. A trust was to be formed to take care of his requirements, and monies coming from the communes in Europe were to be channelled into it. His millionairess and her friends would manage the trust, he said. As it turned out, not one trust but two were necessary to fulfill this instruction: the *Rajneesh Modern Car Collection Trust* and the *Rajneesh Jewellery Trust*.

A little later in the year, Bhagwan told Sheela that he would leave his body on Master's Day, 6 July, but did not reveal in which year, saying only that there was much work to be done. How long he stayed with his people would depend on how hard they worked. He spoke to her of an Armageddon scenario that only his people would survive because only he could guide them in making the necessary preparations. When the time was right he would explain how to prepare the underground refuge where his people would be safe until it was time for them to emerge and begin the new age of the new man. It sounded like science fiction to me. I didn't give it much thought as he was clearly talking about the dim distant future, but even so a part of me felt relieved to think that Bhagwan would take care of me and my children when the time came. Later he gave instructions as to how his legacy was to be managed after his death, naming many of his bodhisattvas to what were to be key positions in the new order of things. He also gave precise instructions for his funeral service and ordered that a crematorium be built.

One night in the summer of 1984 I was called from my bed and told Sheela needed me in Jesus Grove, which was the name Bhagwan had given to her house. In India I had learned the Indian way of making depilatory 'wax' with sugar and lemon juice cooked slowly to a honey-like consistency. Sheela must have caught wind of it because when I got down to the house I found she was going somewhere the next day and wanted me to wax her legs. A few weeks later Sheela directed me to move into her house. I was flattered. Whatever misgivings I had about living in such a busy household were quieted by my pride. It was like being invited to live in the master's house.

As with all the accommodation I was ever assigned in the commune, I shared a small room with another person, but this time I had a bed instead of a mattress on the floor. The room was at the far end of the house in the new wing, quite removed from Sheela's room, but from that day on I was at Sheela's beck and call, as were all those who lived in her house. The house had been extended a number of times and was like a small hotel. Thirty or forty people lived there, all of them in some way or another of service to Sheela. A few others lived in A-frames nearby.

Initially great pains were taken to apply for all the necessary permits and planning permissions; applications were meticulously prepared and queries answered. But as difficulties arose Bhagwan was of the opinion that things should be built as needed, and the county planning office could ask questions later, should they become aware of it. This attitude led to surprise inspections by county officials, and games of hide-and-seek and placing obstacles in the paths of county planners trying to carry out their inspections. It happened more than once that heavy machinery 'broke down' in inopportune places, forcing officials to continue on foot, or turn around and go home.

In August 1984 the City of Rajneeshpuram annexed land without the consent of the county. Shortly afterwards the county took out an injunction against the city, in an effort to force it to withdraw to its previous boundaries. Bhagwan had long since set his sights on controlling the planning process at the county level, but the injunction irritated him so much it now became top priority. He began pushing Sheela hard to come up with a scheme for taking over the county, in much the same way as had been done with the city of Antelope. A county election was set for November and

Rajneeshees should win it, he said. He even dictated speeches that the Rajneeshee commissioners would make when elected. But producing six thousand voters out of a hat to win a county election is not the same thing as winning a council election in a ghost town in the Oregon desert with a handful of voters. Try telling that to an angry master who won't take no for an answer.

At the time I moved into her house Sheela was becoming more and more manic. She no longer slept without medication and called daily meetings, demanding action and immediate solutions to the escalating problems. She had a devoted nurse attending to her day and night, who supplied her with medications to put her to sleep, to wake her up, to get her through the long days, and to deal with the throat infections and other physical problems that came in the wake of the unrelenting demands on her body. Bhagwan told Sheela the body was just a vehicle to support the spirit and she shouldn't hesitate to take whatever drugs were needed to keep her going and get her work done. The work was the most important thing. And that went for everyone else too.

Sheela assigned me to a newly formed group whose mandate it was to guard Bhagwan's house. We were led to understand that there was danger of the INS making a raid and snatching Bhagwan away. I took it very seriously and was honoured to defend my master. The security force was trained by two former members of the South African armed forces. They were very professional. We learned all there was to know about the care and use of the predominantly Colt revolvers and Uzi semi-automatics at our disposal. I had the advantage over most people of already being familiar with the use of firearms, which would lead Sheela to boast that I was their best marksman. Her glib tongue gave me an undeserved reputation that was to haunt me in the years to come.

Bhagwan's compound was already encircled by a mesh fence augmented by an electric fence, and armed guards stood at the gate. Now a watchtower was built directly above his house for the exclusive use of the new security force, which was separate from the gate guards and other security services. Security force members stood guard in the watchtower for two hours at a time, in shifts that moved forward an hour every twenty-four hours, all the while keeping up the long hours in their normal place of work. So if my shift was from 1 am to 3 am, I would set the alarm for 12.15 am, get up and get dressed, drink a quick cup of coffee and drive up to the house in time for the changing of the guard at 12.50 am. There were always two people on every shift. The compound was floodlit and with the help of binoculars we maintained watch in and beyond it. At the end of the shift I would drive back home and go back to sleep until it was time to get up and go to the office. The next evening my shift would begin an hour later. And so it went.

I became increasingly sleep deprived. I kept up a good face but I was beginning to fall apart. One day I was sitting with a group of colleagues discussing a legal problem when I lost it. I became very angry with the office manager. She was a gentle woman and not the kind of person one would normally be angry with. I stood up and shouted at her, then ran off in tears to my room. Sheela's nurse came and gave me a tablet to take and told me to sleep it off. I slept for three days, waking only to go to the bathroom and drink glasses of water. On the evening of the second day the personnel manager came to tell me it was time to get back to work, but in a rare display of disobedience I ignored her and slept for another thirty-six hours. Only then was I ready to get out of bed and return to my desk and the two-hour stints in the watchtower.

Earlier in the year Roger's parents had flown from Australia to see him and his new wife and the children. Not long after returning to Australia his dad fell ill with cancer and Roger and his wife flew to Esperance to see him. While his dad was dying, his mum was also diagnosed with cancer. Roger was back at the ranch when the news came that she was failing. He came to see me to tell me what was happening and to ask if I had money I could give him for a fare back home.

To support Roger's application for a business visa when he first came to the Big Muddy, it had been decided that the money we had donated should be used to open a bank account in our names, at a bank in a nearby town. However, it was made clear to us that our donation had been accepted and the money no longer belonged to us. The accounts department then used the account for its own purposes, occasionally asking me to sign withdrawal forms. When Roger asked if I had any money I told him I didn't, but afterwards I went to talk to Savita. She told me there was about fifteen hundred dollars still on the account and at my request agreed that Roger could have it. But when he went to the personnel department to ask for permission to go to Australia, his commitment was called into question. He seemed to be putting his family before the commune, he was told. He had recently been in Australia and should he decide to return there again so soon, it would be better he leave his mala at the office. Upon his return he could decide if he still wanted to be a sannyasin. This was a veiled threat of excommunication. Roger did not want to put his commitment to Bhagwan in question, and besides, his children lived in the commune. He hesitated for some days, until finally the pull to see his mother won out and he simply got a lift to Portland and flew out. When he arrived in Perth he called home to Esperance to tell his mum he would be there in a couple of hours, only to be told he was too late. His mother had just died. After her funeral he returned to the commune, but he never forgave himself for having hesitated those few days.

One day at a routine practice on the rifle range I was informed that I was to attend extra training sessions as we would shortly be giving a demonstration of our skills to the press. The demonstration of firepower was Bhagwan's answer to the escalating tension. I am no longer sure of the exact incident that led to his decision to have his security force demonstrate its capabilities to the world, but it was at the time when an attempt to win control of the county by busing in thousands of potential voters was dangerously taxing the patience of all concerned.

The scheme was euphemistically named the 'Share-a-Home' project. If I were asked to pinpoint the beginning of the end, I would have to say the Share-a-Home project was it for me. The idea alone was insane. In an America-wide action, homeless people were recruited from the streets of major cities and bussed to Rajneeshpuram with the promise of being incorporated into the community. At enormous cost, thousands of homeless people were transported across the country into Rajneeshpuram, where they were housed, clothed, fed and given medical care. What is wrong with that, you might ask. Firstly, they were deceived into thinking they were being given a new start, when in fact they were pawns in a reckless political manoeuvre. And secondly, no thought was given to the people themselves and as to why they lived on the streets.

It very quickly became clear that we had imported a hornet's nest into the very heart of the community and we were in no way equipped to deal with it. The majority of those who came were men with severe mental and emotional problems. A good number were Vietnam veterans who had returned from active service only to find that their government and countrymen saw them not as heroes but as embarrassing reminders of an unpopular war. Most were alcoholics and drug addicts, and every one of them, men and women alike, had serious medical problems. Add to all that the natural cunning of those who have to fight to survive each day and you have a volatile mixture.

In no time at all there was a brisk trade in contraband among the newcomers. Winter coats, cigarettes, warm boots and socks, medication; you name it, they were stealing and trading it. They joined the sannyasins at drive-by and were instantly dazzled by the Rolls-Royces and the diamonds glistening on Bhagwan's wrist. Sheela had already taken the precaution of having all the public phones tapped, and when Bhagwan heard that phone calls were being intercepted that indicated the makings of a plan to steal his jewels, he told Sheela to seize the instigator and have him drugged to find out what was going on.

I was often called out in the night or early morning to soothe a severely mentally disturbed person who was out of control because the medical staff were not aware of their condition and the person had run out of medicine. In a fit of psychotic rage a man of considerable size rampaged through the streets one day, stopping cars, dragging out the people sitting in them and throwing them to the ground. When Sheela tried to intervene he picked her up by the neck and threatened to break her head off. He was finally sedated and driven off the ranch and set down somewhere where he would be someone else's problem. Many quickly tired of the novelty of the city of red-clad residents in the middle of nowhere. Hardly had they arrived than they expressed their wish to go back to the cities that were home to them. So we had the absurd situation of bus loads of new people arriving, and bus loads of those who had taken a ride across the country, seen a few new places, been given a warm coat and a warm meal, leaving. Some didn't even wait for a bus and simply walked out, stopping in neighbouring towns to beg or steal a little something for the road. When the county refused to allow a group of the newcomers to register to vote, it quickly became obvious that the whole exercise had not only been in vain, but it had blown up in our faces. That it was costing an enormous amount of money and taxing our human resources to the limit, without producing the desired results, displeased Bhagwan very much. He told Sheela to get rid of them. By way of punishing the local community he ordered that the homeless be taken by bus to Portland and dropped off there. Some were not even taken that far and were dropped off in the Dalles, the seat of local government. This created an untenable state of affairs for the police and the residents of those cities. The situation was explosive.

It may have been Bhagwan's reaction to documents leaked from the governor's office that was the trigger that led to the demonstration of firepower. The documents outlined discussions of the 'Rajneesh problem' and a tentative plan to send in agitators to Rajneeshpuram to start a riot, which would then be used as a pretext to send in the National Guard. Whatever the cause, Bhagwan decreed that we should strike fear into the hearts of anyone who might be considering using force against the city and its inhabitants. The demonstration was to send the clear message that we would answer violence with violence and would be no pushover in the event of an attack. It was to be a warning not to mess with us.

The press was notified and the appointed day dawned cold and grey. I remember it well because, despite rugging up against the cold, my hands and feet were freezing and numb within minutes of standing out on the rifle range. Everyone wore brown padded overalls, a knitted cap, sunglasses and gloves. The intention was that we look sinister and threatening, and we did. It was not possible to recognise anybody or to distinguish men from women. Under the direction of the trainers, we went through our paces, shooting at stationary targets, throwing ourselves down in the mud to fire at moving targets, drawing the pistols on our hips with a speed that would have won the approval of Jesse James. That night every television station in Oregon carried the story, illustrated with footage of obscure figures firing semi-automatic weapons in a barrage of gunfire. The lines were drawn. From here on in, both sides in the conflict gave no quarter.

In December the Attorney General's Office filed a lawsuit in Federal Court charging that the City of Rajneeshpuram violated the constitutional separation of Church and State, arguing that it was a religious city while all its inhabitants were of the same religion and all its institutions were run by the religious inhabitants. Of course it was a little more complex than that, but that was the gist of it. It was a brilliant tactic that went for the jugular. Some of the lawyers were of the opinion that the corporations needed to be restructured before the case could be adequately defended. Sheela and Savita were strongly against such a complex solution. There was so much controversy among the lawyers about the best line of defence that Bhagwan called them all to his house to speak to them. He told them that the attorney general was right in saying there was no separation of government and religion at Rajneeshpuram, and urged them to be creative in finding arguments to support the insupportable. He told them the story of an attorney who went into court in the morning and argued a case with great skill, only to be told at the lunch break that he had argued for the other side. Unperturbed he returned to the courtroom in the afternoon and argued brilliantly for his client, refuting his arguments of the morning and winning the case.

The legal department was stretched to its limits and had replaced the purchasing department as the largest department on the ranch. There was the on-going, complicated litigation over land use; a large Rajneeshee suit against the INS trying to force a decision on the sannyasin visa applications languishing in their Portland office; and a number of smaller, less complicated but nevertheless troubling proceedings. The city and each of the corporations had been named as separate defendants in the Church-and-State case so it was necessary to produce separate motions for each of them. It was not uncommon for a group of us to work through the night preparing motions for one or more court hearings the following day. More than once I showered and changed after a sleepless night in the office, to accompany the lawyers to the courthouse for a hearing or filing of motions.

The pressure was building up to unbearable proportions. It was chaotic and frightening and sleep was becoming a scarce commodity. I felt I was caught in a whirlpool and I could hardly catch my breath. I never complained or gave voice to my fears. Everyone else was in the same boat and I forced myself to keep going. Bhagwan had said, 'Out of chaos stars are born', and in my childish magic-thinking I comforted myself that it was all a test and I must persevere. But I was desperate for peace and quiet, and sleep. And worse was still to come.

18

Early in 1985 police entered the school in Antelope unannounced and served papers on my daughter Kylie and a number of other young girls, naming them in a lawsuit charging that they had been sexually abused by unnamed commune members. Kylie had just turned fourteen. The suit had been brought by a woman from a nearby town who was well known for her outspoken condemnation of Rajneeshees. I was outraged that she should use the children to further her malevolent campaign against the community. I never for a moment imagined there was any truth to the allegations.

On that day whatever fragile threads of empathy I still had for the local people snapped, and with them something inside me. Those people 'out there' all merged into a faceless monster that was threatening my child. I was filled with cold fury and ready to kill any of *Them* who would dare lay a hand on her. In that moment I crossed the threshold into madness. It had been a gradual, insidious, almost imperceptible process over many years that finally silenced the still small voice of reason inside me.

Another mother might have packed up her things and taken her child out of there instead of fantasising about killing someone. But I was by this time so identified with my life as Bhagwan's sannyasin in his city in the desert that such a sensible solution did not enter my mind. At that time it was simply unthinkable. Bhagwan and Rajneeshpuram were my world. There was nothing outside of it. There was no place out there. Roger and I had long since gone our separate ways and there was no partner or moderating friend to counsel caution and point out that Kylie's safety and wellbeing were obviously of paramount importance.

To Bhagwan and Sheela and the lawyers, the lawsuit was just one more in a never-ending succession of lawsuits. Motions were written and filed and with time it seemed to lose its threatening nature, but I was ready now to do whatever had to be done to protect my child, my master and my community. In my mind it was now a life and death struggle for survival.

One aspect of the antagonism between Sheela and the members of Bhagwan's household was Sheela's undisguised dislike of Bhagwan's doctor and his dentist. She considered them both incompetent, if not downright dangerous. She complained that the doctor was a kind of mad scientist and maintained that his ineptitude would be the death of Bhagwan. Bhagwan did not share her concerns and was in fact perfectly happy with both men. They were first and foremost his disciples and when he let them know that he wanted them to administer laughing gas to him for an hour every day while he dictated a book or two to them, they were only too happy to comply. Neither thought to question the master's wishes nor to warn him of the possible consequences of inhaling so much laughing gas over such a long period of time. Like me, they must have thought Bhagwan knew best, even when it came to their own areas of expertise. I never took Sheela's complaints very seriously. They were simply background noise. But then something happened that made me sit up and take notice.

Sheela was in Australia at the time and she called every day to hear what was happening in Rajneeshpuram. On this particular day she was told that an outside doctor had visited Bhagwan in his house. A dental surgery and medical facility, complete with a fully equipped operating room, had been installed in Bhagwan's house and all his medical requirements were taken care of by his personal doctor and dentist, both of whom lived in his house. If an outside medical expert had been called in something must be seriously wrong.

Sheela called her husband Jay and told him to go and see the doctor who had visited Bhagwan. He should take me with him as the representative of the Church concerned for the health of its spiritual leader. Our instructions were to find out what was going on with Bhagwan.

The doctor was very direct. Bhagwan was suffering from blood poisoning, brought about by two different situations. Bhagwan had his own private swimming pool at his house and it was his habit to go swimming every day. After swimming, the doctor explained, Bhagwan's ears were rinsed with Listerine mouthwash, 'to dry them out'. The alcohol in the Listerine had dried out the walls of the ear canal so dramatically that they had cracked, allowing bacteria that normally live in the ear canal and are perfectly safe there to enter the bloodstream, where they were never intended to be. At the same time Bhagwan was undergoing multiple root canals. The activity of the dentist (whom the doctor described as 'a butcher') had opened up more opportunity for infection, with the result that Bhagwan had developed blood poisoning. The doctor was very angry with Bhagwan's dentist and doctor. He said

Bhagwan's doctor was completely incompetent, that any fool knew that Listerine was for gargling, not for pouring in the ears.

So Sheela was right! She had been saying for years that Bhagwan's doctor was incompetent, that he would kill Bhagwan one day, and here was a specialist saying essentially the same thing. It was the turning point. From that day on I no longer dismissed Sheela's complaints about the doctor. Now I took them seriously.

Bhagwan never swam again, preferring to give the swimming pool over to the people in his household, a gesture that annoyed Sheela very much.

One evening Sheela called me into her room and said there was another tape from Bhagwan's room she wanted me to listen to. What I heard was incomprehensible to me. Bhagwan was speaking with his doctor. He was asking whether it was possible to bring on death so that it would be painless and dignified. The doctor told him three drugs were needed. They should be administered intravenously, in a particular order. The first was morphine. Morphine would put the person into a beautiful space and slow the breathing. A sufficiently large dose of morphine would slow the breathing to the point of stopping it. The second drug was curare, which would produce total body paralysis; and the third was potassium chloride, which would then stop the heart.

Bhagwan told him to order enough of the three drugs for three people. I couldn't grasp what was going on but my heart hurt in my chest. I was not a rational human being in those days. I was a devout sannyasin trying desperately to shore up my increasingly unstable 'perfect' world from the onslaughts of a confusing and threatening reality. I did not understand about the loneliness and depression that can visit a reclusive guru and I did not want to know that Bhagwan intended to orchestrate his own death. I shut my eyes tighter than ever and covered my ears even more determinedly.

Today I venture to guess that the two other people Bhagwan had in mind were Vivek and Sheela. They were the two people who knew him best of all. They could reveal the most about him, and do the most damage to his image. Bhagwan paid a lot of attention to his public image. There were the dozens, if not hundreds, of books of his discourses that had been published in India, plus large coffee-table photographic accounts of his life, the ashram in India and the community in Oregon. He chose the photographs to be used and stipulated the title and layout of each book. Bhagwan also liked to dress up and pose to have his photo taken. The thousands of tasteful images of him in all manner of elegant costumes with carefully chosen props illustrate one of the ways in which he filled his days, and the extent to which he kept his seamstress and his court photographer busy.

His public appearances were always carefully orchestrated. He attended to every detail: where he would enter; how he would enter; what kind of chair he would sit on and where exactly it should be; microphones; music; his clothes, and the clothes of his dancing girls, if they were part of the show. So much energy did he exert in creating and refining his public image, one could be forgiven for thinking that he had dedicated his life to deliberately and carefully creating a legend.

Sheela's nurse monitored the order from Bhagwan's doctor for the three drugs. When they arrived, the doctor reported it to Bhagwan, who told him to bury them in a safe place in the garden until they were needed.

19

As preparations got under way for the Master's Day festival in 1985, the organisers began running into trouble with local government authorities over permits. Previous festivals had been carefully planned to meet the necessary standards and things had gone smoothly. This year the local authorities were stalling and the permits were not forthcoming. Time was running out and tempers were short when it was announced that there would be a public hearing in the Dalles to consider the issue. Sheela instructed me to accompany the Rajneesh attorneys and planners and engineers to the hearing. When we arrived we found the hearing had been moved from the planning office into the courtroom in order to accommodate the large number of people who had turned out for it.

The courtroom was packed. Apart from one pew at the front that had been reserved for us, every seat was taken and people stood packed in around the walls. The air was thick with sullen hostility. After the opening remarks people were invited to speak. I sat in the front pew listening to a steady stream of people come forward and voice their opinion that permits for the festival should be denied. Many spoke about when the Share-a-Home participants had been set down in their town. All the while, in the rows directly behind me, women were knitting. Their knitting needles clicked with an intensity that called to my mind a scene from a movie about the French Revolution. Women had sat knitting and chortling as the aristocracy were dragged off to the guillotine. I began to feel a strange mixture of fear and outrage.

When it came my turn to speak, I took my place next to the Rajneesh attorney at the table. As I began speaking, the thought that the commissioners were intending to deny the permits suddenly seized me and I exploded with rage. There was an element of fear of what I perceived to be the lynch mob behind me, but of far greater weight was the fury at the thought that these people would dare to thwart Bhagwan's festival. The press would carry the story the next day, referring to me as 'little Sheela'. I did in fact do a Sheela. Casting aside all caution and logical argument, I launched an attack on the women knitting behind me, followed by a vulgar personal attack on one county commissioner after another. Pandemonium broke out and the commissioners adjourned to deliberate as to whether or not I should be arrested. I went outside to call Sheela to ask her advice. I should let myself be arrested if need be, she said, but we were to get those permits. She was pleased with me for putting those people in their places, she said.

When the commissioners returned they stipulated that the hearing would continue on condition I sat back on the pew and did not speak. If I spoke I would be arrested and the hearing would disband. The Rajneesh attorney urged me to assent. I was actually shocked by what I had done and, although I put on a very haughty demeanour, I was glad to withdraw to the pew, leaving my companions to win the day with rational arguments.

Those Rajneeshees who had a public role were kept supplied with good clothes. Whenever I attended a court hearing I borrowed nice clothes from a room set up for the purpose in Jesus Grove. Otherwise I got what I needed from a large storeroom where clothing for members of the community was kept. There one could obtain anything from a new dress or a new blouse, work overalls, socks and underwear. With time it became increasingly difficult to get a new item of clothing. One was put through the third degree as to why the new item was needed, what it was replacing and where the old item was. More often than not one was given a used piece of clothing in exchange for the old, until the time came when there was only used clothing and nothing new at all.

Not long after the festival permit hearing I ran into Peter in downtown Rajneeshpuram. He was a tall, thin sixteen year old. I noticed he was wearing sneakers with gaping holes in them and told him to go to the storeroom to get some new shoes.

'I've just come from there,' he said, 'they have no shoes my size.'

No shoes for my son! I went up to the storeroom to find out what was going on. The woman in charge told me they only had the shoes that were on display and there were no plans to buy any more. I was angry. I went to see Sheela. She said she would take care of it but that there was no money left to buy shoes for the working people and they would have to make do with what they had. I was consumed by a feeling of impending doom. All this work to build a Buddhafield, and there was no money left to buy shoes?

By this time Bhagwan was speaking publicly again. He came down to Buddha Hall every day and gave a discourse, just like in the old days. Well, almost. Gone was the austerely dressed sage of Pune. Now he wore fantastic flowing robes with matching caps and sparkling jewels on his wrists. His chair was grand and throne-like and sat atop a raised podium. He was guarded by a bevy of armed guards who stood around the periphery of the hall, constantly scanning the assembled crowd sitting on the floor. To make up for the menacing guards there was music and dancing girls, who pranced at Bhagwan's side, keeping time to the music and his vigorous two-handed conducting of them, before he sat down, and began to speak. Two discourses stand out for me from those days of 'neo-discourse'. The first, which still haunts me today, was actually a series of discourses over a number of days in which Bhagwan talked about a voluptuous middle-aged woman from his household and her attempts to seduce a teenage boy. It was a hilarious story that recounted the boy's disinterest in her, his preference for Asterix and Tintin comics instead, and of the feminine wiles she had to resort to in order to have her way with him. Everybody laughed uproariously at Bhagwan's ongoing account of the drama as it unfolded. When I realised the boy was my sixteen-year-old son I was at first too shocked to know what to think. I had always believed the community to be one big family that took care of its children, and in fact the public relations department boasted that the city was drug-free and the children were safe wherever they went. But then I told myself Peter was a young man now and if Bhagwan thought it was okay then it must be all right. So 'surrendered' was I and so completely without a mind of my own, I joined in the laughter and felt proud that Peter should have come to Bhagwan's notice and that Bhagwan should talk about him at such length. What Bhagwan failed to mention was that the seductress gave Peter genital herpes, which was to plague him for the rest of his life.

The other discourse I remember was the one in which Bhagwan announced to everyone's great mirth that actually he had been having us on all along and he was not celibate at all. He presented the news wrapped in a package of jokes that had people rolling in the aisles. I laughed with everyone else and repeated my mantra that Bhagwan was perfect and whatever he did was perfect too. He could change his story any time he wanted to.

'Truth is what works' was the first commandment of Bhagwan's creed. He never felt in any way bound by what he had said yesterday. If it was expedient, he would say the opposite today, and something different again tomorrow. He was above the normal rules of language and society. He was in a league of his own.

20

An older woman, Mrs Byron, had been a resident of the ashram in Pune, and as soon as housing was available she was invited to the ranch. She had not found the Big Muddy a congenial place, especially as she had a physical condition that required her to walk with a cane. So she went back to her home in New Mexico. Mrs Byron had lent the ashram in Pune a substantial sum of money and the day came when she sent a formal letter asking for its return. When Sheela took the letter to Bhagwan he said that under no circumstances was the money to be returned. So Mrs Byron sued Rajneesh Foundation International. Bhagwan treated the case as a personal affront and refused to listen to counsel to return the money, saying they were to argue that it had been a gift to him.

The case was referred to as the 'Helen Byron case'. I was first notified of it in May 1985 when I was informed that as treasurer of Rajneesh Foundation International I was to appear in federal court to testify that the money in question had been a donation. I was to do this by verifying that the book-keeping records were original and genuine. I was not told that the records had been tampered with, but I could see that for myself and was aghast that I was to present them as authentic. Were we so arrogant as to think we could pull the wool over the eyes of anyone who opposed us? Or were we like drowning men, desperately clutching at straws as the waters engulfed us? I was certainly one of the latter. I took the stand very unwillingly, though as usual I did not protest. When asked if the records before me were bona fide I answered 'Yes'. The court ruled for the defendant and ordered RFI to pay compensatory and punitive damages in the amount of one million, seven hundred thousand dollars.

When the dust had settled from the grotesque attempt to take over the county, a perfidious new set of game rules were in place. Just when and how they came into being I do not know. The initiated were few, but their numbers would grow. In January 1985 the planning office in the Dalles was set on fire and many records were destroyed. In summer the previous year there had been an outbreak of salmonella in the Dalles. These two seemingly unrelated events would one day be shown to have their roots in Jesus Grove, where a small group of sannyasins had been conscripted to use guerrilla-warfare tactics against the commune's perceived enemies. I cannot say with certainty how much Bhagwan knew of their activities.

My only personal experience of what might be considered his endorsement of such clandestine activity was a tape Sheela played one evening to twenty or more of us. It was the tape of a conversation she had had with Bhagwan in which she had asked him to what lengths his sannyasins may go in order to protect him. Bhagwan answered to the effect that an enlightened being such as himself was a very rare thing and that if ten thousand people had to die in order to protect the enlightened one, then so be it. He also said that if there was an attempt to seize him, his sannyasins were to form a massive human shield around him, which left open just which ten thousand people he had in mind: *Them* or *Us*?

Preparations for the Master's Day festival had begun when I became privy to the existence of this clandestine group, although what exactly they were doing did not become clear to me until some time later. Almost without noticing what was happening I became embroiled in an intense, macabre game of mental violence in which people were called into Sheela's bedroom to talk about killing people thought to be a threat to Bhagwan and the commune. No one asked me if I wanted to be part of the group. I was simply called in to find people would be gathered there, sometimes more of them and sometimes less. I no longer walked out when I heard things I didn't want to hear. I stayed and listened.

It was like some sort of surreal cops and robbers game. Someone was looking for inspiration by reading John Le Carré novels and they put forward the poisoned-cane-in-the-crowd suggestion. Sometimes the enemy was *Them* outside, and sometimes it changed to Vivek and Bhagwan's doctor. It was never very clear who was an important enemy and who was not, but the number of enemies seemed to grow every time I found myself in that room. I listened a lot, and thought a lot about who might be a real danger to Bhagwan. Once there was talk of buying guns that could not be traced, and the man reading the Le Carré novels said he thought Texas would be a good place for that. There were some comments about me being a good shot and the one to pull the trigger. I didn't volunteer anything but I thought about Kylie and the lawsuit and thought a gun that could not be traced would be a good thing to have.

One day a call came to the office that Sheela wanted to see me downstairs in the restaurant. An old work colleague from the booking office in Pune, who was now managing the restaurant, was there with her. She was not someone I had seen in the intense discussions in Sheela's bedroom. Without further ado Sheela said she had a job for us. We were to drop whatever we were doing and go out of state to buy guns that couldn't be traced to the community. We were to go to Texas, as my colleague came from there and knew her way around. We were to see Sheela's housekeeper about some non-sannyasin clothes and she would arrange for money. We were to leave as soon as possible.

She could have been ordering a burger and chips with a shake on the side. 'This is the order. Fill it fast.'

My companion and I were both dedicated sannyasins who had always worn the red colour and our malas. We did not want to leave the city in fancy dress on some mission impossible, but neither of us breathed a word of dispute. We had our orders and we marched. The housekeeper took us to a shed in the yard that turned out to be full of regular street clothes and we selected what we would need. I talked to the Le Carré fan about what kind of guns we should buy. He thought pistols would be easier to come by and to transport.

'Don't take the plane home,' he said.

Someone showed up with a bundle of cash. Two women came to give us advice about using a different name every time we moved hotels or booked a flight, and leaving all our ID behind and using only cash. All the time my stomach was turning over so badly I was nauseous and kept having to run to the toilet. I was at the centre of a hive of activity, and yet I didn't seem to be present, as if I were watching someone else who looked like me make all these preparations.

When we left the next day Sheela was not around. We drove to Portland and spent the night in the Rajneesh Hotel, and early next morning someone drove us to the airport. We wore orange raincoats over our clothes so people at the hotel wouldn't see that we were wearing regular street clothes. We booked a flight to Houston under assumed names. I had never been anywhere else in America except when I touched down on the east coast on my way to Oregon. Since being in Oregon my radius had extended only as far as court hearings had required. I had never used American currency, booked a hotel or ordered a meal in America. What I lacked in practical knowledge and experience I made up for in dedication to Sheela and Bhagwan. I did not like the job I had been given but if it was something I had to do in order to protect Bhagwan and the community then I would do it. On that count I think my companion felt the same way. She took care of finding a motel when we got to Houston and we agreed that she should do all the talking and paying for things.

It is indicative of our naivety that the first place we enquired about guns was in a gun shop, of which there was no shortage in Houston. The storekeeper explained that there were ID requirements to buy guns in Texas. We went back to the motel and mulled over the problem. My companion thought perhaps we might be able to buy a gun without ID in the bad part of town, but we didn't know where that was and were afraid to find out. That evening we went to a country and western dance, Texas style, in the hope of finding a wallet or purse lying around. I was overwhelmed by the drawling cowboys and the crowds and smoke and we left soon after we had arrived. We then spent a couple of days wandering the streets with our eyes cast down looking for a sign from heaven in the form of a lost purse full of ID lying on the pavement. We were beginning to get desperate.

One evening we went to a restaurant. The lights were dim and it was smoky and my companion succeeded in picking up the purse of a lady at the neighbouring table. We took it to the powder room and removed the driver's licence, then we paid and left. We were petrified and imagined with every step we took that a policeman would lay his hand on our shoulders. We walked a long way before we felt calm enough to take a taxi back to the motel. Neither of us had ever done anything like this in our lives and we didn't know whether to laugh or cry. We felt like naughty children. The lady was from out of state so her driver's licence was of no use to us.

It was a relief somehow. On the one hand we saw ourselves almost as knights on a mission, but on the other hand we were just plain scared and wanted to be back at the ranch. We decided we couldn't do what was asked of us and would return home. For the first time in days I felt calm and slept like a baby. Next day we went to a mall and I called the ranch and asked to be put through to Jesus Grove. Careful not to use my name I let the person who picked up know that our shopping trip had been unsuccessful and we would be coming back. I was told to wait while advice was sought. There was a message for us, she said when she came back on the line: we were not to come back empty-handed.

My stomach turned over. Dreams of imminent return disappeared in a flash. The game was getting serious. If we wanted to go home again we had to get those guns. Crestfallen and sobered, we decided to leave Texas and go to New Mexico, where my companion had once lived. She had a cousin in Albuquerque, she said. So that's where we went. We booked into a motel and went to visit her cousin. She told him a story about being in town looking for investments, and he arranged for a friend to lend us a car. Then my companion went into a gun shop and found out that to buy a gun in New Mexico all one needed by way of ID was a birth certificate and a rent receipt. Determined now, we spent the next two days in the library studying microfilm of birth and death announcements in old newspapers until we found what we were looking for. It was the birth announcement of a baby girl born in about the same year as my companion. The announcement included the names of both parents, and the mother's maiden name. A few months later a notice in the obituary column of the same paper showed that the baby girl had died. My companion went to the registry office and applied for a birth certificate in the name of the dead baby.

The rest was easy. A receipt book bought from a stationery shop produced the rent receipt. Armed with her new ID, my companion visited three gun shops and came back with five revolvers and five boxes of ammunition. As she drove us back to the motel I shredded the ID and threw it out the car window. We were nervous but excited that we had succeeded in our assignment and could go home at last.

Remembering the advice of the Le Carré man, we decided I should transport the guns back to Portland on a Greyhound bus and my companion would fly back to Texas to visit with her parents for the couple of days it would take me to get back. I called the ranch to give the time the bus would arrive in Portland. The Le Carré man met the bus and relieved me of my burden. I saw the revolvers again a few days later when he took me to the rifle range to test fire them, but after that I never saw them again. I didn't know where they were kept, nor did I want to know. I threw myself back into my work in the office. The whole thing had never happened.

Or had it? Hardly was I back in the office than I was told to go to Portland, where I was met by a sannyasin dressed in 'blue' and taken to an apartment. She indicated it was a safe house for a small group of sannyasins like herself who were involved in undercover activities. She invited me to help myself to a set of street clothes from the cupboard. There was something she wanted to show me, she said. We were picked up by two other sannyasins in blue and driven out into the country. On a quiet country road the car slowed down and my companions pointed to three letterboxes by the road-side. On one of them was written the name *TURNER*.

'His house is just down here,' said the driver and turned into a small laneway.

One of the women was telling me excitedly how she had found the house, but I was hardly listening. As the car did a U-turn and drove back out onto the road, the driver indicated towards a stand of trees and said he thought hiding in one of them might be the way to go. Turner was a name that had come up in Sheela's bedroom. Something to do with a grand jury and the INS investigation into Bhagwan's visa status. I wasn't sure, but I understood he was one of the more dangerous enemies as he was working against Bhagwan himself.

Returning to downtown Portland, the driver drove into a public parking station and up a few floors into a parking bay. We all got out. One of my companions indicated an empty parking bay across from us and said this was where Turner parked his car. These people had done their homework! I was beginning to get into the spirit of it. I imagined using one of the untraceable revolvers to shoot him as he stepped out of his car. No, that would never do. The sound of the gunshot would reverberate through the parking station and there was a guard downstairs. Ah yes, the guard. We decided to check out possible escape routes. As we stepped into the elevator, the guard stepped out. I cancelled the gunning-him-down-in-the-parking-station idea, and we left. The next morning one of the women took me to McDonald's and we sat there in our blue clothes and makeup, drinking coffee and watching the exit to the parking station to get a glimpse of the 'enemy'. To complete the picture of the undercover cold-blooded killer mixing with the crowd, I smoked cigarettes for the first and only time in my life. It was straight-out of Hollywood, except that it was horribly, horribly real.

21

The festival had begun and things were going well. The news was out that Bhagwan was talking again and the population of the city had swelled to an estimated fifteen thousand people as sannyasins flew in from all over the world to hear him speak. It was a rare opportunity to make money. The casino was doing a roaring trade and raffle tickets with one of Bhagwan's Rolls-Royces as the prize were selling like hot cakes. Who wouldn't want to win a car that the master had sat in and driven? The winner gave it back, which was lucky because we couldn't really afford to be giving away Rolls-Royces.

The throng of people and the excitement of the whole festival atmosphere pushed the cares of the last few months aside and gave the impression that the world was in order again. It was a ray of light in a dark, threatening sky. And then the sky closed over altogether.

It was evening. The next day was Master's Day, 6 July 1985, the climax of the festival. The phone rang in the office. I picked it up and a voice said I was to come down to Jesus Grove right away.

There were twenty or more people there when I arrived. Sheela looked exhausted and pale, but determined. When she was satisfied we were all present, she began to speak.

'Tomorrow is the day,' she said. 'Tomorrow the doctor will inject Bhagwan with the drugs and he will die. We have to do something.'

There was horrified silence. Tomorrow Bhagwan would die? My mind was racing. I could see the doctor digging the drugs out of the garden. In my desperation I never thought to question that it was Bhagwan's own decision to die. Or where Sheela had got her information that it would happen tomorrow.

Sheela was talking again. She was saying we had to do something. It was now or never. We had to get rid of the doctor. Who of us would save Bhagwan?

There was silence in the room. No one spoke. The silence seemed interminable. Slowly, ever so slowly, sounds formed in my throat and a disembodied voice came out of me and said,

'I will do it.'

Everybody looked at me.

'I will do it,' I repeated more firmly, and I was aware of an overwhelming feeling of reckless disregard for my own safety and an absolute determination to save Bhagwan's life. It was as though by saying those words I had thrown a switch and all my natural instincts to preserve and protect myself were turned off. I was filled with all the fervour of a saintly knight going into battle for the Lord. I was Joan of Arc herself. I would die to save Bhagwan if need be.

Sheela looked pleased.

'Good, Shanti B. You can do it,' she said.

It seemed Bhagwan's demise was to take place sometime during the following day, but not before the grand Master's Day celebration in Buddha Hall in the morning. Short of raiding Bhagwan's house and killing the doctor in his bed, the only opportunity to dispose of him would be during the celebration itself. The murder weapon would be, appropriately enough, a syringe filled with poison. One woman suggested she sit behind me so I could pass the empty syringe to her once the deed was done. Once that was decided upon, a clamour broke out as people discussed who should be where in Buddha Hall and who should not be there at all.

I withdrew into my shell and let them talk. I was in a bubble, like a fish in a fishbowl, looking out at them, hearing the noise but not translating it into something understandable. Later, when they had all gone, I sought out Sheela's nurse and got what I needed from her, and I made my own arrangements about what I would wear in order to conceal the syringe and just how I would act. I was very secretive. Afterwards people would realise they did not even know what poison I had used, or what moves I had made, or how I had done it. They would think they remembered me practising using the syringe on an orange, whereas in actual fact I practised on Sheela's nurse when we were alone in her room. I did not talk about it. It was my martyrdom and, like the saints of my childhood, I suffered it in silence for my God.

The syringe was filled with adrenalin. When I jabbed it into the buttock of the doctor as he sat there innocently enjoying the deafening music and the singing and swaying of ecstatic Rajneeshees delighting in the presence of their very own master on Master's Day, I believed it would kill him. Thankfully I was mistaken. Injected into a muscle, the small amount was not really dangerous, although he got such a terrible shock at my attack that he almost died of fright. Of course he realised that I had stuck him with a needle and he reached back and grabbed my hand. There was a bit of a struggle and the syringe came out, the needle scratching my hand as it did so. I managed to slide the syringe back to the woman sitting behind me, before the doctor stood up and staggered towards the back of the hall. I followed him, feigning concern. And then the celebration was over and Bhagwan drove away and people were leaving and I turned and walked away. I walked through the crowd and out of Buddha Hall and all the way back to Sheela's house. No one walked with me. I was alone in a very lonely world and that's how I wanted it.

I hardly felt my body. It seemed to be floating above the ground. I felt strangely invincible, as though what I had done would have no repercussions for me. Why should it? Nothing had happened. I was not afraid. I was simply returning home after a routine day of doing my duty. But deep down I had imploded. My world was blown to smithereens. I had tried to kill a man.

The doctor was taken by ambulance to hospital in Bend. He did not tell the administering doctors what had happened to him. He sent a message to Bhagwan instead, an indication of his absolute devotion to his master. As far as he knew I had injected him with a deadly substance and he might be about to die, but he told Bhagwan what had happened, not the treating doctors. It was he who was the true disciple. Faced with death, he was ready to die rather than risk the secret entrusted to him coming to light. When he was released from hospital some days later the diagnosis read: 'The patient was suffering from a valium/alcohol reaction'.

When Vivek relayed the doctor's message to Bhagwan, he summoned Sheela to his house. He told her she was to have me drugged and beaten to find out what had happened. Of course she had no intention of doing such a thing and instead defended me strongly, casting aspersions on the doctor and questioning his mental state. When she returned from Bhagwan's house she directed that I be moved into a room next to hers. It took a couple of days to invent a story about a safety pin in the doctor's pocket, but Bhagwan seemed satisfied with the explanation and spoke no more about it.

I was in a state of suspended animation. Nothing seemed quite real any more, except the crushing pain in my chest at the knowledge that I must leave the commune. I went through the motions of living but felt I was dying. To leave the master felt like a living death. The thousands of stories I had heard of masters testing the worthiness of their disciples swirled through my head. And where would I go? I had nothing in the world outside the master and his commune – no money, no friends, no life. My little family had disintegrated. My children had been abandoned to the commune years ago. I had not answered my parents' letters, and had not had any contact with my siblings. All I knew was that I must leave. I must leave the place where I had broken the immutable law. *Thou shalt not kill* was branded in my soul and my soul cried out in anguish at what I had done. It didn't matter that I had not succeeded. It had been my intention, and even in my madness I knew I had gone beyond the pale.

I did not recognise the person I had become, and I was afraid of her. I wanted to run as far away as humanly possible, but in my dreamlike state my legs were like lead and would not obey my command to set themselves in motion.

22

It is safe to say that those who were privy to the attack on the doctor were also in shock. I detected a note of 'thank goodness it was you and not me' in their solicitous attitude towards me, but I could see the horror written on their faces. For all the schemes that had been discussed in Sheela's bedroom, it was the first time anyone had actually laid a hand on somebody. All the while we had been working on scripts for B-grade movies, now suddenly, like a Frankenstein monster, one of those scripts had come to life. A pall of silence hung over the whole incident. It was not talked about, least of all by me. Sheela tried to rally us but nothing was the same any more.

A trusted intimate and her partner stole off the ranch in the middle of the night. They sent a letter through the post with the keys to the car they had left parked at Seattle airport, and the watches they had received from Bhagwan with his image on them. The faces of both watches were smashed.

Even outside enemies failed to rouse the group. People were reticent and uncooperative when called to Sheela's bedroom. When she attempted to resume discussions of plans to kill Mr Turner, the personnel manager broke down completely. I was called to Sheela's bedroom to find the personnel manager prostrate on the floor, weeping uncontrollably, sobbing that she couldn't bear to hear talk of killing people any more. Sheela asked me to talk to her. The words poured out of me like water when a dam bursts. I told her she was not to worry, that no one would be hurting anybody any more, and certainly not me. It was finished. Over. Sheela watched me but said nothing. It was the first time I was able to give words to what was happening inside me. Afterwards I found I could breathe a little easier again. There were not many people in the room but they joined with me, voicing their agreement that there would be no more violence.

Sheela herself had lost her drive. She travelled a lot at this time and when we gathered in her bedroom the talk turned to tentative plans for the group to leave, and to live and work together somewhere else in an effort to get the community out of debt. A noble, surreal, absurd idea mirroring the state of our collective minds. By way of doing something, CVs were written and photos taken.

It was September 1985, two and a half months after the attack. I had been away for two days attending a court hearing. I returned to the ranch in the evening and went to find Sheela to report on the hearing. Sheela was in her room, sitting on her bed, and an unusually large number of people were sitting or standing around. Some of them were crying. There was a lot of tension in the air. I looked at Sheela enquiringly.

'I'm leaving,' she said. It was the catalyst I had been waiting for. If Sheela could leave, I could leave too. It gave me permission to go.

'If you're leaving I'm leaving too!' I said without a moment's hesitation.

I was shocked to hear myself utter the ultimate sacrilege. For weeks I had carried it in my breast like the fragile thing it was, but to give it form in the shape of words was to give it life, to make it real.

Sheela did not go to see Bhagwan to tell him she was leaving. She wrote him a letter which Savita took into him, and listened to his response on the bug. Bhagwan said if Sheela wanted to live in Europe that was fine but she was not to take any money from the European communes and was to sign formal letters of resignation from her many positions, and he asked Savita to be his new secretary. She was so shocked at his apparent indifference to Sheela's leaving, she could not answer.

Within hours of Sheela's announcement more than twenty people had voiced their intention to leave. In all the years I was with Bhagwan hardly anyone who had been with him for any length of time left him by themselves. It was almost always a pair who left. Alone one did not seem to have the strength to leave. Now it was not just a pair who wanted to leave, but a whole group. The thought of leaving the master and the place we all called home was daunting and we looked to each other for support, herding together like a flock of frightened animals, not daring or wanting to go our separate ways. Jorg, a member of Sheela's household, offered to buy air tickets for those who had no money. He thought Germany would be a good place to start as it was one of the few countries that would allow people of many different nationalities to enter and stay for three months without visas. It was agreed that we all meet up in Germany, where we could take stock and examine the possibility of working at something together to support ourselves.

Many were not in a hurry to rush off but wanted to take time to ensure that they would be leaving their workplaces intact and in good hands. I was one of these. The decision had been taken and voiced and now I would tidy up and go. Next morning I went to see my children to tell them I was leaving and to ask if they would come with me. They went to consult with Roger and their friends, before coming down to Jesus Grove to tell me that Peter had decided to stay with his father and Kylie would come with me.

Sheela left with a small entourage after a twenty-four-hour whirlwind of packing, answering people's anxious queries, telling people not to cry, and signing dozens of documents the legal department and her secretary brought to her. The listening station in her house was dismantled and she took with her the most critical tapes from the tapping of Bhagwan's room. Crying, flower-throwing sannyasins were at the airport to wave goodbye when she left. Sheela and her companions flew to Portland in the commune plane and then took a commercial flight to Europe.

That evening Savita went to see Bhagwan and declined his offer to be his secretary, saying that she too would be leaving once she had seen to it that financial matters were in good hands. She told him others would also be leaving and he asked her to prepare lists of suitable candidates for the various positions that would need to be filled.

I was walking down the corridor to my room after saying goodbye to Sheela when my gun-buying colleague from Texas stopped me to ask when I was leaving. When I told her I was planning to leave in a few days she begged me not to delay.

'You have to go now!' she said. 'Remember Bhagwan wanted to have you drugged and beaten. It will be too dangerous for you now that Sheela is no longer here to protect you.'

I felt a cold shower of fear wash over me. I had forgotten all about that. I went to see Jorg about tickets and arranged for Kylie to bring her things to Jesus Grove, and then spent the next few hours saying goodbye to colleagues and my American husband, and to Roger and Peter and the kids my children had grown up with in the ashram in Pune.

I had lived in the master's presence for eight years and even as I made preparations to leave I was still telling myself I was not really leaving. Only my body was leaving, my soul would remain with the master. I even told people I would come back from time to time for festivals, and in a way I believed I would. I wrote to Bhagwan thanking him for all he had given me and for all I had learned in his presence, and I returned the little amethyst ring he had given me at the beginning of the ranch project. Many years would go by before I freed myself from the nagging suspicion that I had failed the ultimate test the master had set for me. A part of me feared that I had not shown the courage necessary to deserve the master's staff.

How often had I heard Bhagwan tell the story of the fierce compassion of the Zen master who, seeing his disciple walking along the path, brought his rod down on the young man's head and killed him? The master knew that the shock of that blow would induce enlightenment in his disciple in the instant before death. The disciple was ready and the master had seen it. Had I missed? Had I run away from the master's rod? Was he truly a great master? Had I not had the good fortune to be born at all, to be born in the form of a (wo)man, to be born in the time of the buddha, to have met the buddha, to have become a disciple of the buddha? To throw away such a priceless gift was to be cast into darkness for lifetimes to come. Who knew if such a rare opportunity would ever present itself again? I had listened to these stories and dozens like them for years and years and years. They were a part of me, like the blood that flowed through my veins. The messages they carried were in every cell of my body. They were not something I could sort through in a few months or a few weeks, and certainly not in the few hours it took to say my goodbyes and leave.

Kylie and I left Rajneeshpuram early the next morning, driving in darkness to Portland in time to catch an early flight to Zurich. As the plane took off I could hardly believe what I was doing. I had done the unthinkable. I had left the master. Kylie and I shared one small suitcase and I took with me another, as yet invisible, carry-on. When I eventually unpacked it I found there all the problems I had brought with me when I became the master's devotee, plus many, many more.

23

Kylie and I travelled from Rajneeshpuram to Zurich with two Swiss sannyasins who had been visiting their master. The woman was the director of the Rajneesh centre in Zurich and had just spent three months at the ranch as part of a programme to allow European sannyasins to spend time in the Buddhafield. She took Kylie and me with her to the centre when we arrived, where we were greeted with open arms. Beds were prepared for us and tea was made. As we drank our tea, people came in and out of the living room, hugging us and chatting excitedly. Then the telephone rang.

The phone call ended and everybody except Kylie and me was quietly ushered into another room where there ensued a subdued discussion. We drank our tea in happy silence. People began moving back into the living room. The same people who half an hour earlier had greeted us with such warm-hearted enthusiasm now walked past us or stood looking at us with veiled eyes and hard faces. They were barely recognisable as the same people. Everything about them was menacing and I instinctively put my arm around Kylie. The centre leader pushed her way to us and turned to face the sullen crowd.

'What are you doing?' she said forcefully. 'So there was a call from the ranch saying that Sheela and other people have left the commune, and you are to have nothing to do with them? Have you no minds of your own? Look at you! If this is what sannyas is all about I want nothing to do with it.'

And so saying she took the mala from around her neck and threw it down on the table.

In the shocked silence that followed this sacrilege, she turned to Kylie and me and said urgently,

'You must leave. Come with me.'

She ushered us past the threatening groups of red-clad figures, her silent fury challenging them to dare raise a finger against us. She escorted us hurriedly out the front door and into a car, running back inside to get our little case before throwing it in the trunk and driving away. Night had fallen. She drove us to a hotel. On the way she explained that Bhagwan had spoken out against Sheela at discourse that morning. He said Sheela and those who left with her were evil and accused them of having tried to murder his doctor. I listened in disbelief and a wave of panic washed over me. I couldn't comprehend that Bhagwan would do such a thing.

Bhagwan's verbal attack took everybody unawares, although if any one of us had been thinking straight we could have seen it coming. The majority of those intending to leave were still in Rajneeshpuram. People like Savita were intending to remain in the city for a few weeks to come. They were now faced with a similar situation to the one Kylie and I had experienced, only on a much bigger and more dangerous scale. Bhagwan had told the assembled sannyasins that Sheela's gang, as he called it, had not only tried to kill his doctor but had also plotted to kill him. He called a press conference later in the day and publicly invited law-enforcement agencies down to the city to investigate his allegations. It took them a couple of days to recover from the shock enough to respond to his invitation. When they finally arrived, they were kept at a distance from his house. Bhagwan sent a message through his lawyers that the police should speak with his sannyasins. He knew nothing at all, he said, but was simply repeating what others had told him.

Bhagwan's accusations started a frantic scramble by those leaving to destroy evidence of wire-tapping and other illegal activities. I was told later that the Le Carré man threw the revolvers bought in New Mexico into the lake. There were a few ugly incidents involving angry sannyasins, but everyone who wanted to leave got out without injury.

With typical shrewdness Bhagwan wrapped his attack in the mantle of outraged decency. That others of us who left with Sheela were caught up in the hurricane of his rage was more by accident than design. The real object of his wrath was Sheela, his other half. While Bhagwan played at being God, withdrawing behind closed gates and surrounding himself in an aura of mystery and holiness, he sent Sheela out into the world as his emissary, arming her with an impertinent and disrespectful tongue. In short, she was the mercurial element, the mischief-maker. Like a jealous lover he now sought to destroy her completely. His task was made all the more easy because Sheela had played her role for him with flair and enthusiasm. Though most had fawned on her in the commune, she was always a controversial figure. In the world at large she was both admired and loathed. There were no half measures with Sheela – she was either loved or hated, nothing less.

If Sheela could leave Bhagwan, anybody could leave him. That was made painfully clear by the fact that more than twenty people left with her, many of them people who had been with Bhagwan since the early days in India. And then there was the question of the noose that was tightening around the community, the result of years of flagrant disregard for the law and the customs and feelings of others. It is typical of Bhagwan that in attacking Sheela and blaming her for all that was wrong, he was seeking to make capital out of an already desperate situation. He was ready to condemn Sheela to the stake if it meant he could maintain the status quo. Perhaps it was not too late to stem the tide he himself had set in flood. But jealous rage addled his brain. His passion possessed him and he made deadly mistakes.

The worthy men and women of the law-enforcement agencies who responded to his call did not limit their enquiries to Sheela's affairs. Before long the commune was in uproar. Couples who had married so the foreign partner could stay in America came like lambs to the slaughter to talk to the police. Bhagwan was telling them to cooperate, so they cooperated. At discourse each morning Bhagwan poured more fuel on the fire meant to incinerate Sheela. He wove a fabric of truths, half-truths, blatant lies and pure fiction, creating more and more fear and uncertainty and outrage. When he transformed the mortgage and corporation debts into one lump sum and described them as millions of dollars of cash that Sheela had taken with her, angry sannyasins ransacked their own shops in their own city. He dealt the fatal blow, however, when he said he had never wanted a religion, that it was Sheela who had insisted on it. He invited his sannyasins to wear whatever coloured clothing they wanted and to take off their malas. He incited them to have a ceremonial burning of Sheela's official satin robes and the Book of Rajneeshism at the newly built crematorium. As they sang and rejoiced as the flames licked around the funeral pyre of robes and books, they could not know that they were burning their own hopes and dreams, and that the song they sang was the swan song of the commune.

This ceremonial burning of the religion of Rajneeshism removed the grounds for the visa which allowed Bhagwan to remain in the United States of America. His visa was conditional upon his being a religious leader. Now that the religion was no more, his visa became invalid.

Were these really errors of judgement on Bhagwan's part? Or was he simply behaving like a spoiled child throwing a tantrum because the game was not going the way he wanted it to, in his paroxysm striking out in all directions and destroying the game itself? There are those who will say this was the whole point. He was not really angry, he was, in his wisdom, showing us that nothing is permanent, and by avoiding attachment in the first place we can avoid the pain of disappointment and loss. These kinds of arguments are like mazes – you can easily get lost in them. They lead to a dead end or, at best, back to where you started.

Six weeks after Sheela and the rest of us left the commune, Bhagwan left too. Having created complete mayhem, and aware of his imminent arrest for immigration fraud, Bhagwan boarded his private jet and flew away. He left behind a sea of shattered dreams. The commune disintegrated. Thousands of people who had invested all their wealth and energy in what they believed would be their home for the rest of their lives found themselves homeless and destitute. It is a tribute to the calibre of so many of the people who followed Bhagwan that most of them picked up the pieces and began the difficult task of building a new life from scratch.

24

Most of our small group eventually met up in a village in the Black Forest in southern Germany. We were like fish dynamited out of the water. None of us had lived in the real world for years and we were all in shock to suddenly find ourselves not only catapulted out of the Buddhafield, but with our master like an unleashed ogre snapping at our heels. A couple of our group were catatonic. They lay on their beds all day looking at the ceiling, unable to laugh or cry or even speak.

Since attacking the doctor I had remained completely dissociated from my feelings. I was somewhere in outer space and felt as though I had landed on an unfamiliar planet. Kylie and I slept late every morning, our room blackened by the wooden shutters I rolled down every night. We went for long walks in the forest each day, suspended between what we had left behind and an unknown future.

In Rajneeshpuram Bhagwan was attacking us on a daily basis. One girl had only got as far as Portland before deciding to return to the commune, where she unburdened herself and confessed her wrongdoing, first to Bhagwan and later to the police. Then the mayor and his girlfriend also returned to Rajneeshpuram, first trying to be good disciples and work for the master's cause, but then bowing to the inevitable and supporting the police enquiry. The international press followed developments with interest. Sensational stories appeared in major newspapers and magazines all over the world.

Needless to say, the press were looking for Sheela to hear what she had to say about Bhagwan's allegations. We were not long in the Black Forest when she was contacted by Stern, a popular German weekly magazine. Stern wanted an exclusive interview. Representatives came to the holiday house where we were and a contract was made. Not only did the magazine pay a generous fee, but in order to protect the exclusivity of the story, Stern agreed to take care of the entire group until the story went to press. We in turn agreed not to speak to any other representatives of the press. In an effort to make us invisible, Stern bought each of us jackets to cover our red clothes and transported us by bus and ferry to the island of Juist in the North Sea. There they put us up in a very gracious hotel on the beach, and the business of writing a story began in earnest.

Two Stern journalists interviewed Sheela over a number of days. Then the photographer came and she posed nude for him, and all in all everyone was happy. But before the story could go to press, we woke up one morning to find the street in front of the hotel swarming with journalists. In a wild flurry of activity we packed our bags and were smuggled out through the hotel's cellars to covered horse-drawn wagons waiting in a laneway behind the hotel. They transported us to the airport at the other end of the island where there were planes waiting to take us back to the mainland. From there we were taken by bus and train to Siena in Italy. We lay low there until the Stern story broke, and then we were returned to the Black Forest.

On 28 October 1985 plain-clothed policemen knocked on the door of the holiday house and were shown into the living room, where many of us were sitting discussing the news that Bhagwan had just been arrested trying to flee America. The policemen indicated they had arrest warrants for Sheela, her nurse and Shanti Bhadra and asked us to identify ourselves. They explained they had a request from the US Justice Department for our arrest and extradition to America to face charges of attempting to murder Bhagwan's doctor.

25

Everybody acted very politely and calmly, as though friends had dropped over to ask us out for supper. I hugged Kylie and assured her that I would return soon. It was clearly a misunderstanding and had nothing to do with me. She hugged me tightly and smiled wanly, as much as to say, 'Just when we finally had time together, you are going away again.' I didn't feel afraid. It was as though my emotions were on hold, or frozen, just as they had been the day I attacked the doctor. Even when I was locked in a prison cell it all seemed like an odd game of charades being played on this strange new planet I had landed on.

The next day we were taken for arraignment and then transferred to the women's detention centre in Bühl. The three of us were imprisoned together, in a large cell overlooking the exercise yard. None of us spoke a word of German, but many of the guards spoke English and some of the inmates too. It was a small prison where women were kept pending trial or resolution of their cases. The population stayed at two dozen or less while I was an inmate. There was Hofgang before breakfast every day and I soon got into the rhythm of rising early and going outside to walk round and round in the walled exercise yard with the handful of other inmates who had left the comfort of a warm bed to spend half an hour in the bracing air.

Kylie came to visit. She had coloured her hair bright green and was dressed all in green. She wanted to make me laugh, she said. She sat on my knee, a beautiful svelte fourteen year old, almost as tall as me. We held each other and she asked me what she should do. Returning to Roger and Peter in Oregon was not a viable option, so I told her to go to my parents in Australia. They had been notified of my arrest and I knew they would not hesitate to take care of her.

When I realised it was possible to order wool through the guards, I purchased wool and sat on my bunk and knitted. I knitted a sweater for Kylie and a vest for Peter and one for my father, and a cardigan for my mother. I knitted for hours every day, as though I was trying to gather the threads of what had been my life and knit them back together again. Although Sheela was my mentor and friend, I soon tired of being locked up in a small space with her all day, particularly as she talked incessantly of her love for Bhagwan and how she was the only one who really understood him. That, and the fact that inmates who worked could shower five days a week instead of once a week, moved me to ask for a job. I was assigned to the laundry.

The prison laundry washed for the women inmates and also for men's prisons in the area. Upon arrival in Bühl we had been issued with seven pairs of spotlessly clean underpants, seven undershirts, three shirts, three pairs of trousers, a pullover, seven pairs of socks, shoes, bright chequered bed linen, clean blankets, towels and washcloths, and an array of clean, ironed tea towels and cleaning cloths. Once a week everything except the blankets was exchanged for clean items. Most things were washed at 95°C and, after being dried, everything was put through a large roller iron and folded neatly. It was a pleasure to receive the new issue of clothing every week, and the crispy fresh bedsheets. It was hot work in the laundry but it was winter and the work atmosphere was pleasant. At the end of the day we were taken to shower, before being returned to our cells in time for supper.

Sheela's nurse joined me for a while, until Sheela recalled her to type her memoirs. The nurse would rush out every morning to secure the typewriter and then sit on the toilet seat with the typewriter on the table in front of her to record Sheela's musings. They were very repetitive. Sheela clung to the story that Bhagwan was a great master, that she loved and trusted him absolutely, that he was testing us, and that only she understood his vision. Part of me believed her, for I was in no way thinking clearly for myself. Even so, another part of me was very sceptical. Bhagwan had just betrayed her royally and I was having trouble making sense of that part of his vision, no matter how hard I tried.

Savita arranged lawyers for each of us, and borrowed money to pay for them. We protested our innocence to our lawyers. Bhagwan was making it all up, we said. That was the party line. Although we were locked into the same cell together, we three women never talked about the offence we were charged with, except to agree it had not happened. There was nothing more to discuss when nothing had happened. Sheela thought that in America lawyers were duty-bound to tell the court if a client admitted their guilt to them, so it was safer not to be too honest with lawyers anywhere, just to be sure. No fear of that as far as I was concerned. I was not being honest with myself, let alone anybody else. I was in complete denial.

I had grown up in denial of everything about myself that could possibly be called bad or sinful. So when I attacked a man with the intention of killing him, that act was so impossibly huge, so devastating, it was automatically denied. It had to be. I could not possibly have done that terrible thing. Of course a part of me knew what I had done, but as with all bad things I pushed it so far from me that it did not seem to have anything to do with me. I was removed from it. I could never do such a bad thing. It had not happened.

I know this will be hard for people to understand. They will say, 'She did it, so of course she knows what she did.' But such people underestimate the power of the mind to rationalise and paint reality in colours that correspond to a belief system. I grew up with the clear understanding that to kill someone was the most terrible thing anyone could do; it damned you to hell for all eternity. It was an unthinkable act. So when I attempted the unthinkable, my mechanism of denial went into overdrive, and stayed there.

The news the lawyers had was not encouraging. America and Germany were parties to an extradition treaty, and if the charge was an offence with a possible sentence of one year or more imprisonment in both countries, extradition would be pretty much automatic. Attempted murder fell within the treaty guidelines. Savita contacted a lawyer in Chicago. When we got news that Sheela faced twenty years imprisonment in America I cried angry tears and cursed Bhagwan. Strangely enough I did not cry for myself and the years of imprisonment I was facing. Just as I had been focused on Bhagwan and his safety and happiness, I now focused all my concern on Sheela. I seemed not to exist for myself.

Sheela's lawyer fell in love with her. He neglected his other clients and came every day to sit holding her hand for hours in the visiting room. It was a little like two people sitting in a kayak gazing into each other's eyes while the kayak is careening towards the falls. It went over them on 22 January 1986. On that day, the Higher Regional Court in Karlsruhe ruled that we were to be extradited back to the United States of America. A few days later we were taken by military helicopter to Frankfurt airport and handed over to US marshals in dark overcoats and sunglasses for transportation to America.

26

The handcuffs went on the moment our German escort departed. Up until that moment we had not been handcuffed at all. Our new attendants would make up for that oversight in the long hours to come. We each had three escorts and were separated and taken on three different flights. A whole section of the plane I was on had no other passengers other than my three attendants and me. I was handcuffed for the entire flight, and in fact until my escort delivered me to the Multnomah county prison in downtown Portland a day later.

I no longer remember the route we flew, but I remember looking out the window at snow-covered Mount Hood and being mystified to see it again so soon. The rest is a blur, until I was locked in a small concrete cell. The bed was a raised concrete slab along one end with a mattress on top. The only other furniture was a stainless-steel toilet and hand basin. There was a fixed window above the bed. I was many floors above the ground. It was dark outside. A single light bulb burned over the doorway. The cell was filthy and the bedding I had been issued was torn and a dingy grey colour, though I could see that it had once been white. My prison wardrobe was a suit such as nurses and doctors wear in hospitals, which smelled of stale perspiration. I had sandals on my feet. People were shouting and screaming and beating on their metal cell doors. I was sure I had been locked in a mental asylum and decided they must be trying to break me. Three months imprisonment in clean, quiet Bühl had not prepared me for this.

The light over the door was never turned off. I thought they would have their way and I would go crazy. The next morning a metal grating sound in the door was followed by the sound of inmates moving around outside. I went to the door and realised it had been opened not by a person but via a central control. I went looking for cleaning cloths and a bucket of soapy water to clean my cell. The other inmates laughed at me. There was no such thing. Once a week the mop came round, they said. It took me a while to figure out that I could use a sanitary pad as a cleaning cloth, wetting it in the hand basin and wiping down the walls and floor with it. By the time I was finished I needed a second one to clean the hand basin and toilet. For the entire time of my stay in the Multnomah prison, I used two sanitary pads every day to clean my cell. Nobody noticed my unusually large demand for them so it was never necessary to explain that I was not in fact haemorrhaging but had assigned the pads another use.

The lawyer who had been arranged for me by Sheela and Savita came to see me. His name was Frank Stoller. I denied any knowledge of the charge, protesting my innocence and putting it all down to Bhagwan's temper tantrum at our leaving. I told him about the hospital's diagnosis of the doctor's condition. Frank thought the chances of an acquittal were good, particularly as Bhagwan's doctor was no longer in the country and it was a very good guess he would not return. He encouraged me to go to trial. I did not tell him it was not my decision to make. I was still passionately defensive of Sheela and was not about to do anything that might jeopardise her safety.

I was arraigned in the Dalles County Courthouse, the same courthouse where less than a year earlier I had raged at local people and the county commissioners. Frank and I sat at the same table I had sat at then. The prosecution argued that bail should not be granted because there was a danger of flight. They showed the judge photographs of what they said was the underground escape route I had used to escape from the ranch. They said the escape route was accessed through a secret panel in Sheela's bathroom and came out on the county road. The photographs were passed around. I was stunned. I had never seen wherever it was the photos were taken, and I had not escaped through it or any other 'underground tunnel'. I had no idea what they were talking about. I whispered to Frank that it was pure fiction and wanted to stand up right there and then and tell the judge that they were making it up. Frank put his hand on my arm and told me to keep quiet. I sat there indignantly thinking Bhagwan had been right about one thing. He had been right about *Them.* They would stoop to any lies and low tricks to have their way.

Later Frank gave me witness statements which indicated that, on Bhagwan's instructions, Sheela had in fact had an escape route built, in anticipation of an INS raid. Bhagwan was to be whisked by car to her house, enter through the secret panel in her bathroom, and down a flight of stairs into a comfortably furnished underground room where there was food and medical supplies. He could hide there indefinitely until the coast was clear, and then walk out through a kind of culvert to the pick-up point on the county road, from where he would be driven the few hundred metres to the airport. She had shown him the set-up when it was finished and he had gone down the steps and sat in the room, and approved of it. I remembered then that there had been some earthmoving activity behind Sheela's house at one time, but I had not asked what it was about or taken a look to see for myself. Bail was set at one million dollars.

Once in America, Sheela was charged with many serious state and federal offences. I was only too happy to have her take control of the defence team. She was now my new master, and I relied on her to guide me safely through the confusing and frightening world in which I found myself. Besides, she was in great danger, I reasoned, so I would let her decide what should be done and just stay out of the way until her affairs were settled. After all, I had only one charge and she had multiple charges. Sheela's nurse had also been charged with multiple offences, so clearly I would also wait until her affairs were settled too.

After Bhagwan had abandoned the commune and flown away, his jet landed in North Carolina to refuel. Tipped off by an anguished sannyasin who watched him fly away, authorities monitored his flight path. Armed law-enforcement officers stormed the plane when it touched down, arresting Bhagwan and his entourage. The prison where he was kept was inundated by an avalanche of telegrams and letters and flowers such that the authorities, not wishing to have a martyr on their hands, cut a deal with his lawyers in double-quick time. Those Rajneesh corporations involved abandoned all claims to the money and jewels impounded in North Carolina. Bhagwan was returned to Oregon where he appeared in federal court and pleaded guilty to immigration fraud. He was sentenced to ten years imprisonment and fined four hundred thousand dollars. The fine was paid immediately and the prison sentence was set aside on condition he leave the country. He and his entourage, which included his doctor, left the court building, drove to the airport and flew away in his private jet. By the time Sheela and her nurse and I arrived in America, Bhagwan and his doctor were no longer in the country.

I spent practically all the time in my cell reading. Meals were generally a bland greyish mush with no recognisable relationship to meat or vegetables or anything else edible, and which tasted just as bad as it looked. I couldn't believe the staff ate the same thing. Often all I could recognise as food were the white bread rolls and the apples and oranges that accompanied the main meal of the day. I traded the other girls my meals for their oranges and apples, and my bread rolls for library books.

Inmates could go to the library once a week and were allowed three books each, but the way I was reading, three books were not enough. On library day girls who had never read a book in their lives started going to the library with me and signing out books like *War and Peace*, *Wuthering Heights*, *Bury My Heart at Wounded Knee* and *The Grapes of Wrath*. I made my selection and each of them signed out one or two books. During open-cell time they would drop the books over to me. They themselves were content to watch the TV running continuously on the pole in the centre of the cell block.

The only fresh air available was on the two days a week when inmates were taken to a covered caged area on the roof. I eventually fashioned a blindfold from a washcloth and a strip of plastic torn from a plastic bag to wear against the light that burned continuously in the cell; I even got used to the screams and door hammering of new arrivals who were locked into cells and left cold-turkey to deal with their alcoholic or drug-induced delirium; but there were times when I didn't understand how my body could go on living in such unnatural, inhuman surroundings. For years afterwards I would be seized with panic if I had to sleep in a closed room where a light was burning, even if the light was only the smoke alarm or the power light on an electrical appliance.

Every couple of weeks I was transported to the tiny local lock-up in Hood River. It consisted of only two cells that opened onto a small recreation room with a table and chairs. Although the windows were covered and I could not see outside at all, I always looked forward to being spelled there. The windows opened enough to let in fresh air and there was no light burning in the cell. There was also a real shower that I could stand under without having to hold a button down to get water. There was a real bed and the cell was always clean. I was locked into my cell every evening and the door was unlocked again every morning at 6.30 am and stayed open for the rest of the day. I was always the only inmate. Even the food was real food there.

I was kept well supplied with books and read my way through the long quiet days. That little lock-up was a haven for me. Only once did I have reason to regret being in such a small prison. It was when Peter flew over from the east coast to visit me. He was eighteen years old and was denied entry because he was a minor not in the company of a lawyer. He wept bitter tears when he was turned away, and so did I when I was told. He stayed in Portland and came with Frank to see me there when I returned. It was the first time we had seen each other since I had left Rajneeshpuram. He had suffered through Bhagwan's character assassination of me, his ultimate betrayal of his sannyasins when he flew away and left them, and the subsequent annihilation of the commune itself.

The half-hour we had together was barely long enough for me to tell him I loved him and to ask how he was and what he was doing. He said he was living with Roger and his wife out east. He was looking for a job, but it was proving difficult because he was loath to mention that he had his training and work experience in Rajneeshpuram, which had become a dirty word all over America. He asked me about the charge and I told him Bhagwan had made it all up. And then he asked how I was and I said I was fine. Then the visiting time was up and he had to go. We hugged each other, and he left. On subsequent visits we sat with a soundproof glass wall between us and spoke through a telephone headset. We touched hands on either side of the glass in greeting and to say goodbye. It broke my heart every time, but I never let on. I pretended I was okay in a futile attempt to ease the anguish I saw in his eyes.

The defence team negotiated plea bargains for us. A plea bargain is a particularly American thing. More than eighty percent of criminal cases in America never go to trial but are dealt with by plea bargain. It involves the attorney for the defence bargaining with the prosecution, much as one might bargain for a car or a carpet. He might say,

'Look, she will plead guilty [thereby saving the State the cost of a trial] if you agree to drop other charges [if there are any] and/or ask for a lesser sentence.'

Government witnesses also have lawyers whose bargaining chip is the information their client can provide about other defendants. The process may go on for weeks, if not months. When all the details are finally agreed upon, a plea agreement is drawn up and signed by all parties to the negotiations.

Sheela's plea bargain was a very complicated affair as there were so many things to negotiate and there were agreements to be reached in both federal and state courts. In addition, her outcome was to influence mine and her nurse's. For example, Frank argued that I was not to serve as much time as Sheela. By mid-July everyone was in agreement. There was one slight hiccup when Mr Turner, who was a party to the negotiations, wanted Sheela to plead guilty to conspiracy to murder him and accept a further six months on top of the time she was already facing.

All sentences on all charges were to be served concurrently, which meant that if Sheela were sentenced to five years on one charge and five years on another charge, she would serve just one five-year sentence. What Mr Turner was proposing was that in return for clearing up the last loose thread by pleading guilty to the conspiracy, she would serve an additional six months on the maximum sentence that had already been agreed upon. She adamantly refused, insisting there never was a conspiracy. So Sheela's federal plea agreement did not carry the usual stipulation that no further charges could be brought at a later date.

On 22 July 1986 Sheela, her nurse and I appeared in state court and pleaded guilty to the attempted murder of Bhagwan's doctor. We all entered *Alford pleas*, in which the defendant pleads guilty to the charge but says they didn't do it. They say they are pleading guilty in order to limit the possible penalties against them (were they to go to trial and be found guilty by a jury), but actually they are not guilty. In the case of an *Alford plea* the defendant is not required to make a statement of facts, as is the case with a straight guilty plea. As far as I was concerned, there were no facts to make a statement about. It had never happened.

The judge accepted our pleas and passed sentence. Sheela was sentenced to twenty years imprisonment and her nurse to fifteen years. I was sentenced to ten years imprisonment.

The State of Oregon had at the time a matrix system for the use of the parole board in calculating the actual time a person was to serve, taking into consideration factors such as seriousness of the offence, previous record and age. The prosecution approached the parole board on my behalf and requested that the time I was to serve be set at the lowest end of the scale. In a letter to the parole board they wrote:

[The accused] was a member of a cult for nine years. She engaged in criminal conduct at the instigation and prodding of others. She was subjected to peer influence and group pressure of unremitting and extreme character over a significant period of time. In a very real sense, her criminal conduct was encouraged by sociological phenomena and group dynamics that distorted her moral priorities. *[She]* was not responsible for the instigation and planning of the attempted murder, nor has she been proven to be involved in any other criminal activity . . .

[The accused] is responsible for a criminal act of a most serious nature. We do not recommend this minimal mitigation in fixing her release date because her crime was excusable or because her participation in a murder plot is insignificant. We believe, however, that the cause of justice in this case requires recognition of the significant differences between [her] conduct and that of her co-defendants.

The parole board agreed to the request. Although I had no federal charge, it was decided I should serve my time in a federal penitentiary (FCI) in California with Sheela and her nurse.

27

People said that FCI Dublin was financed by the newspaper baron William Randolph Hearst when his daughter Patti was sentenced to imprisonment. I guess what they were trying to say was that it was one of the better prisons. Each cell had a large window without bars. We couldn't open the window but it was set low enough down that we could look out. Each cell was originally built to house one person. Most were already housing two, and during my time the last of the women still alone in a cell were assigned a second person to share their precious space. There were three cell blocks set apart from each other in a large open area. This meant that to go to the cafeteria, or to work, we walked outside in the fresh air. And at given times of day it was possible to exercise in a large open sports field. If you were to forget the high razor-wired fences and overlook the small windows in each cell door, it could at first glance have looked like a university campus. In those days men were housed in one cell block and women in the other two. Sheela was in one block and her nurse and I were in the other, so we only got together with her when the cell blocks were unlocked. Although I still looked to her for guidance, I was aware of a sense of relief when it was time to return to our respective quarters.

Within days of arriving in Dublin, the three of us were taken under the wing of a woman called Liz who had already been incarcerated for a very long time. Most people in prison don't talk about why they are there so there are always lots of rumours going around. By the time Sheela, her nurse, and I arrived our reputation was already established as dangerous, tough dames to keep clear of. There were rumours about Liz too, but she herself never referred to her life before prison.

She was intelligent and she knew her way around. She worked as the inmate supervisor in the data-input office and suggested it would be a good place for the three of us to work. It was clean, safe work (unlike the furniture manufacturing workshop on the compound) and we could be together. Sheela and her nurse were all for it but there was a catch. I couldn't type.

'Don't worry,' said Liz, 'you'll learn.'

So we applied for work at the data entry office and were invited to come for a proficiency test. The supervisor handed us a text and disappeared behind the glass partition where the mainframe computer recorded the input of the dozens of terminals in the room. It also recorded the speed with which the data was entered on each individual terminal. Liz assigned Sheela and her nurse terminals on the wall. She gave me a terminal at the very back of the room.

I had never studied a keyboard close up before and was disconcerted to discover that the keys were not in alphabetical order. Liz sat down at the machine as if she were showing me the job. She said words I didn't really hear because I was mesmerised by the speed with which her hands were racing over the keyboard as she spoke. She stopped abruptly, stood up and indicated for me to sit down.

'You space the words with this one,' she said hitting the space bar. 'Just begin.'

I started searching for letters as she walked away. It seemed an eternity before she came back. She stood there for a moment at my shoulder. Then her two hands reached over and played another salvo on my keyboard, while she continued to stand there as though she were simply observing. As suddenly as she had begun she stopped and wandered off down the aisle, stopping to say a word or two to the people she passed. For the duration of the test, she wandered back to where I was searching my keyboard again and again, and each time, under the guise of showing an interest in my work, her hands would race across the keyboard with dizzying speed.

I got the job. That evening I enrolled in the office skills course to learn to type. There was just one supervisor. She assigned me a typewriter, a place to sit and a book divided into lessons, and returned to her desk. I did lesson one. In the weeks that followed, daytimes were spent picking away at my keyboard in the data-input unit, and evenings spent in night school working my way through that book. By the time I left data entry I had attained the maximum wage of $1.10 an hour.

Wages were used to buy basic necessities like toothpaste, soap, shampoo and hair conditioner. Then there were the luxury items like Cup-a-Soup, hair curlers, perming lotion and emery boards. It was considered a real treat when avocados were available in the commissary. Avocados meant salsa was on the menu for midnight snacks, a welcome change to the clandestine cheese sandwich toasted on the ironing board with a hot iron.

One morning I woke with my belly full of tears. I carried them around with me until I remembered my dream of the previous night and they spilled over. I had dreamed there was a brilliant white gold light. It was so bright I could hardly keep my eyes open. Suddenly I realised it was Rosemary. The moment I recognised her, her life played before me, starting when she died and running backwards. It played fast, in the blink of an eye, and I saw that she had lived her life to the full. She had done what she set out to do, and she had done it well.

For the first time since her death, I was overwhelmed with grief that Rosemary had died. I longed to hear her harsh monotone voice again and to have her throw her arms around me. I was brokenhearted that I had not gone to see her when she was dying, and that I would never see her again. I sat at my keyboard with the tears running down my face. When people asked me why I was crying I told them my sister had died.

Through an arrangement made with Sheela's lawyer, and with Savita picking up the tab, it was possible to use the payphone in the prison to call overseas. I used to call Kylie once a week. Although my parents had welcomed her with open arms, they were overly protective of her. This natural tendency of theirs may have been exacerbated by their advanced age and the responsibility they felt towards her because of my being in prison. But Kylie was not used to being asked where she was going and when she would be back, and having to explain herself if she was out longer than expected. After a time she went to Esperance to stay with an aunt and her family. There too she felt restricted and finally returned to Germany to the dwindling group of renegade sannyasins with whom we had lived before my arrest.

One day when I called and asked to speak to her, there was an awkward silence.

'Kylie has run away,' I was told. 'The police are out looking for her.'

Without stopping to consider what may have compelled her to run away, I hung up and made a phone call to Peter, who very reluctantly told me where she was. I called to the group in Germany and let them know where the police could find her. It is one of the ugliest episodes of my life and one I deeply regret, that I did not see my child crying out for understanding but instead sent the police to bring her back. And once she was returned I did not ask her what was wrong. I chastised her vehemently instead, and when she answered back and said she didn't want me as her mother, I asked the personnel manager to slap her face for me, not once but twice. It was the beginning of a period of complete estrangement between Kylie and me that would last more than a year, ending as it did when she came to see me almost every day pending my release.

From a prison cell in another country I was trying to be the mother I had not been for her for the last eight years. Sensing the futility of what I was doing, I became more and more desperate every time she voiced her dissatisfaction with her living arrangements. I had heard that some of the kids had begun taking drugs after the commune collapsed and that some were now heroin addicts, and I was afraid to let her go to America where Roger and Peter and many of the commune kids were now living in California. In truth all she wanted was to be with her father and her brother, and when she ran away that was where she was headed.

Through all this Sheela was coaching me from the sidelines, telling me I should forget about her. But even in my very messed-up state I knew that Kylie was my daughter and, although I might be making a complete botch of being a mother to her, I would always be her mother. I contacted Roger for the first time since leaving the ranch and asked him to come and see me.

It was a terrible visit. I had asked him to come on Saturday so we would still have Sunday to visit if we needed more time. He came on Sunday afternoon with only an hour and a half of visiting time left. I was already angry with him for not having contacted me since my arrest, and when he came so late I was even more angry with him. He cried and was nauseous and had to go to the bathroom. As usual I felt contemptuous of his weakness. When he returned I explained that as I was not able to care for Kylie myself, he needed to take responsibility for his daughter. As it turned out he was doing just that and was already making arrangements for her to join him in America.

Many years later I would learn that Kylie had been treated badly by the very person I had asked to slap her face. When Kylie returned from Australia, the personnel manager treated her like Cinderella, bossing her about and even confiscating the little money she made working in a bakery. No wonder she ran away. But I was still light-years away from myself, and Kylie would have to live as many years again before I would have eyes to see her pain. My eyes were still squeezed tightly shut and I was holding my breath waiting for the bad things to go away, especially this bad thing called imprisonment.

It was a long breath but I made it. Twenty months after being arrested in Germany, I was taken in chains to San Francisco airport and put on a plane to Australia. Mum and Dad were there to meet me at the airport in Perth. For all the callous indifference I had shown towards them, and then my much publicised arrest and imprisonment, it was remarkable with what joy first Dad and then Mum took me into their arms again, and with what joy I fell into those arms. It was such a relief to know they still loved me. Twenty-one years had passed since I had left home as a new bride. I returned to my parents' house destitute, with only the clothes I was wearing. Like the proverbial prodigal child, I had squandered my wealth and the gifts I had been given, and I had lost my husband and children. My parents took me in and cared for me. Dad opened a bank account for me and Mum took me shopping and bought me clothes and shoes, and took me to the dentist and the hairdresser. I spent my days cooking and gardening with them and allowed their gentle goodness to wash over my bruised soul. All the running away, all the groups and commune living had not produced an independent human being. On the contrary, I was a helpless child in a forty-two year old body.

Germany

28

I had a huge legal debt. Savita had covered it from money she had borrowed but the debt had to be repaid. The first instalment came from a couple of interviews I did when I first came home. I wince to think of them now, for I was still in complete denial of any wrongdoing on my part or on the part of my co-defendants. A listener to a radio interview took umbrage at my defence of Sheela and called in to say he had a mind to set fire to my parents' house, with me in it. It was the first time the impact of my actions on my family really came home to me. They had had to deal with inquisitive neighbours and the press, but an overt threat against them of this kind awakened memories of similar rhetoric from the past. It was as though I had tainted them in some way. It shook me terribly.

After I had spent six months in Australia with my parents, potting up herbs and selling them at weekend markets to earn a little income, Savita invited me to return to Germany where she had bought a small juice bar she thought I could manage. It would depend on me being given a working visa, she said. Dad wasn't sure. I had been gone so long and we were just settling into a semblance of family life again. But I was restless. I still felt very connected to Sheela and the people who continued to support her. I ran up huge phone bills in my need to maintain close contact with them. Savita's offer sounded ideal. Mum didn't hesitate.

'Go to Germany,' she said. 'It will be good for you.' And so it was that I packed my bag and went, thinking that I would return in a year.

Once in Germany, Savita accompanied me to the office where working visas were issued, and explained that she needed someone to manage her juice bar. The man behind the desk asked me how long I would like to stay. I said a year. He said I would need two years to learn the language, and wrote me out a visa for two years.

Of the original group of more than twenty people who had left Bhagwan, only three remained. In the time I had been away the others had all gone their separate ways. The remaining three had an apartment in Baden-Baden, where two of them worked. I joined them there. Savita, and now myself, travelled to Karlsruhe to work, Savita to a bistro she managed at the time, and me to the juice bar. It was a drive of perhaps half an hour on a busy autobahn. The days were short and the nights were long. It was always dark when we drove back and forth. I was barely six months out of prison, and I think it is safe to say I was still in shock from the whole Bhagwan experience. And now I was in Germany. I had inadequate clothing for the cold. I could not speak or read the language. The traffic drove on the right-hand side of the road, and it was fast! On the autobahn between Karlsruhe and Baden-Baden I lived in terror of missing the turn-off and driving on into the darkness until I reached the end of the world, or ran out of petrol. Either scenario was horrible to me. It was the long dark nights that threw me. I felt as though I was living in perpetual darkness. I am sure it was a reflection of my inner world. I felt lost, all the time.

I was running a juice bar for the first time in my life in a country where I didn't speak the language. It was called the Saftladen, which literally means 'the juice shop'. But Saftladen has another meaning in German. A place is referred to as a *Saftladen* when it is badly managed, or rundown, or the staff are rude and unhelpful, or it just doesn't live up to standard. Customers in my Saftladen were afforded friendly service and good food and the place was clean, but they did have to order by pointing to the drink or snack they wanted on the menu card. I learned what everything was the first day and I would make up the order, smiling all the while to distract them from thinking too much about this odd Australian woman running a juice bar in the middle of Germany, with a vocabulary of *Guten Tag, Danke schön* and *Auf Wiedersehen*. Many of the customers came from the nearby university and most of them spoke English far better than my stumbling German. Being true Europeans at heart, they gave every indication of finding the whole ludicrous situation perfectly in order.

It was in those dark early days that I first met George, doctor of mathematics, computer scientist, logician and hermit. Later he would confess that for some time he had been visited by the absurd notion that he would meet his partner in a juice bar. This feeling had become so strong that he had actually sought out all the juice bars he knew of in the city, though he was unaware of the existence of the Saftladen. The young men and women working in those juice bars caused him to shake his head at his own foolishness, and he dismissed the whole thing as misguided fantasy. So when a colleague invited him to come to lunch at the juice bar run by 'two friendly English girls', he agreed without giving it a second thought.

George says that the moment he saw me he knew he had found me. He was in shock for days, his logical mind telling him it couldn't be so. I was not so quick to recognise him, or even to really see him. I was still struggling out of my dream world and could not see beyond the next juice. I was completely oblivious, concentrating on understanding and filling customers' orders, and simply getting through the day. For they were long days, and at the end of a day of pressing orange and grapefruit juice by hand with a lever press, preparing muesli and fruit pulp, and Pellkartoffeln with quark, the machines had to be cleaned and the floor scrubbed and it was 8.30 or 9 pm before I got home for dinner. On Sundays I slept.

It was not only my busyness that prevented me from noticing George. It was also my conviction that only a sannyasin would understand me. In fact I was in a relationship with a sannyasin. When Savita confided to me that she had fallen in love with a mad scientist and her boyfriend of many years was beside himself, I entered into a relationship with the boyfriend in a display of misguided solidarity with both of them. He was known as James, though that was not his real name. I had not been with a man for many years, not since the Frenchman who called me a nun. James was affectionate and I was in need of that; he in turn was comforted, and Savita was free to pursue her new love. It seemed perfectly logical to our sannyasin way of thinking. We had to stick together.

With the coming of spring things began to change. Days were longer. Now it was daylight when I made the trip back and forth to Baden-Baden, and for the first time since arriving in Germany I began to get my bearings. I began to relax. I was at ease with preparing the different items on the menu, and a woman came in to help with the lunchtime rush. George was a regular customer. He began writing down a German phrase of the day for me to paste on my side of the counter where I could read it before trying it out on the customers. At first it was simple phrases like *Guten Tag. Was hätten Sie gern?* (Good day. What would you like?). The door would open, I would take a quick look at my prompt, look up and smile and say, 'Guten Tag. Was haetten Sie gern?' Or he wrote *Schönes Wochenende* (Have a nice weekend) or *Fröhliche Ostern* (Happy Easter). When I told him people asked the difference between the two dried fruit 'energy balls' and I didn't know how to explain that there was no difference other than the one was rolled in coconut and the other in sesame seeds, he wrote down *nur die Oberflaeche ist verschieden* for me to paste on the counter.

Never taking offence at my flawed pronunciation, customers were delighted at my tentative efforts to speak their language. They talked right back, pointing and gesticulating to emphasise their point. At first it was all incomprehensible sounds, but then I began to recognise isolated words, and then phrases, and then whole sentences! I could understand what people were saying long before I could speak fluently myself, and there were many times when I felt frustratingly mute because I couldn't find the words to express myself. But more and more I could find the words, and almost without noticing, I was speaking German. It was all pretty basic small talk, but it is to my customers that I owe my introduction to the German language. They good-humouredly laid the foundations that would later allow me to read Goethe and Thomas Mann in their native language, and to communicate my thoughts and feelings freely to the German friends who would come into my life.

Organising ourselves like a mini commune, our little group in Baden-Baden worked long days and put everything we earned into a common fund. Savita continued in her role of managing financial matters, and on Saturday we gave her our weekly earnings and accounted for our expenditures. After expenses were paid, the rest went towards supporting Sheela and her nurse, who were still in prison, and towards repayment of our loan. Savita managed the finances with great care. When we three women were arrested, she had borrowed five hundred thousand Deutschmarks from a generous German heiress. It was understood that it was to be used to cover our legal costs and the initial care of the group that had left Bhagwan, including buying businesses we could work in. The loan was interest-free and was to be repaid in full, five years hence. The group agreed to take joint responsibility for the repayment of the loan and Savita placed her signature on the contract.

In her wisdom she left about a quarter of what had been borrowed in the bank as a security blanket, painstakingly adding to it whatever small savings could be made from the combined income of the group. As people left, the number of people remaining to cover the debt diminished, until eventually, after yet another defection, there were only three of us, and the two women still in prison. There was never any mad money to spend. We never went to the movies or ate out. We bought everything in bulk from a self-service wholesaler. Savita and I often removed vegetables from the crates of produce tossed into the garbage bins after a night of trading at the markets. We took our finds home to the kitchen in Baden-Baden and were proud to be so thrifty. We kept very much to ourselves and had hardly a friend in the outside world.

It must be said that, for all the rigour of those early days managing the Saftladen, working so single-mindedly at the task helped me get my feet on the ground again. I would still need some time before I began to take root there, but my feet were back on planet earth. And despite the similarities of hard work and no money to the life we had known in Oregon, some things in our mini commune were different. I maintained close contact with my family, and at the end of the first year I flew home to my parents for a visit.

It was at about this time that newspapers carried the story that Bhagwan had announced that he no longer wished to be known as Bhagwan. He had already taken the precaution of changing the names of his doctor and Vivek after they had left the commune with him. Now he changed the name by which the world knew him. Henceforth his name would be Buddha, he said. Buddhists all over the world protested vehemently, leading him to say a few days later that it had all been a joke and actually he wanted to be called Osho.

It was an important step in the process of repairing the damage done to his image by the events in Oregon. With one broad stroke he made it all disappear. He painted it over with a new name. The name Bhagwan disappeared completely from the dozens of publications of his discourses. They were reprinted under the new name of Osho. Even the text was changed. Questions that had once been asked of Bhagwan appeared in the new generation of reprints as questions addressed to Osho, my own question included. All over the world Bhagwan books disappeared from the shelves of bookstores and were replaced with Osho books. It was a brilliant manoeuvre, carried out with typical attention to detail.

A year later, in January 1990, he was dead. A few months earlier Vivek had been found dead in a hotel room in Pune. The authorities said it was suicide. Bhagwan died in his ashram. Cause of death was reported as heart failure. He was fifty-nine years old. His doctor and faithful ministrant was with him. Ready as I had been to throw away my life that Bhagwan might live, I was strangely indifferent to the news that he had died.

29

Although I only saw George when he came to the Saftladen, when Sheela was to be released from prison and would be coming to join us in Baden-Baden, I felt the need to tell him about my past before she did it for me. He was the only customer I told. We sat on the window sill outside the Saftladen after the lunchtime rush and I told him I had been in the ashram in India and the commune in Oregon. I told him I had been in prison, and that Sheela was coming. As always, I protested my innocence. He listened and did not appear shocked or horrified, and he came as usual the following week.

One of the first things Sheela said when she met George was, 'Shanti B is an excellent shot!'

I cringed. The name, the subject. They were from another time and seemed to have no place in my life any more. Sheela would always persist in using my sannyas name, but for me the name was now associated with another person.

Sheela's parents came to visit once she was free. She left for Japan with a rich German sannyasin the day after they arrived, leaving them in our care until she returned. One day her father called us all together in the living room and urged us to follow her without question.

'Sheela has the vision,' he said.

I was aware of an unwillingness in myself to go along with this proclamation. After managing the juice bar for a year and a half, I was beginning to develop a little independence and self-confidence. I did not understand this at first and sought to pick up where we had left off. I was genuinely delighted that Sheela was free and we were together again, and yet something had changed. She was as charming and outrageous as she had always been, but I could no longer find the same enthusiasm for following her caprices.

When Sheela began talking about buying hotels and restaurants again, as she had done in the days before her arrest, Savita left the group, saying she no longer wanted to be a part of such grandiose schemes. She took another apartment in Baden-Baden and handed over to Sheela the management of the loan, including the savings she had conscientiously built up towards its repayment. The Saftladen was signed over to me and I was granted a visa allowing me to be self-employed. I missed Savita a lot. She had been the steadying influence in the group and when she left I felt abandoned and was angry with her.

There were new demands on my time now, and on the money from the Saftladen. Sometimes Sheela would want me to drive her somewhere and I would have to arrange for someone to take my place in the juice bar, and pay them to do it. She needed cash and would ask me to bring money home from the till. The Saftladen was small and couldn't maintain those kinds of demands on a regular basis. I told myself it would all work out and sought to enjoy the time with Sheela, but all the while the Saftladen was losing ground, and me along with it.

Sheela thought I needed to be jazzed up and organised a new haircut for me. Then, taking advantage of the winter sales, we went shopping to buy warm coats. In a shop in a village near Baden-Baden we discovered two very nice, elegantly cut woollen coats. They were of excellent quality and were half price. One for me, and one for Sheela. We didn't have any money with us, so the shopkeeper agreed to lay them aside until Sheela returned the following day to purchase them. I was very excited. A woollen coat! And such a lovely one! I would be warm at last. The next day in the Saftladen couldn't go by fast enough. I was looking forward to returning to Baden-Baden in the evening and slipping into my new coat. When I got home, Sheela excitedly announced that she had the coats and that she had found an even better one for me. She handed me a loosely woven object which revealed itself to be a short jacket of large sloppy cut in extremely bright colours.

'It's perfect for you,' gushed Sheela, 'and it only cost twenty Deutschmarks!'

I put it on. It hung on me like a gaudy rag. And the other coats? Yes, she had them, said Sheela, but when she saw the short jacket she thought it was so perfect for me that I should have it, and she would make use of the other coats herself. She would be needing them, she told me. Her public role required her to be well dressed. I swallowed my disappointment and tried to convince myself that she was right. But I was angry, and a storm of confusion and resentment swirled around in my head. I said nothing.

Deciding we needed two cars, Sheela traded in the station wagon and bought a bargain Ford and a tiny bright yellow Fiat. Needless to say, the Fiat was for me. Even with the passenger seat taken out, two boxes of bananas and a crate of oranges pretty much filled it.

It had a loose electrical connection somewhere which shook apart from time to time when driving, causing the motor to die, usually at the most inopportune times. The good thing was that it was such a small car I could hop out and easily push it off the railway tracks or intersection or bridge it had just stopped on.

The Ford was a bargain because it had been modified for its previous owner whose right leg had been amputated. It was an automatic, but the brake was where the clutch should be, and the accelerator was where the brake should be. I drove it only once, and never again!

When Sheela's nurse was released I could leave the two of them to run around the countryside while I concentrated on the Saftladen again. They returned from a trip one day to announce that Sheela had found a perfect little stone house for us in a nearby village. We could live there and it would be an investment for our old age. I should take out a mortgage with the bank to finance the purchase. The bank baulked. Although George saw Sheela only rarely in the Saftladen, he found her charming. I had of course often sung her praises to him; I had told him how she had managed the building of a city in the desert, and he admired her entrepreneurial spirit very much. When I told him about the property she had found and my difficulties with the bank, he offered to put up the security. The bank was happy with that, until Sheela returned from the notary with only her name listed on the deed papers. My name was not on the document, and the bank refused to go ahead with the loan. It was Sheela's lawyer who ultimately secured the loan, and who was left with the figurative millstone around his neck.

While Sheela was living in Baden-Baden and busy negotiating to buy property, her father was in the habit of strolling around the local park. With his long flowing beard, and dressed in a traditional Indian dhoti kurta, he looked for all the world like Bhagwan. People began to notice him, and her. The press asked for interviews. She appeared on television to talk about plans to buy a restaurant adjacent to the local TV station. Because I had a work visa she used my name as the future 'owner' of the restaurant and I received a letter from the police asking me to come in for an interview. The letter said they had reason to believe I was acting as a front for Sheela. George accompanied me to the interview to help with possible translation problems, and I came away with a stern warning. Sheela's careless boasting had nearly cost me my visa. I couldn't stand it any more. I just wanted to run the juice bar and create some security and order in my life. I didn't want to live in chaos any longer.

I told George I needed to get away for a few days to think things through as I wanted to make some changes in my life.

'You can come with me to my house in the Black Forest this weekend,' he said.

I protested that I needed to be alone to think things through. He said his parents lived in the granny flat on the ground floor, but that he was a hermit and there was plenty of space for me to be alone, in the house and in the forest. I shook my head. No, I needed to be alone. On Friday he popped his head around the door of the Saftladen.

'I'll pick you up after work tomorrow,' he said. 'The Black Forest is the best place in the world to think.'

As we drove up the curving roads that would take us up above the clouds I felt nervous and insecure. I had not been anywhere with a regular person in years. I really didn't know how to behave in the world and I still believed I could only relate deeply to someone who had been a sannyasin.

By the end of the weekend I had walked miles through the forest and knew what I had to do. I needed to leave Sheela, the relationship with James and the little group in Baden-Baden, and move to Karlsruhe where I could be close to the Saftladen. On Monday I answered a newspaper ad for a room in a student house near the university.

'Don't you think you're a bit old for a student house?' said George when I told him. 'There is a spare room in the house where I rent my apartment. Would you like me to ask the landlady if you can have it? I'll pick you up after work and take you out to have a look.'

It turned out to be part of the little apartment George rented, which was in turn part of a stately house. The landlady said she would remove the furniture she was storing there, we agreed on a price, and I moved into the room, and into George's life. The day I moved in I took the tram out to the apartment, carrying everything I possessed with me in a small sports bag.

I hung a photo of Sheela in the kitchen and spoke with her almost every day on the phone, but my focus was the Saftladen and getting it back on its feet. When the opportunity came up, I relocated it to a more central position in a courtyard off the main street. A new modern art gallery had opened in one of the buildings around the courtyard, and I secured space in the entrance to the gallery for the juice bar.

By now George and I had become a couple. On weekends we left Karlsruhe and drove to the house in the Black Forest. George had built the house so his parents, who had never owned a home of their own, could retire there. In a neighbouring village a friendly car dealer sold me an old Renault R4 for a very good price. I put the passenger seat back in the Fiat and sold it for a song to a customer for his student daughter. The Renault was essentially a motorised tin box on wheels, but it was my dream car. I could load and unload it easily, and transport all the crates of fruit and vegetables I wanted to. On his first visit to Germany, Peter sat next to me as we drove down the autobahn at the Renault's maximum speed of one hundred and ten kilometres an hour, engine and road noise making conversation practically impossible in the unlined tin construction. He looked at me with a pained expression and shouted above the noise,

'How could you do this to me, Mum? All my life I have dreamed of driving down a German autobahn, but in this!'

One evening in August 1989, James called from Baden-Baden and asked me to drive to Lake Constance with him. An American woman who had been in the group that left Bhagwan wanted to meet us there. Alma was living in Berlin. Although I had had no contact with her since my arrest four years earlier, James had kept in touch. She said she had something important she wanted us both to know.

We met at a place overlooking the lake. Alma had a friend with her. It was the heiress who had lent the money to Savita. Alma told us she had been contacted by the FBI. They wanted her cooperation in the Turner affair. They were saying that if she didn't cooperate she would get twenty years on the charges pending against her. Turner? I couldn't remember who that was. She reminded me that Mr Turner was the United States attorney whose house she had taken me to and whose parking space she had pointed out to me. It all seemed so long ago.

'But nothing happened,' I said weakly, aware of a coldness creeping in around my heart, unable to grasp that some menace might still be hovering around out there.

It seemed that Alma and James and another woman had become friends while they were involved in clandestine activities originating out of Sheela's bedroom. When we left Bhagwan, their friend was the one who had got as far as Portland but then decided to go back. She had become the first government witness, receiving full immunity in return for her testimony, as a result of which Alma and James were subsequently charged with arson and burglary, and Alma with wire-tapping. Now those charges were being used as a lever to pressure Alma into cooperating as a government witness.

I couldn't believe that there was any real threat to me. I had done my time. I had been in prison in America for almost two years and there had never been any hint of a new charge. I had abandoned all that madness and left the commune, and even the country, as had others who had been in some way party to it. Nothing had happened. There was no threat to anyone any more. George and I had just got together and my life was beginning to take shape again after the whole ghastly nightmare. I don't remember much more about the meeting by the lake, other than I cried at the thought of the past coming between George and me, without having any clear picture of what that might mean.

When James and I told Sheela what had happened, she agreed there was nothing to worry about, repeating the tried and true, 'But nothing happened'. George was worried at first, but I kept repeating the mantra. We didn't hear anything more from Alma and after a while the fear subsided and then disappeared altogether.

In an effort to be closer to her lawyer, Sheela leased a small pub near his home. She would often call me on weekends and ask me to come to the pub to help. I didn't like the place at all. I couldn't stand the smell of old cigarettes and beer, and the strident voices of those who had drunk too much. I would much rather have stayed with George in the peace and quiet of the Black Forest, but I always went when she called. She and her nurse had moved into the living quarters above the pub, and it wasn't long before Sheela was sitting outside on sunny afternoons talking to the press again.

One night, very late, the phone rang in the apartment. I staggered out of bed and picked it up. It was Sheela. She and her nurse had been shopping in France, she told me, and on the way back into Germany they had been stopped at the border and Sheela had been told she could not re-enter Germany. They had driven further along the border and tried to enter at another point, but she was expected there and stopped again. She and her nurse were in a hotel in France. I should call her lawyer, she said, and have him sort things out. I told her there was nothing to be gained by waking him at midnight. She should get some sleep and I would call him in the morning.

This incident did in fact mean that Sheela could not re-enter Germany. She decided she would hand-knit exclusive pullovers and vests to support herself, and to that purpose the Saftladen and the pub contributed the start-up capital for the purchase of yarns. Her nurse drove back and forth across the border bringing her raw materials. When it became clear that her visa situation was not about to change, she asked that her belongings be delivered to her too. One weekend George drove with me to the pub so I could help Sheela's nurse pack up her clothes. He watched in disbelief, and growing irritation, as we packed box after box of fine clothes and shoes and a total of five woollen coats from the overflowing cupboards. Even I was stunned at the amount of clothes Sheela had accumulated in her relatively short time in Germany. Perhaps it was her way of finding her way back into the world after three years of imprisonment. Or perhaps she knew my trick of squeezing my eyes shut and pretending nothing had happened, or changed, and she continued to live in the memories of what she would later describe as the happiest days of her life. Whatever it was, barely a year before the loan was to be paid back in full, Savita learned that the entire capital and savings she had given into Sheela's care had been spent.

When she decided to have village women in Portugal knit the sweaters, Sheela moved to Portugal to supervise the enterprise. She still called and asked me to do things for her, like selling her sweaters at the markets, but the enforced physical distance between us was loosening the last ties, and I found I was untangling myself and could say no. Her nurse had already made the break. When Sheela went to Portugal her nurse returned to America. She met up with an old beau from college days and they soon married and settled down together.

There were two critical factors on my side at this time. One was the fact that Sheela could not enter Germany, and the other, of no less importance, was that I had George by my side. His quiet steadiness had a stabilising effect on me. After a lifetime of blowing around like a leaf in a capricious wind, I was beginning to settle into myself and to take root in the earth at last, and I liked it. I had developed what could almost be called an allergy to chaos. I began to understand that my friendship with Sheela was one I could no longer afford to maintain if I was to foster stability in my life.

When Sheela returned to France from Portugal in late autumn, I drove there to see her. I told her our friendship was at an end. We had been through a lot together, but now it was over. I said I would have no further contact with her; there would be no more phone calls and no more money. It was over. She cried and said I was her last friend. Then she pulled herself together and became the saleswoman for her own exclusive line of knitwear. She opened the array of suitcases she had brought back from Portugal and showed me her wares. Perhaps I would like to buy one for myself, and one for George? I declined. We said our last goodbyes and I left. The next day I took down her photo from the kitchen wall.

When winter came, George and I went shopping to buy a woollen coat. It was a classic loden, beautifully cut, elegant and warm. We had a ceremonial burning of the twenty-Deutschmark harlequin jacket. George said he had never liked it either.

30

All this time Peter and Kylie were living in America. After an initial period of turmoil, they had settled down in California. They no longer lived with Roger, but shared living space in separate houses with their friends from the commune. Kylie had completed her high school certificate and was producing artworks and jobbing in restaurants to support herself. When Peter began working in a print shop, she got a job in the restaurant across the road so she could give her skinny brother generous portions when he came in for lunch every day. I was of course prohibited from entering America to see them. We exchanged sporadic letters and occasional phone calls (which were still very expensive in those days), but it wasn't until George and I got together and I distanced myself from Sheela that they came to Germany to visit.

Kylie came first, bringing me one of her art pieces to hang in the Saftladen, and then Peter came. In some ways it was as though we had never been apart. We simply picked up where we had left off so many years before. We didn't talk about the past, and if something did come up, I was still in a state of denial and kept to my version of the story. Their friends were by and large the same friends from commune days and I was always conscious that whatever I said could innocently find its way back into the sannyas milieu. I was deeply distrustful of sannyasins and, in fact, of just about everybody.

When I planned my annual trip home to visit my parents, George said he would like to come too. What he didn't say was that he wanted to meet my parents. He wanted to know where I had come from. So in February 1990 we flew to Australia together and spent four weeks with Mum and Dad. It did not escape my notice that my mother, normally reserved when meeting someone new, threw her arms around George the moment she met him. My father also found an immediate friend in George. They went out of their way to make him feel welcome. Mum made pasties and they drove us out into the eucalyptus forests and around the coast for picnics in true Paul style. My brother and his family joined in and took us to their favourite coves and the best of the local wineries. George ran on the beach every day, and swam in the ocean, enjoying the wide open spaces and easy uncomplicated lifestyle. He sat in the garden, smoking his pipe and reading, reaching out to pluck grapes from the great bunches hanging on the fence, or eating loquats and seeing how far he could spit the big brown seeds across the garden.

George and I walked along the Busselton jetty many times during our holiday and I recounted to him the happy memories the jetty held for me. We sat down and dangled our legs as I had done so often as a child and I was aware of how good it felt to have George to share my life and my memories with.

Shortly after our visit to Australia I told George I had attacked and tried to kill Bhagwan's doctor. He was the first person I ever told, and in telling him I was admitting it to myself for the first time. We were in the house in the Black Forest. It cost me a real physical effort to speak each word, and as they stumbled out my body began to shake. It took all my strength to will the story out into the open. My jaw was shaking as though I had fallen into an icy sea and I could hardly speak. George listened quietly. When I was finished he reached out and took my trembling hand and said,

'Come, let's go into the forest.'

My body was shaking so badly I could hardly get my coat on. He put his arm around my shoulders and held me close as we walked. We walked in silence. It was only when the shaking finally subsided more than an hour later that we turned for home. And only then did George speak again.

'I knew,' was all he said, and hugged me even tighter as silent tears ran down my face.

A characteristic of George's that not only endeared him to me but was also critical for me at this stage, was that he was patient and respectful. He was not opinionated and did not pry or prod or tell me what to do. He gave me time to work things out for myself. He waited until I was ready to talk about things, and then he was a good listener. Even when he saw through the dynamics of my relationship with Sheela, he did not urge me to end the friendship. He simply waited until I came to it myself.

In the summer of 1990, George received notification that he had been accepted for a post at a European Commission research centre. He had applied for the job a year earlier when he was still a hermit, and in fact it had been so long ago he had almost forgotten about it. It would mean leaving the university in Karlsruhe and moving to Italy. He asked me if I would consider selling the Saftladen and moving to Italy too. It was an easy decision. I wanted to be where he was. Lago Maggiore sounded like a beautiful place to live, and

I was sure I could learn Italian just as I had learned German. I began looking for someone to take over the Saftladen, and together we made lists of things to do. One morning at breakfast I said almost to myself,

'I must go to the dentist before we go to Italy.'

'Yes,' said George, 'and we must get married.'

We married on 10 August 1990. It was a Friday. I hung a note on the door of the Saftladen that said: *Wegen Familienfeier heute geschlossen.* We kept it a secret from everyone except our parents and Peter and Kylie. I had an almost superstitious need that there be no discordant note disturbing the harmony on our wedding day. I did not want anybody to know who might even think an unpleasant thought about our union, let alone say it. And from his point of view, George wanted it to be between us, and without any fuss, so only George's parents, my friend Susanne, and George's friend Kurt, were present. Afterwards we drove to *Der Grüne Baum,* a lovely hotel in the foothills of the Black Forest, and celebrated with a festive lunch.

When I went downstairs to the ladies' room, George's mother followed me and tried to bless me right there outside the toilets. She was a devout Catholic and it troubled her that we had not been married in the church. She didn't dare try to bless George for fear of rejection, but reasoned that if she blessed me that would count for both. I said I would be happy to receive her blessing, but asked her to wait. I wanted to talk to George, who I was sure would have no objections to motherly blessings. After lunch we took our guests for a walk and found a comfortable bench on the edge of the forest where they could sit in the soft summer sun, while we sat in the meadow before them and read aloud from the Song of Solomon, finishing with:

> *for lo, the winter is past,*
> *the rain is over and gone.*
> *The flowers appear on the earth,*
> *the time of singing has come,*
> *and the voice of the turtledove*
> *is heard in our land.*

Then we approached George's mother and asked for her blessing. She made the sign of the cross on each of our foreheads and spoke a blessing over us. Now we were married in the eyes of heaven too.

We planned to be in Italy by 1 October, the day George was due to begin his new job. There was a lot to be done preparing the Saftladen for sale. On 12 September Susanne took care of the shop while George and I drove to Bonn to apply at the Australian Embassy for a new passport in my married name. It was a beautiful day and as we drove home we congratulated ourselves on having ticked off yet another item from our to-do list. Tomorrow was the meeting at the bank to finalise the sale of the Saftladen and we would be able to tick that off the list too. On the way back along the river Rhine, George left the main road and drove to the nine hundred year old Benedictine monastery at Maria Laach. It was the first time I had seen anything like it. An old stone wall ran right around the property, and as we walked through the grounds it was tangibly a place that was loved and cared for. As we entered the old Romanesque basilica through the ancient wooden doors with the signs of the zodiac carved around their borders, I was struck by the uncluttered, simple beauty of its lines. We sat down on a pew towards the back. It was warm and peaceful, empty save for the sarcophagus of its benefactor. We sat there hand in hand, gazing up at the great mosaic filling the dome above the altar. I was filled with gratitude for the man at my side and for the way my life was taking shape. Tears welled up in my eyes. It was as though twin springs had just found their way to the surface. They flowed down my face like two rivers and would not be stemmed.

Early next morning, 13 September 1990, four weeks after George and I were married, two men and a woman walked into the Saftladen. One of the men went into the gallery to look around, but I paid attention only to the man who approached the counter.

'Guten Morgen,' I said smilingly. He took a wallet from his coat pocket, opening it as he held it out for me to see.

'You are under arrest,' he said, 'charged with conspiracy to murder the US attorney for the district of Oregon, Mr Charles Turner.'

31

I couldn't understand how my legs were still holding me up. The man walked around the counter to handcuff me and said I was to lock up the shop and go with them. Just walk out like that? Disappear without trace? George would come to pick me up in the evening and wouldn't know where to find me. No one would know where I was. I said I wanted to call my husband. He said I could not use the phone. I stood my ground and insisted one of them go upstairs and call Susanne down from her apartment. The woman went to get her, and the man warned me I was not to say anything to her about why I was going with them. As the woman came back with Susanne in tow, I raised my hands to show her the handcuffs around my wrists and said I had to leave with these people. Poor Susanne. She looked so bewildered, but her practical nature came to the fore and she said she would take care of the shop until I came back. I told her I might not be coming back. One of the men said,

'Oh don't say that.'

Numb as I was I turned to him and said bitterly,

'I know this game. I have played it before.'

It is hard to put on your coat when your hands are handcuffed. The man who had clipped them on draped it over them so they were discreetly covered, and we walked out to a car parked around the corner. I don't know where they took me. I couldn't see or feel. I was in such shock I could barely function and slipped into a dreamlike blankness. In my mind's eye I could see a monstrous machine. Like a gigantic steam roller. Now it had been set in motion, it had a momentum of its own. It was dark and menacing and rolled slowly but inexorably forward crushing everything in its path.

I was locked into a cell where I sat on the bunk with closed eyes and repeated George's name softly the whole day. I wanted so much to ease the shock when he would find me gone. With closed eyes I sat with him again in the church at Maria Laach and walked with him in the forest. I was so happy to have my wedding ring. It became his hand in mine. When I kissed it I was kissing him, and when I rested it against my cheek, my cheek rested on his shoulder.

I couldn't eat, but I made myself drink. As happens in times of great shock, I had to pee and poo again and again. The toilet had no flush of its own. It was flushed from outside by the guard. I was embarrassed to have to ask him to flush it every time he came by. It was late in the night when he came with a message to say George had called and said he would see me in the morning. I wept to know that he had found me. Then I lay down and slept.

The following morning I was taken for arraignment. As I stood there outside the judge's chambers, still in the clothes I had slept in and surrounded by four policemen, George suddenly appeared at the end of the corridor and came striding towards me. He walked straight up to me as though I was waiting for him in the park. The policemen did not exist for him, and they seemed not to see him at all. They parted as though moved aside by an unseen hand. He took me in his arms and held me, and for the first time since my arrest I knew I was not dead. He opened the plastic bag he had in his hand to show me the muesli he had made for my breakfast, Thomas Mann's *Joseph and His Brothers* (which I had just begun to read), my reading glasses, a photo of us on our wedding day, a photo of my children, and one of my parents. He had thought of everything. I thanked him for the muesli but told him I would not be able to keep it. I slipped the photos into the book and held it in my hand, together with my reading glasses. We stood there together, my head resting on his chest. The door to the courtroom opened and the four policemen suddenly became aware of his presence. They ordered him away from me, and escorted me into the courtroom.

The arraignment judge said I was to be confined to the women's prison in Bühl. The guard who processed me on arrival said I could not keep *Joseph and His Brothers*, but would have to apply to have it sent in at a later date. I protested that it was a religious book, based on the biblical tale of Joseph. She was sceptical and called up to the office. While she was on the telephone I remembered that Joseph was also thrown into prison twice, and it was the second time that the angels started pouting and complaining among themselves about God's behaviour. It was at the beginning of the fourth segment, which I had read as a separate book, not realising at the time that there were three others before it; an oversight I had just begun to remedy. In a way it was comforting to have read the fourth book first because I knew that the tale had a happy ending. I smiled wanly at the desperation that found solace in such things. The prison director said I could keep the book. He had seen me as I came in through the front gate.

Although it had been five years since I had been an inmate there, he recognised me. Somehow it was a consolation to see him, and to recognise other guards too.

I was assigned to a cell with a young woman asleep on the top bunk. As the door closed and the key turned in the lock, I sat down on the edge of the bottom bunk. A terrible panic began to rise slowly from the deepest recesses of my belly. Like a bubble it moved up through my abdomen and across my heart, getting bigger and bigger, crushing my organs against my bones. Just as it threatened to overwhelm me completely, I felt someone stand at my left shoulder and throw a long cloak around my shoulders. It fell around me, wrapping me completely in its soft blue folds. In that moment I knew that, no matter what happened, I would not be harmed.

That night I dreamed that I was standing on the jetty. My light summer dress fell loosely about me. It was a warm, still day. Sunlight sparkled on the water and I rejoiced in the delicious warmth that enfolded me. A mischievous breeze played with my dress. It rippled across my body mirroring the ripples running across the water. I smiled contentedly.

A little down the bay a young woman was waterskiing. She turned and moved towards the jetty. As she approached I began to feel agitated. She could not possibly intend to ski under the jetty. Impossible! The piles and timbers are much too close together to allow a speed boat through, let alone a skier in tow with a wake like a tidal wave. But that was exactly what she seemed to have in mind. Boat and skier headed straight for the jetty at breakneck speed. Head thrown back and laughing gleefully, the girl disappeared in a cloud of spray under the jetty and shot out the other side.

I watched in awe, mesmerised, as she turned full circle and advanced again. The roar of the motor filled the sky as the girl shot under the jetty a second time, not far from where I stood at the junction. I gazed enchanted at the figure on her watery throne as she reappeared and moved away.

But suddenly the tow rope was no longer in the girl's hands; it was looped around her waist. It tightened, as a fishing line does when a fish takes the bait. For a moment she stood stock still on the water. The straining rope held her there, and then violently demanded her return, tossing her up into the air and hurling her backwards.

My heart stopped. My blood froze in my veins. There was no sound. The pull of the rope around her waist folded the girl in two. She hung in the air, a bizarre rag doll suspended in nothingness. The shattering, terrifying explosion as she ricocheted into the piles exploded into the silence. She hung there for a moment, wrapped around the pile like a wet beach towel, before soundlessly slipping down into the water and sinking beneath its shining surface. The silence was deafening.

I stared in horror at the place where the girl had sunk. Nothing moved. I looked desperately around. The jetty, always so full of people promenading and fishing and riding their bikes, was empty. With mounting horror I realised that it was I who must do something. I knew the girl was dead. No one could survive an impact like that. She must be horribly mutilated, bleeding, sinking to the ocean floor.

I was already running along the jetty to the place where I had seen her sink. I didn't hesitate now. I jumped over the side. The shock of the cold water cleared the fear that was fogging my brain. I swam strongly to where I had last seen the girl. I could see her hanging in the water like washing on a line, about two metres down. I was already kicking my way down to her, stretching out my arm to cup the lifeless chin in my hand.

Turning towards the surface where the sun sparkled and danced on the water, I kicked my way upwards, lifting the limp form with me. Gasping for air, I broke into the sunlight and raised her head above the surface of the water, gently moving it to my shoulder so I could take up the limp body in my arm. As I did so, her face rolled towards me. I stared in disbelief. There was not a scratch on it. No blood, no bruising, no ugly gaping wounds. The eyes were closed, but the face radiated a luminous glow. As I stared, the eyelids flickered. They opened and two dark brown eyes like two inexhaustible wells met my gaze. In a moment of shocking recognition I knew her. It was me.

32

When George and I married I had closed the door on my past and turned towards what promised to be a brighter, sunnier future. During my first arrest and imprisonment I had successfully avoided being honest with myself about what had happened. The second arrest was an unmistakable signal, confirmed by my dream, that in order to move forward in my life I had first to deal with the past. I instinctively knew that I must turn back and open the door I had closed so tightly shut. Having finally acknowledged that I had tried to kill a man, it was no longer an option to pretend that I was an innocent victim of grave misunderstandings. It was now imperative that I be as honest with myself, and my lawyer, as I possibly could. But I dreaded going back there. It was such a dark place for me, full of painful memories of my frightening slide into irresponsible, ugly madness. Up until this point I had managed to keep them pretty much at bay, and many of those memories were still shadowy figures cloaked in the mists of time, and denial. Now the time had come when I must approach them more closely and look at each of them directly and honestly, with open eyes.

Everything was familiar about being imprisoned in Bühl again, and yet it was different. This time I had George by my side. Known to his family and friends as a quiet, peaceful person, with my arrest George suddenly became an enraged giant of a man. People did not always understand the fury with which he went forth to do battle. Like his namesake of ancient legend, he set out to slay the dragon. No monster was going to steal his maiden from him now that he had finally found her. If sheer will power can move a mountain, then George's will was going to move it. He gathered other knights to him to help him in his task. The first to join him was the lawyer, Michael Rosenthal.

Michael is very tall and skinny and I liked him the moment I met him. When he asked if he could smoke a pipe and pulled out Early Morning, the tobacco George smoked, I knew we were going to understand each other. Michael said the higher regional court was surprised, and displeased, to be asked again for my extradition to the United States. The chief justice had recognised my name as the woman the court had extradited five years earlier and the court had sent a letter to the US Justice Department asking the reason why the intent of the conspiracy was not carried out, and why the conspiracy, which had been known about in 1985, was only now becoming the subject of new criminal proceedings. The court also asked what had happened to Mr Turner and why the already known charge of conspiracy to kill him was excluded from my plea bargain when I was in custody in the United States; why was I not prosecuted at the time; and was there a statute of limitations that would bar prosecution?

In my first meetings with Michael I tried to give him a picture of myself, of life in the commune, and of what had happened. He asked a lot of questions in an effort to understand how I had ended up in prison not once but twice. At that time I was still unclear about the motivating forces in many aspects of my life. I still held Roger responsible for the breakdown of our marriage and remained convinced that I had gone to Bhagwan because I was a seeker. But even with my limited understanding of the emotional issues and the impact of my unconscious, I was still able to tell the story and relate my part in it. It was with a deep sense of relief that I found I could talk to a virtual stranger about things I had previously only spoken of to George. I had not been aware of the degree to which they had weighed on my heart.

At the end of October a letter was delivered to the higher regional court with the answers to the questions it had asked of the US Justice Department. Unlike all previous cases against Rajneeshees in the commune, the conspiracy case was being prosecuted out of Washington DC, not Oregon. The letter from Washington DC pointed out that I had only made a plea bargain with the State of Oregon, whereas the present charge came under the jurisdiction of the federal government of the United States.

Michael explained that this idea of dual sovereignty is inconceivable under German law, where the obligation to investigate the truth applies to the 'whole criminal act'. The 'criminal act' is comprehended as the historical facts of the whole case, in its context within the whole picture. For German courts, therefore, it is not considered acceptable to repeatedly reproach an individual with what is essentially the same story.

The reason given as to why the case was not brought when I had first been extradited was that, although it was known about, there had not been enough evidence to make a case. It had been necessary to enlist the help of further government witnesses, and that had taken time. Further, as to the statute of limitations, while there was indeed a five-year period allowed in which to bring charges in a case, the act of transporting the guns and travelling to the intended victim's house had happened on or about 20 June 1985 and the indictment had been returned on 25 May 1990, three weeks before the statute expired.

The letter went on to say that although Mr Turner had not been harmed, under American law a conspiracy is complete when there has been an agreement between two or more persons to commit a crime, and there has been at least one overt act committed by one of the co-conspirators.

Michael told me Alma had become a government witness. In return for her cooperation and willingness to accept a prison sentence of two years for her part in the conspiracy against Mr Turner, all other pending charges against her had been dropped. Following her testimony before a grand jury, an arrest warrant had been signed for my arrest, and the arrest of six other people.

I was genuinely confused as to why there was a case at all. In my mind there had only ever been what I called 'loose talk'. I had not associated buying the guns with a threat to Mr Turner, but the case now pivoted on those guns and I was deeply implicated.

'But they were never used. I didn't even know where they were stored,' I protested to Michael. 'Nobody was hurt. Mr Turner only became aware of there having been a threat at all after we had left and Bhagwan started attacking us.'

The indictment alluded to the attack on Bhagwan's doctor and accused me of not only having transported the guns but also of volunteering to be the assassin. I was awarded the dubious honour of being placed second only to Sheela in order of importance and accountability and was portrayed as one of the five most powerful women in the commune. The trap had been carefully laid and now it had snapped shut. A lawyer Michael contacted in America talked to the prosecutor's office there and was told I would get 'double figures', which in federal court, unlike the sentencing matrix in state court, meant what it said. The situation seemed hopeless. Michael told me about a partner he had worked with when he first began practising as a criminal defence lawyer. The more experienced man told him that being a defence lawyer was a bit like doing battle with a toothpick against an opponent with a pitchfork. It was his way of telling me the odds were heavily against us.

But then he smiled brightly and said, 'But you know, I hate to lose!'

That night I dreamed I was walking by myself in the Black Forest. I walked along a path that took me out of the shadows and into a large clearing. The sun was shining and the flowers in the meadow were dancing in the sunlight. In the middle of the clearing another path intersected the one I was treading. A group of four people approached the junction on the other path, and as I came closer I saw that they were the four government witnesses. We met at the junction and greeted each other affably, old acquaintances smiling in recognition. The girl from Texas put her arms around me and kissed me on the cheek. We exchanged pleasantries briefly and then continued on our separate ways.

After an agonising decision to go ahead and take the new job in Italy, George was taking care of the sale of the Saftladen, finishing up at the university, and packing up the apartment. He wrote to me every day. Visiting times in the prison were strictly limited, and visits were only half an hour long, an impossibly short time to give expression to all that was in our hearts. On his first visit to me in Bühl, George wanted to arrange for me to have my own clothes. I assured him that the conditions of my imprisonment were not in themselves bad. I had my coat to wear when I went outside each morning, and otherwise it was better to wear what was issued. It was adequate and was laundered every week, and I did not wish to appear different or more privileged than other inmates, who were all wearing clothing issued to them, and many of whom had very little in their own lives. I had him, and that made me rich beyond all measure. We made a pact that we would take care of ourselves until such time as we could take care of each other again.

For me that meant, first and foremost, getting up every morning to take advantage of Hofgang to walk in the walled courtyard in the fresh air, and the occasional shower of rain. Imprisonment has a deadening effect on the body and the spirit. It is as if a thick fog rolls in, clouding the mind and making the body as heavy as lead. A terrible lethargy drags at you and all you want to do is pull the blankets up over your head and sleep. My cell mate could sleep the whole day, waking only to eat something or talk a little, before going back to sleep. It is like a sleeping sickness. I was still reading *Joseph and His Brothers* and when Joseph talked about going down into the land of the dead, I began to think of prison as the land of the dead.

I asked for work and was assigned the job of cleaner. It was the perfect job for me. I moved a lot, sweeping and washing stairs and mopping and polishing the wide hallways. I worked alone, so I had time to think, and during the breaks I jotted down notes of things I wanted to remember to tell George or Michael. And at the end of the day came the blessed shower.

The cell I shared was one of three in a small area on the ground floor. The main cell block was on the first floor. The only other inmate in our mini compound was alone in one of the other cells. She was one of those who had made a new life for herself in East Germany following the troubled times of the seventies. As a result of the wall between east and west Germany coming down in 1989, her identity was revealed and she found herself in prison. She was mostly kept in isolation, but was permitted to walk in the Hof with the rest of us, and most evenings our cell doors were opened and we would be free to come out into a small communal area. We found we had a lot in common. Well educated and facing years of imprisonment, she too had been young and idealistic when she went down the wrong path and was now having to open the door to her past and make the painful journey back into its murky depths. We would sit on the wide window ledge talking about our experiences and exchanging insights. She spoke very good English and whenever Michael sent me a letter she made an excellent translation from the German to be sure I understood clearly everything he had written.

Sometimes my cell mate woke up to join us for our soirée and then we would get out the biscuits and boil water for tea with a tiny immersion heater, and have a picnic. My cell mate was a good-natured young woman who had a problem with alcohol and lived on the streets. She confided in me that she had stolen something openly from a local supermarket so she would be arrested. Winter was coming and she needed a warm shelter and food to tide her over the cold months. She was perfectly happy, even content, with her cramped winter quarters. When I made out my order for fruit and tea from the commissary every week, I invited her to add her own requirements to my list. Her requests were very modest, and always the same: one packet of cigarettes, one packet of Werther toffees and one packet of Prinzenrolle biscuits. She managed things carefully so that she was never without.

On a visit, George told me that Sheela had telephoned him at the house in the Black Forest. He said she was living in Switzerland. Her husband was Swiss and she had Swiss citizenship. Although she was one of the named defendants in the conspiracy case, she was not at risk as the Swiss do not extradite their own citizens. She was worried about me, he said, and would call every Saturday to ask after me. I asked him not to take her calls. Shortly before George and I married I remember thinking that I would have to choose my friends more carefully in the future. For me Sheela was simply bad news.

33

In our first meeting I had told Michael about the attack on Bhagwan's doctor and how it had shocked me into realising I had crossed a threshold I could never cross again; from that moment on I had known I must leave Bhagwan, and the commune, withdrawing completely from any further involvement in acts of violence against others. He asked me if I had told anybody that, and I told him about the personnel manager's breakdown and my declaration to her.

On 1 October George started his new job in Italy; the same day, unable to come to Bühl to tell me himself, Michael wrote me a letter. In it he said that the higher regional court had taken an extremely unusual decision. To his knowledge it had only ever happened once before in an extradition case. The court had decided to examine the facts of the case.

Under German law, he wrote, there is provision for those who have been involved in a conspiracy but withdrawn. If a person withdraws from a conspiracy of their own volition, the person is not held accountable. Or if a person tries their best to hinder the fulfilment of a conspiracy, even if the purposes of the conspiracy go ahead, there is no guilt.

When next he came to Bühl to see me, Michael explained that under German law a criminal case is not adversarial. Normally there are no witnesses for the prosecution or expert witnesses, neither is there 'defence' evidence. Instead there is an obligation, 'by virtue of one's office', to investigate the truth. During the judicial inquiry this is the responsibility of the office of the district attorney, and during the trial it is the responsibility of the court of justice. The law clearly states that the police and the office of the district attorney must investigate all exculpatory facts too, and the results of the investigation must be recorded in full.

For this reason the questions of why the actual crime was not carried out and why the accusation was not raised in 1985 were of great importance. Because nothing had happened it would be reasonable to think that the conspirators had given up the plan. The conspiracy would then, under German law, be exempt from punishment and as a result the dual criminality requirement for extradition would not be met.

German authorities and courts expect a complete and true representation of the facts from the requesting state, but as American law does not recognise withdrawal, there had been no investigation in that direction and no mention made of it. For this reason the German court felt itself bound to investigate the facts of the case in order to establish whether or not the withdrawal clause in German law applied to me. The court was not trying my case but it needed more information in order to reach a decision on the extradition request.

A month later I received an invitation to appear before the higher regional court in Karlsruhe. Michael explained that the German judicial system requires judges to conduct their own investigation into the facts of a case rather than to rely on the prosecution's version, as happens in the British and American judicial systems where judges are moderators between prosecution and defence and, at trial, the jury. Judges in Germany question the accused themselves in order to reach a judgement as to what happened.

Michael said our situation was fraught with danger. I would appear before a panel of three judges, all of whom would ask me questions. The judges themselves would take notes of my answers and their notes would be compiled into a single document which would be sent to the prosecution in America for comment and rebuttal. If in the future the higher regional court decided to extradite me, my statement would have preceded me and, as there is no provision for withdrawal under American law, I wouldn't have a leg to stand on in an American court. I thought about what he said only briefly, but I knew what I had to do.

'I'll speak to them,' I said, 'I have nothing to lose. If I don't speak to them, they will be obliged to extradite me.'

'All right,' said Michael, 'but I want you to know one thing. The chief justice will lead the panel. If he thinks you are guilty he will extradite you. He would extradite his own grandmother if he thought she were guilty.'

The night before I was to appear before the court I had a dream. I was sitting on a simple straight-backed chair. A second empty chair was next to me. All around me was nothing but emptiness. Out of this misty emptiness a man approached me. His manner was noble. He asked if he could see my files. My legal files were sitting on my lap. I said yes. He sat down next to me and I gave him the files. He took them on his lap. He opened the first one and began to study it. I sat there quietly, looking ahead. Then another man approached me out of the mist. His manner was gentle.

'I can see you are worried,' he said, 'but you mustn't worry. Everything is going to be all right.'

Irritation rose up in me. 'Who is this person?' I wondered to myself. 'Of course I'm worried. I have every reason to be worried. Who does he think he is to tell me not to worry?'

He looked at me and, as though reading my thoughts, he repeated,

'I can see you are worried, but you mustn't worry. Everything is going to be all right.'

34

On Friday 23 November 1990 I was driven to Karlsruhe for my appointment with the higher regional court. As my two guards and I mounted the sweeping staircase to the first floor, a man stood at the top of the stairs looking down at us. As we approached I recognised him as the man in my dream who had asked to see my files. He greeted me by name and asked the guards to remove the handcuffs and to remain outside the room he ushered me into, asking me politely to wait until I was called.

Michael came to fetch me. The courtroom was empty save for the three judges sitting at the bench, a man who was introduced as a German prosecutor, and a woman who was there to translate. The person who shortly before had asked me to wait sat in the middle at the bench. He was the chief justice. I felt my fear fall from me and a quiet trust take its place.

The chief justice invited me to answer in English if it were easier. I was grateful for the offer. Later I would write to my father that I had the feeling of being in the presence of wise men. Right from the beginning it was clear that they genuinely wanted to know what had happened. They were not asking trick questions and laying traps for me to fall into, or putting words into my mouth. They asked about my life and my family, and how I came to go to Bhagwan in the first place. They asked where my children were, and when in answering my voice broke, they asked me not to distress myself and suggested we take a break.

And then they asked specifically about the case in question. In all things I answered honestly and openly. I explained about the extreme pressures that had built up outside the commune, and of the growing discontent and jealousies within the commune itself, culminating in my attack on Bhagwan's doctor. It was the first time I admitted publicly to attempting to murder him.

An hour and a half later there were no further questions. I was asked to return to the waiting room. A few minutes later Michael came in and said the chief justice had told him he could apply for bail. He was incredulous. He said as far as he knew bail was never granted to people in extradition custody.

On Tuesday 4 December, the day after Peter's twenty-second birthday, I had just started work when I was summoned to the prison director's office.

'What is the name of your lawyer?' he asked.

'Rosenthal,' I said.

'He is on the phone,' he said, handing me the handpiece.

Michael wanted to know where my passport was. I told him it was in the house in the Black Forest.

'Darn,' he said, 'we need it, and George is in Italy.'

'No he's not,' I said, 'he has special leave to allow him to vote in the elections. He is there today.'

'Bye,' he said abruptly, and hung up.

Guessing why Michael would need my passport but not daring to believe it, I worked like a navvy that day. After completing my usual work, a fellow inmate and I changed all the mattress covers in the cells. It was strenuous work but I was glad of it as it kept me almost too busy to think. But as four o'clock approached I knew I would miss the deadline. At four o'clock the guard changed and the director left for the day. Once the night guard came on, the prison was locked down and no one came in or went out. I went to the wash room to rinse out my cleaning cloths before going to take a shower. A guard who had got wind that I might be released commiserated with me that I would have to spend another night in prison. As I came out of the wash room I saw George disappearing into one of the visiting rooms. My heart jumped into my throat.

The director then came out of the visiting room and motioned to me to come. He had not left the prison but had waited in order to let George, with a local judge in tow, into the building so that I could leave. Without his presence, it would not have been possible at that hour.

The judge said I was to be released on bail and explained the terms of my release. I was to reside in the house in the Black Forest; I was to report to the local police station once a week, and I was not to leave Germany. I agreed and signed the necessary paperwork.

The director sent one of the guards with me to my cell to get my things, and then downstairs to exchange the prison clothes for my own. I was dirty and sweaty and I had not had a haircut in months, but I didn't care. George was standing in the hallway waiting for me when I came back upstairs. At that moment my friend of three months of evening conversations came out of her cell to collect her supper. A flash of understanding crossed her face. She hesitated for a moment and then ran down the hall to us. No one tried to stop her. George and I hugged her. Then we turned to leave. The door opened and I walked across the threshold on George's arm.

35

We walked out into the night. I was in a daze. We hugged and cried and then George led me to the car and we drove towards the Black Forest. I must have dozed off and woke as the car came to a halt. We were parked under a sign that said *Der Grüne Baum*.

'Oh look,' I said sleepily, 'it has the same name as the hotel where we celebrated our marriage.'

George chuckled. It was the very same *Grüne Baum*!

'My bride,' he said as he opened the car door for me, 'let us celebrate our marriage again.'

The last time I had been here was as a bride and I was a little ashamed to be so unkempt. The owner greeted us warmly as we entered, apparently oblivious to any shortcomings in my appearance. We ordered local pheasant and while we waited for it to arrive George told me the story of his day.

After getting Michael's phone call, he had called his friend Kurt, grabbed my passport and run out the door. Once he was out of the Black Forest and onto the autobahn to Karlsruhe, he drove, he said sheepishly, faster than he had ever driven in his life. Kurt was waiting for him outside the courthouse with the bail money, and George ran in to deliver passport and bail to the prosecutor, only to be informed that he was out of the office for the next hour. The two men went to a nearby restaurant for a bite to eat, and were back on the doorstep an hour later. George handed my passport and bail to the waiting prosecutor, who thanked him and said he would take care of the paperwork and I should be out in a couple of days.

'A couple of days! But I would like to get her today,' said George. He explained that he had to return to work in Italy the following day and couldn't be there to pick me up in a couple of days.

The prosecutor looked thoughtful and wondered aloud if it might be possible to finish the paperwork and have a special courier take it to a local judge in Bühl, who could then go across to the prison to complete the formalities. He was concerned that it was already early afternoon and that the courthouse and the prison would close at 4 pm. Suddenly he looked up at George and said,

'You can take it! It will be close, but if you can find a judge in Bühl who can go across to the prison with you before 4 pm it should work.'

He rapidly put together a bundle of papers and sealed them in a large envelope which he handed to George, having first explained carefully to him what he was to do with them. George ran out the door and headed back along the autobahn. When he arrived at the courthouse in Bühl it was closed and there was nobody around. He knocked on the door and called out. Eventually the janitor came and, in response to George's urgent request for a judge, indicated that there was a judge still upstairs in his office. George ran up the stairs two at a time. The judge was congenial and listened to George's request. He didn't know, he said, it was all most unusual and he had never done anything like that before. George tried to explain what needed to be done, but he would not be hurried and pulled down a law book to see if he could find procedures written there. It was 4 pm when George in desperation suggested he call the court in Karlsruhe. He did, and was connected to the chief justice himself. The chief justice explained what he needed to do, and George and the judge went over to the prison. But it wasn't over yet. George passed security and was allowed in, but the judge was denied entry because he didn't have any identification with him and there was nobody left back at the courthouse who could vouch for him. Just when it seemed the whole exercise had been in vain, one of the guards came to see what the fuss was about. She recognised the judge and he was permitted to enter.

George's story was a perfect illustration of the determination he exhibited in his battle for his wife. It was a determination that people responded to with kindness and cooperation and I was touched to learn of the many people who had supported him that day, any one of whom, in going by the book, could have sent him away empty-handed.

It was midnight by the time we drove up to the house in the Black Forest. We drank a cup of tea together, but then George left to continue driving on to Italy, where he had to be back in his office first thing in the morning. Thankfully this time the separation would only be for a couple of days.

And so began a period of respite. I was comfortable and able to move around, and George and I could communicate freely with each other. On weekends he drove back from Italy, arriving home late on Friday evening and getting up at four on Monday morning to drive back again. Sometimes he came home very late, needing to stop and put on snow chains for the climb into the Black Forest, and once he was caught in a snow drift for hours. We spent the weekends together, and I could sleep in his arms, but I was on bail pending the decision of the court, and the threat of extradition was as real as ever. It was our constant companion and many's the time we held each other and cried at the thought of what might happen.

In a very real sense George gave me physical and emotional security of a kind I had not known before. Feeling safe in the love of my mate, and no longer required to focus my energy on working long hours at a job, I now found myself with a unique opportunity to look more closely at myself and to ponder my predicament.

I began to see that I had grown up denying the greater part of myself. My inner child, with its black and white view of the world, denying the black and determined only to be white, had been driving my every move. I had conscientiously denied anything that did not fit into my simplistic view of the world, and when my lopsided world began to topple, I ran off to create a new one. What an arrogant child I was to think I could cast off my European/Christian heritage and replace it with a completely different culture. Understanding neither and trying to replace one with the other were costly mistakes. Only now was I beginning to get a hint of the extent of the damage that had been done. There was still a long way to go. When one has lived in denial for so long, there is a lot of mucking out to do.

I once helped muck out a stable where three horses had been housed throughout the winter. It was tedious, time-consuming work and, once the surface was scratched, it stank into the bargain. When I began my own mucking out, it was not a matter of a few months, it was forty-five years worth.

Slowly I began to understand that as long as I was in denial about something, it did not exist for me, so it was not possible for me to examine it. My denial made it invisible and inaccessible to me. In the peace and tranquillity of the Black Forest I gradually learned to ask the right questions of myself, and to answer them honestly. It was a kind of treasure hunt, like the paper-trail game we had played as kids. Each question led me to the next clue, which led me to the next one. As an adult, the treasure hunt is perhaps better likened to peeling an onion, for whilst continuing to reveal ever new layers for perusal, it generates a lot of tears.

'I was a seeker' was no longer an acceptable answer to the question 'Why did I go to Bhagwan?' It implied that I was special. It implied that not everyone is a seeker. It was an attempt to cloak what had happened in a shroud of spirituality that would excuse everything. But that gossamer veil was no longer big enough to cover the pain and anguish that my 'seeking' had inflicted on the people I loved, particularly on my children. As I began to bring light into the darkness, I started to see the extent of their suffering, and it was almost unbearable for me to face.

With time I would ask myself, 'Why did I marry Roger?' and for the first time I began to look at our relationship in a different way. Instead of blaming him for everything as I had always done in the past, I began to look at our marriage as it had really been: the love I had for him, the good times and the bad times, and my part in the dynamic that destroyed it. It was at this time that I realised Roger had had a nervous breakdown at Coral Bay, and that I had discarded him instead of supporting him through it. I wrote him a letter apologising for what I had done.

The God of my childhood only loved us if we were good; if we were bad he became angry and revengeful, a childish image of God which Bhagwan had in the end filled to perfection. It was during this period of aloneness and stillness that I had the revelation that what the nuns and the hellfire-and-damnation missionaries had told us was wrong. The God they described was none other than a conglomerate of their own reactions to disobedience or perceived wrongdoing among their charges, and their own all-too-human desires to be powerful and to be honoured and obeyed without question. But God, whoever or whatever mysteries were concealed behind that misused name, was not so small and petty, but a vast ocean of love supporting and carrying us through life. Although facing years of imprisonment in a faraway country, I felt held and protected and was strangely at peace.

Following my meeting with the three judges, a document was prepared with my answers and submitted to the prosecution in America, with the request that a response be forthcoming within six weeks. After a number of requests for extensions, the response came back in late May 1991. It came in the form of a one-hundred-page rebuttal by the four government witnesses denying all knowledge of any statement by me that I had withdrawn from the conspiracy. One glaring omission in the very formalised questioning of their witnesses was the government's avoidance of any mention of the personnel manager's breakdown, an omission that raised questions in the minds of the German court as to just how genuine an effort had been made to seek the truth. Further, although two government witnesses lived in the same city as Sheela's nurse, who was mentioned as having been present at the breakdown, no attempt was made to contact her and ask questions of her.

Nevertheless, it was the word of four government witnesses against mine and the situation looked grim. The personnel manager was also named in the case and was fighting extradition from her home in South Africa. Michael contacted her lawyer in the States with a view to having her come to Germany to appear before the higher regional court. The court itself offered her a guarantee of safe passage in Germany if she agreed. Her lawyer let Michael know that she would not come as it would compromise her own situation, but that she might be able to make a written statement about the circumstances of her nervous breakdown, in return for a written statement from me. Michael submitted a list of questions that the court would like to have answers to. There followed some correspondence, with increasing demands made of me, interspersed with long periods of silence. The court was becoming impatient, seeing itself duty bound to reach a timely decision. To indicate the types of answers the personnel manager would give to its questions, Michael made the faxes from her lawyer available to the court.

He also asked the court to invite Sheela's nurse to appear before them to answer questions. She was not directly involved in the case so was not threatened by the outcome. In fact she was specifically protected from further prosecution by her earlier plea bargains with both US state and federal authorities. In other words, she could afford to be honest without fear of prosecution. She was living in America, but the court agreed to ask her to come.

Unlike the American legal system where witnesses are prepared and their answers carefully worded and rehearsed, sometimes in pretend courtroom scenarios with professional trainers, the German system demands that witnesses relate their story themselves, the way they remember it. American lawyers turn pale at the thought of presenting a witness over whom they have no control, with no way of knowing what the person might say. In Germany it is the norm.

Brought up in the American system to say what your side wants you to say, Sheela's nurse tried in every way to avoid saying anything she thought would be detrimental to me. When the hearing was over and she met with Michael outside the courtroom, she burst into tears because she thought she had let me down. She had related the scene of the personnel manager's breakdown; but under the persistent questions of the court, she had finally admitted that I had been chosen as the would-be assassin. She could not comprehend it when Michael tried to soothe her by saying she had done the right thing in telling the truth.

On 9 July 1991, ten months after my arrest, the higher regional court in Karlsruhe denied the request for my extradition to the United States on the grounds that the charges against me did not meet the requirement of punishability in both countries. In its findings the court found that, although I had been involved in a conspiracy to murder Mr Turner, it was satisfied that I had withdrawn from that conspiracy. Further, as I was to have been the assassin, my withdrawal meant the collapse of the conspiracy itself. Under German law there was therefore no guilt and I was exempt from prosecution.

36

The United States government sent a formal letter of complaint to the German government about the higher regional court's decision. The department of foreign affairs referred the complaint to the court, which responded, reiterating the reasons for its decision. The upshot was that I was only free within Germany. Outside Germany an international arrest warrant waited for me. I could not join George in Italy, and I could not travel to Australia to see my parents and family. Convinced that the whole thing was a misunderstanding on the part of the American prosecution, George hired a lawyer in America to try to sort it out. He continued to travel back and forth between Italy and the Black Forest, our life together still reduced to weekends.

When the implications became clear to Peter and Kylie, they began making regular trips to Germany to see me. One day as Kylie and I were walking in the Black Forest she told me that when she was seventeen she had returned to the ashram in Pune to see Bhagwan, who at that time was again residing in his house on the compound. While she was there, a girlfriend discovered she was pregnant. When Kylie heard her friend would have an abortion and sterilisation, she decided to go with her and be sterilised too. Kylie was sterilised. I wanted to cry out, but instead I made some inane comment about being sterilised myself. That night I cried myself to sleep on George's shoulder. It was I who had taken my daughter to live in a community that condoned sterilisation. That it should have such terrible consequences as this was like an axe blow to my heart. And I wept the more, knowing that she would one day regret her impulsive solidarity with her friend.

On another visit Kylie again came from Pune where she had been hospitalised with a severe infection. She was very thin and had shaved off her hair. It broke my heart to see her so fragile and desperate. Dim memories surfaced of Rosemary when she was so sick in hospital and her hair had been shaved off to accommodate the spinal taps. I took Kylie to the dentist. When he looked into her mouth and saw that her eye teeth had been removed, he said bitterly,

'Who did this?' She told him they had been removed by Bhagwan's dentist because her teeth were crowded. He was contemptuous.

'We always protect the eye teeth,' he said. 'They are very deeply rooted and later in life they are often the only teeth left to a person.'

A cold shiver went through me. Where was I when that happened? I had not been there to question the need for the procedure or to take care of her after it was done. Later Kylie told me all four eye teeth had been removed at once and she had been sent home to her room to deal with the pain and swelling alone. I was horrified to realise I had not been there when she needed me so badly.

The dental examination revealed that all four of Kylie's wisdom teeth were infected and had to be removed, first two on one side and, when the wounds had healed, the two on the other side.

For the first time in over fourteen years I could be completely present for Kylie. I cooked her nourishing food and nursed her back to health. It was not always easy. She wanted me to call her by the name Bhagwan had given her and I wouldn't do it. She shouted and cried and said she hated the name Kylie. At night in bed I wept for my child, and in the daytime I took care of her and loved her and watched her beautiful thick curly hair grow back again.

Kylie was a passionate cook. We studied cookbooks together and her enthusiasm for trying new recipes was endless. In preparation for George's return one weekend, we made an apple strudel that involved rolling and coaxing the dough until it covered the entire table, before filling it with nuts and jam and apples and cinnamon and sugar and rolling it up and cutting it into oven-sized logs. We were catching up on the things mothers and daughters do together that we had missed out on. In many ways we were getting to know each other again after so many years apart. It was summer and I rented a holiday house in the Rhine Valley. We went riding through the countryside on our bicycles, walked through the mountains and picnicked by streams, and filled our bellies with the black cherries and apricots and peaches growing in abundance in the area.

When it became clear that my legal situation was not about to change, George began looking for a position that would allow us to live together in Germany. His employer had a number of establishments throughout Europe and eventually he was able to transfer to one closer to home. It was too far from the Black Forest for us to stay there, so we bought a small house nearby and I found work in a local health food shop. After two years of spending only weekends and holidays with each other, we could finally begin our married life together.

It was tricky at first. Small irritations that had been ignored during those precious weekends took on unnaturally large proportions. We found ourselves disagreeing on all sorts of things and having heated rows. I was particularly shocked to recognise old, almost forgotten 'he didn't do this right, he didn't do that right' (translation: he's not perfect) numbers replaying in my mind like broken records. But my arrest and all that followed had bonded us in such a way that we knew we had something worth caring for, even if we were having trouble finding it at that moment.

It had been said of my Aunty Dorry that whenever a plate or cup cracked or chipped she would place it in a box in the garage. Whenever she became very angry about something, she would go into the garage and smash the crockery she had saved for the occasion. I broke quite a bit of crockery, not always waiting until it was chipped or cracked, but it didn't take us long to figure out that neither of us had been in a healthy relationship before. We were repeating old patterns of behaviour we had brought with us. We were going to have to break new ground if we were to preserve and nourish what we had together.

I remember well the day I realised how like the father of my childhood George is. He is tall and thin, wears glasses, has curly dark hair and is a mathematician. One could almost say I had married my father! When I told George this he laughed and said that I was very like his mother when he was a child: short, dark-haired and dark-eyed, and good-natured. Then we both laughed, for in that moment we recognised the relationship patterns we shared, patterns that related to our parents and a child's need to be loved and taken care of. It changed something. We stopped playing mothers and fathers and began communicating like the equal partners we were. I stopped throwing tantrums, and George stopped behaving like a disapproving father. We were on the right track.

The great steamroller rolled relentlessly on and other people named in the case were extradited back to America. Some made plea bargains and two went to trial and were found guilty. All received prison sentences between four and five years. With each new conviction, the case took on more weight and it became more and more impossible to find a solution for me that would not involve my going back to prison. George and I comforted ourselves that we were together and that Germany was a large and beautiful country. Germany and its people had been good to me: taking me in; allowing me to stay and work until I was ready to see the man who would offer me the love and security I needed before I dared to open my eyes and face the world; and then affording me sanctuary when it seemed all was lost. But George's work took him all over Europe and I could not accompany him, and in Australia my parents were getting older and I lived in fear of never seeing them again.

Years passed. George's parents died. He sold the house in the Black Forest and we added another level to our little house to better accommodate the family when they visited.

My process of introspection continued, although somewhat less intensively than the two years in the Black Forest. I read a lot too. A book which moved me deeply was Victor Klemperer's diaries, *Ich will Zeugnis ablegen bis zum Letzten* (I will bear witness until the end). Victor Klemperer was a professor of Romance languages at the University of Dresden when Hitler came to power in 1933. He was of Jewish origin and his wife was not. Within months of the Nazis seizing power, his previously well-attended lectures were empty. Only two students stood up against the boycott of classes of Jewish professors and continued to attend his lectures, until the university cancelled them altogether for 'lack of student interest'.

The diaries are a record of the strength and frailty of human nature; of those who unquestioningly supported the decrees from above, turning on neighbours and friends; and those who in their own quiet way did whatever was in their power to help its victims, be it something as small as surreptitiously slipping a forbidden tomato into Klemperer's hand as he walked down the street. There are the stories of old colleagues who crossed to the other side of the road to avoid him when they saw him coming, and others who deliberately crossed over to greet him and shake his hand. His wife paid a high price for not deserting him. Like her husband she was treated as a pariah and was forced to forgo all comfort and security, but in doing so she prevented his deportation to the death camps.

As I read the diaries I was aware that I wanted to see myself as one of those who would have tried to help, and not one who mindlessly followed a policy that sought the destruction of fellow citizens, some of whom may have been my lecturers or friends or neighbours. I had to pause and remind myself that I had once tried to kill a man, and plotted to kill another, because I was blinded by an ideology and not thinking for myself. I too was enamoured of the idea of a saviour of the world and thought myself to be a warrior in his cause. And I was humbled to realise that I was no different to those millions of people who mindlessly seize hold of a cause and lay siege to others in its name.

One of the most troubling books I read was Hannah Arendt's *Eichmann in Jerusalem: A Report on the Banality of Evil* for it becomes very clear that Eichmann did not fit the popular image of a crazed Nazi monster. He was an ordinary person, an average government employee, a polite and honest citizen, and a good husband and father. He was a conscientious, hard-working man who did not question his political leaders or his superiors but rather applied himself to his work to the best of his ability, meticulously organising the transportation of hundreds of thousands of people to concentration camps and death.

Eichmann's story brought home to me yet again that we all carry the possibility for good and evil within us and it is very often circumstances that decide whether we become murderers or healers. Unless, that is, we are able to rise above circumstances by nourishing honest self-awareness and becoming a truly autonomous person.

In the summer of 1996 my parents flew to Germany to see me. Dad was eighty-nine years old and Mum was eighty-three. We sat around the kitchen table together podding peas from the garden, slicing green beans and pulling redcurrants from their stems. Mum created a fresh flower arrangement every day from the flowers in the garden, and Dad chopped wood and weeded the paths. We walked in the forest and along the river, taking advantage of the benches along the way to rest and contemplate the countryside. One weekend George drove us to the monastery at Maria Laach, and in the evenings we played crib.

It was a wonderful visit. Just being together in such an easy, natural way was balsam to my soul. We did not talk in detail about events that had caused me to be unable to leave Germany. They did not want to know, and I respected that. There had been a time when I had wanted them to know all about me and to listen to my insights, but I quickly realised it was my need and not theirs, and let it go. What was important was that I understood what I had done, and why. It did not matter to them, they loved me no matter what. Dad held my hand all the way on the long drive to

Frankfurt airport when they were leaving. At the airport he held me and kissed me goodbye. There were tears in his eyes and he could not speak, but I knew he loved me and was proud of me. It was the last time I saw him alive.

In 1997 Kylie married her beau Gregory. How I would have loved to be able to celebrate with them and the rest of the family, and to make the wedding cake. But as it was, all I could do was send the recipe for it, and Kylie and Gregory made the cake themselves.

A few months later Roger flew to Germany to see me. We had not seen each other for almost twelve years. He had maintained the boyish charm that had attracted me to him over thirty years before and I was very happy to see him. He had come to Germany because he wanted to apologise for not having stood by me when I was arrested and imprisoned after leaving the commune. He talked about his devastation when the commune collapsed, and said he had come to see that in following Bhagwan he had simply been following his cock. Women had gathered around Bhagwan like bees round a honey pot and, like so many other men, he had been attracted to the swarm.

One day we sat atop a large rock in the garden and he told me he was just beginning to understand the tremendous influence his parents had had in shaping his life, particularly his strong, silent father, and he told me of the circumstances that led up to his breakdown. He was telling me all this for the first time and it shocked us both to realise the extent to which we had been unable to communicate with each other when we were young. Now, so many years later, it seemed impossible that he and I had lived so closely together and yet he could not tell me what was happening to him, and I could not see to ask. Even now we were both oddly awkward together. I still had something of a superior, I-know-better attitude towards him. He was involved in some new growth movement with a female guru and I thought myself to be beyond all that, and found myself being judgemental about some of the things he said, instead of simply being open and listening. Although I had moved away from blaming him for everything that had gone wrong, I had still not penetrated to the core of our relationship. Nevertheless, it was a very heartful visit. He stayed with George and me for two weeks, and I was deeply grateful that he had come so far to speak about the things he had been unable to give voice to in the past. He told me all about Kylie and Gregory's wedding and we laughed to recognise the pride we shared in our children. He had divorced and was planning to remarry and said he and his new wife would be moving to Australia, where Kylie and Gregory were living.

In 1999, in an extraordinary proceeding, a Swiss court tried Sheela on the conspiracy charge. The trial was held at the insistence of the US Justice Department, which agreed to abide by the decision of the court. Quoting extensively from the decision of the higher regional court in Karlsruhe, the Swiss court found Sheela guilty of acts preparatory to the commission of a crime, but imposed no further sentence in addition to that which she had received in her federal plea bargain of 1986, pointing out that the conspiracy was not a new offence but had occurred in the same context as the other crimes committed in the time period covered by the plea bargain. Further, it found that a relatively long period had passed and the defendant had conducted herself well since then.

That same year in early July Mum called to say Dad was in bed and that he had not eaten or drunk anything for two days. Dad never stayed in bed. I knew he was dying and everything in me wanted to get on a plane and go to him and Mum. I felt like a caged animal and paced through the house crying tears of rage and desperation. He died early next morning.

Peter and Kylie flew to Western Australia for his funeral. I wrote Dad one last letter and Peter read it out at the service. In it I thanked Dad for all he had given me and for having stood by me through the darkest nights. And then I told a fishing story that made him laugh every time he told it.

Dad was long since retired from being a school principal and was down fishing on the jetty. He was sitting there with his legs hanging over the edge, pulling up gardies with every throw. A boy of perhaps eleven or twelve came along. He stopped a little way off and watched for a while. Then he sat down and watched some more. Dad always had a special empathy with young people. He knew the boy was longing to feel the weight of a fish on the line and so he asked him if he would like to fish too.

'I sure would,' he said, 'but I don't have a line.'

'You can have one of mine,' Dad said. 'I have plenty here in the fishing bag. And here's a handful of mince.'

The boy had caught half-a-dozen fish by the time Dad began rolling up to go home. He pushed over the last of his mince, telling the boy he had to go as his wife would be waiting for him.

'You can return the line next time you see me on the jetty,' he said, 'I'm down here most days.'

But the lad rolled up too, thanked Dad warmly and said he must be going. As he moved off, Dad said,

'Don't forget your fish!'

'Oh no,' he said, 'you keep them. It was your line and your bait.'

'No, no,' Dad said, 'take them back to your mother. She will be happy to have fish for dinner.'

'I can't,' the boy wailed, 'I'm supposed to be in school!'

After Dad's funeral Kylie wrote me a heartbroken, angry letter in which she said that when she saw his body lying in the funeral parlour it broke her heart to know what she had missed by being taken away from her grandparents when she was a child. Roger's parents had both died while she was in the commune and she was grief-stricken to be confronted with so much loss, represented as it was in the lifeless body of my father.

How I wished I could turn back the clock. But it was not possible. I could not restore the birthright of which she had been robbed. My heart heavy with grief, I wrote back, acknowledging her pain and her right to be angry.

37

Peter and his girlfriend Jennifer married in Germany on 6 July 2000, bringing with them four-month-old Chloe, my first grandchild. They married in Germany so I could meet Chloe and be part of the festivities. It meant that a lot of their own friends were unable to be there, but Roger and his wife came, and Kylie and Gregory, and one of Roger's sisters and her husband, and cousin Moira, and Jennifer's mum and an aunt and uncle, and our neighbours. An old family friend, Elizabeth, came over from Ireland to bless their union.

The young couple married in the forest near our home. They chose a spot under the trees atop a mighty rock pillar, which we would later learn was an ancient Celtic meeting place. As they exchanged rings, the sun broke through the clouds and bathed them in light, and the bells in the nearby chapel began to chime. Elizabeth had brought a Celtic blessing with her, which Roger's wife had put to music, and she and Roger sang it over the newly wed couple.

Kylie came ahead of everyone else and together we planned the catering. We baked bread and froze it and shopped and made detailed daily work plans, and when everyone arrived we produced three meals a day for all the guests for the duration of their stay. Some slept at our neighbours' and some were in a holiday flat, but everyone gathered at our home for meals.

While we were still in the planning stage, Kylie often expressed the fear that I would not have time for her when everyone arrived. The fact that we could only be together when she came to Germany produced a real need to make every moment count. I reassured her that I would be there for her, but by the time the bridal couple and most guests had left, her worst fears had been realised. Playing the good hostess and expecting her to follow suit, I had in fact taken care of everyone else but her. She was deeply distressed and needed to tell me why. We were sitting in the living room, talking about the past few days, when all of a sudden we were back in the ashram in Pune.

Her anguish and pain at my neglect of her as a child suddenly rose to the surface and spilled out. A wave of unexpressed grief swept over her, fed by an additional flood of agony at having been left alone when I was arrested and imprisoned following our departure from the commune. I was overwhelmed with the responsibility for so much suffering. I desperately needed Roger to help me carry the burden and went downstairs to fetch him. He baulked and I became angry and insistent, brushing aside the protests of his wife. It was as terrible for him as it was for me, and we dealt with it in our own ways. He became sick and threw up and I became angry and cold towards him. Despite the insights I had gained into our relationship, I was still unable to approach him as an equal, and my angry demands elicited the response of the frightened child rather than the caring father and friend he was.

However, the ice was broken and Kylie and I were able to acknowledge and cry about the things that had happened to her in the commune as a result of my neglect of her. We talked of her feeling lost and abandoned in Pune when the family scattered; of her missing me and feeling I had deserted her when I did not go to Australia with her and Roger and Peter and she didn't have a mother when all her cousins did; of my never being available when they came from Australia because I was working in Antelope; of suffering through nights of earache alone when all she wanted was to curl up next to me and be comforted; of spending three months in the clinic with glandular fever, cared for by the nursing staff but not by the person she most needed. As I listened I was devastated to realise that I had not registered these things when they were happening, let alone responded to them. It did not seem possible that I could have been so lost in my fantasy world that I had not allowed what was happening to my own child to penetrate into it.

In the moment when Kylie talked about the man twenty years her senior who took her as his plaything when she was thirteen, I no longer knew whether or not I had known. I had been so ready to dismiss anything that did not fit into my perfect world that I had satisfied myself, without ever speaking to Kylie, that there was no truth to the allegations in the lawsuit or to gossip I had heard about her and an older man. And if I had known? Did I simply accept it, as I had accepted what happened to Peter? Now, years later, sitting on the couch in the living room, Kylie said very softly,

'Today I wish it had never happened.' With all my heart I wished it too.

Within a year of his marriage, Peter and his little family moved, to the east coast of Australia where Roger and his wife, and Kylie and Gregory were living. In 2002 Kylie and Gregory began visiting doctors and hospitals and undergoing tests to assess the possibility of Kylie having an operation to reverse the sterilisation. During this time Kylie dreamed that she gave birth to a baby girl and that I was with her. She called me up to tell me. I was so happy to hear that her dream indicated that she would have a baby, I didn't take notice of the rest of it.

'But, Mum, you were with me,' she said. 'You were with me!'

And then I got it.

When they realised that reversal operations are rarely undertaken in Australia, Kylie and Gregory decided to return to Pune, to the same hospital where the sterilisation had been done, and where the micro-surgical procedure of reversal is performed relatively often and the success rate is unusually high. The nephew of the doctor who had done the sterilisation performed the operation. Kylie could not fly for six weeks afterwards. Even while she was still in India recuperating I felt I must do something about getting free, so her dream could come true. She had done something about removing the blockage to her becoming pregnant, and now I must do something to remove the blockage that prevented me from travelling to be with her when she gave birth.

Prior to the trial of two co-defendants in the case, the lawyer for one of them had come to Germany to interview me and it was his name that now came to mind. I called him and asked if he would represent me. There was not a moment's hesitation. 'Yes!' he said, as though he had been waiting for my call. His name was Steve Wax and he explained that he was a public defender and would have to get the permission of the court to take my case. My heart sank. Although I was no longer working, having given up my job to be with Mum who preferred to spend most of her time in Germany since Dad's death, George had a well-paid job and I feared I would not be eligible for a public defender. Steve asked me to send a copy of George's last pay slip, and an accounting of our savings and debts for him to take to the court. This I did and shortly afterwards he called to say he had the permission of the court to defend me, but that he must now seek the permission of the woman he had defended at trial in the same case, and who was now living in England. A few days later he called to say she had refused to allow him to take my case.

For twenty-four hours I walked around feeling I had been kicked in the guts. But then I began to sense that if Steve couldn't do it, there was someone out there who could. Steve called again. He had found someone to take my case and, if I were agreeable, he would go to the court to explain the situation. I readily agreed, and Steve secured permission of the court for Phil Lewis to be my counsel. Although already practising law in Portland at the time when the group had left Bhagwan and the subsequent collapse of the commune had kept pretty much every lawyer in town busy, Phil had somehow been overlooked by Rajneeshees seeking legal advice, which meant that he could now take on my case without any conflict of interest anywhere.

It was an unbelievable relief to be granted a public defender. Over the previous twelve years George had paid out large sums of money to lawyers in efforts to secure my freedom. The average hourly rate of two hundred and fifty US dollars forced us to be as brief and concise as possible in our dealings with them, but even so, reading an email and composing an answer could easily produce a billing of a few hundred dollars, and those hundreds of dollars quickly added up to thousands of dollars.

One of the very first things Phil did after taking my case was to attend the court appearance of the personnel manager who, after twelve years of fighting extradition from South Africa, had negotiated a plea bargain with the prosecution and was now appearing before the court to enter her plea and accept the agreed-upon sentence of one year's imprisonment.

While I was busy writing Phil the story of my life and the case, in my mind's eye I would often see my father sitting on the back steps of the cottage in Busselton untangling a badly knotted fishing line. Dad could be impatient at times, but never when untangling a fishing line. Displaying infinite patience, he quietly and methodically worked his way back through the tangled loops into the heart of the knot. Now, whenever I looked, he was sitting there bent over his task.

One day the thought came to me that maybe my lack of freedom was an outward manifestation of my inner world. A novel idea, but in the instant between the thought arising and my mind discarding it as nonsense, I felt strong. It did not escape my notice and, thinking about it, I realised that if it was something inside myself, then I could do something about it. Instead of being a helpless victim I could take the initiative and take action to change myself. But what action? And what did I need to change?

Through the book *Love's Hidden Symmetry* I was aware of Bert Hellinger's work with family constellations. The concept was not new, but having worked with tribal people in Africa, Hellinger brought another dimension to it and continued to refine it. One aspect of the work is based on the understanding that each family member, past and present, has a particular place in the family which is theirs and theirs alone, by virtue of their birth and/or marriage into the family. If any family member (living or dead) is forgotten or pushed aside or for some reason 'loses' their place, the natural order in the family is disturbed and things start going awry.

Not knowing what else to do, but knowing that I must do something, I decided to start by doing a family constellation. After all, when Mum first came to Germany after Dad died, she told me that the real tragedy of Rosemary's illness was that my oldest sister had lost her place in the family and never got it back.

Up until this time I was the proverbial burned child shunning the flames and had studiously avoided anything even remotely associated with therapy. For this reason I asked a doctor whom I trusted if he knew of anyone he could recommend who did family constellation work. He gave me the name of a naturopath living a few hours' drive away. When I called, Monika said she was conducting a seminar in April. I booked to do it.

At the last minute Mum came with me. On the evening when I was to set up my family constellation, Monika invited Mum to be present. Monika explained that I was to individually ask men and women present to represent male and female members of my family, and to place them in the room as I perceived my family constellation to be. I soon learned that the juxtaposition of each member of the family to the others, the way they are facing or not facing each other, and where they are looking, tells a story. But most remarkably, the representatives of the family members, without knowing anything about the person they are representing, begin to feel as that family member feels.

I selected men and women from the group, one by one, beginning with a representative for Dad, then Mum, then Rosemary, Sue, Mary Lou, me and John, and guided each one to where I felt they should be. My siblings and I were scattered all over the room, looking downcast and distressed. When everyone was in place, I went and sat down next to Mum. She was furious.

'This is terrible! This is not right! I won't stay!' she said, without really knowing what was happening. She was so agitated, it was all I could do to convince her to stay.

As the constellation unfolded it came to light that I was still standing on Rosemary's place, where I had gone to wait for her when she became ill. Now, more than fifty years later, I could tell her in the simple language of that six-year-old child that her sickness took too long; when I needed her she was not there and I was angry with her, until today. In uttering those words, the spell was broken and I could take my proper place between Mary Lou and John.

We kids held hands and beamed from ear to ear. I could see a river of light flowing down from Rosemary, to Sue, to Mary Lou, to me, to John. And I could see that it flowed from our grandparents through the eldest down to the youngest, so that we were all directly connected to our grandparents. I could see Nan beaming at us all, and I knew it was she who had thrown the soft blue cloak around my shoulders to protect me and give me courage that first day back in Bühl.

Everything was spoken in German, but Mum was sitting next to me, smiling broadly and her eyes were sparkling. In that moment I understood that whereas I had always thought she had come to Germany so I could take care of her, in fact she had come to help free me and all her children.

In the days that followed there was a domino effect. I saw that I had spent my life standing in the wrong place. I had stood next to Roger as his mother instead of his wife. No wonder I had always felt bigger than him and ever since his breakdown had always seen him as a child. Suddenly I could see the man. And I saw that I was still standing next to Peter, but could step back to make room for his wife to take her place by his side. And finally, at last, I took my proper place at George's side.

On the drive home I became aware that Dad was no longer sitting on the back steps. I saw that the tangle was out and he had rolled up the line, put it back in the fishing bag, and was gone.

It was Easter Sunday and my fifty-eighth birthday when we returned home. In recognition of my journey into the dreamtime of my family, George attached a large picture of Uluru to the car port, in the blue sky above which he had written 'Welcome Home'. I roasted a chicken in the coals of our wood fire to celebrate and we ate it with our fingers. I did not understand fully what had happened, but I knew it was profound and very important. I had seen it on the faces of my family and I could feel it in my bones.

To let Roger know what had happened, I found a rock and sent it to him, a sign I knew he would understand. It was not just any rock, it was a thunder egg from the area around Uluru. Some people say they are living rocks. With that rock I wanted him to know that I had finally stepped aside from the place of the mother, and in so doing I had finally seen the man he was and had always wanted to be for me and our children.

Two months later, on 1 July 2003, Peter and Kylie called. It was very rare to have them on the phone together, but my joy was shortlived. They were calling to tell me Roger had died. I saw a comet shoot up through the sky from the horizon, its tail creating a circle of shimmering stars in the heavens as it returned from whence it had come.

He was only sixty-one years old. Wiry and active, and apparently as fit as a fiddle, he had suffered a massive heart attack. His wife was visiting her family in the States and it was Peter who found him sitting up in the bathtub, dead, the water still warm, and the cup of tea he had placed on the edge of the bath still hot enough to drink. He was my first love, my first husband and the father of my children. My heart broke, but especially for our children. Finally settled and living within ten minutes' drive of each other, it was inconceivable that their father should suddenly die like that, and me on the other side of the world, unable to comfort them or to pay my last respects. It was one of the worst moments of the now fourteen years that I had been confined to my sanctuary in Germany.

Peter wrote me that during the wake he was sitting on a chair at Roger's feet when Jennifer, pregnant with their second child, came and stood behind him. The child in her belly began kicking him in the back and it struck him that while his father lay dead beside him, new life was waiting impatiently to emerge. Two and a half months later his son was born, and Kylie was pregnant.

Kylie brought her son into the world at home in Australia soon after my fifty-ninth birthday. I was not there with her. Phil and I had talked and exchanged letters, but a solution that would not involve further imprisonment seemed as far away as ever.

38

It was late October 2004. What a wonderful year it had been, I thought to myself as I finished up the last of the chores in the kitchen before going to bed. In summer Peter and Jennifer and the two children had come to visit. Mum was with us at the time and she and ten-month-old Dylan became the best of friends. The visit coincided with Peter and Jennifer's wedding anniversary, so while we grandparents looked after the children, they celebrated at the hotel where we had celebrated their marriage. Things were going well following the move to Australia and Peter was establishing himself as a very able Mac consultant. He and Jennifer were clearly doing well as a couple and he took great pleasure in fatherhood.

Peter always said he had few regrets from the years in Pune and Oregon, insisting that the freedom he had experienced had been very important to him. He said he had grown through the difficulties he had had to face and was happy for the friends he made there. Although they were now scattered all over the world, they stayed in close contact with one another. He never wanted me to feel bad for what had happened, and I never knew whether it was out of love for me or if he truly felt at peace with it all. Perhaps it was a combination of both, for he had grown into a remarkably loving and tolerant adult.

Now Kylie and Gregory and baby Joshua had arrived in Germany and were sleeping peacefully downstairs. It had been a year of visits from my children and their mates, meeting my new grandsons and renewing my acquaintance with my granddaughter. I felt blessed and very content.

I smiled as I looked up at the inscription hanging on the kitchen wall: *No hay mal que por bien no venga*, a Spanish saying meaning 'There is nothing bad that does not bring good with it'.

How true it was for me. There was no doubt that everything that had happened in my life had contributed towards making me the person I now was. If I had not run off to India I would not be this person here tidying up this kitchen, with my husband George upstairs at the computer and the children asleep downstairs. I wondered at the apparent contradiction that the most terrible situations had brought with them undeniable blessings. Had not Joseph pondered the same riddle when he recognised, twenty-three years after his brothers had sold him into slavery, that their violence against him had, in the end, been shown to be a blessing in disguise?

Yes, I said to myself, I had much to be grateful for. I put the porridge on to soak, turned out the light and went upstairs to bed.

The phone ringing on the bedside table woke me out of a deep sleep. I groggily reached over and picked up the receiver.

'Jane, it's Jennifer.'

I was wide awake immediately. George turned on the light. I looked at the clock. It was 2 am. In a voice full of emotion Jennifer told me Peter was in hospital. He had woken in the middle of the night, she said, and sat up smelling burning plastic. He had woken her and she had realised very quickly that something was not right with him. The children were in the next room asleep so she had called a close friend and asked him to come over right away. The friend had driven Peter around the corner to the local hospital, where he was promptly put in an ambulance that set off for Lismore Hospital, an hour's drive away. On the way, he had a grand mal seizure and his heart stopped. It was only due to the fact that medical help was right there that he was still alive. He was in an induced coma, she said, and the doctors were trying to find out what was wrong. She had arranged for the children to be taken care of and was on her way to the hospital.

I was numb as I hung up the phone. I lay back down next to George and wept.

Over the next few days herpetic encephalitis, an inflammation of the brain caused by the herpes virus, appeared the most likely culprit. An MRI scan had picked up a small lesion on the midtemporal lobe which probably indicated infection. Armed with antiseizure medicine and potent antiviral drugs Peter was allowed to go home. In the normal course of events he should have felt better and better as the encephalitis healed. Five weeks went by but he was still unwell. A second MRI scan was ordered. When it came back it showed that the small lesion, which should by rights have shrunk by now, had actually grown. It seemed probable that Peter had a brain tumour, but exactly what kind of tumour could only be determined with a biopsy. An appointment was made to see a neurosurgeon at the Princess Alexandra Hospital in Brisbane.

The moment I heard the news I contacted Phil. Later I would find out that his mother had died of a brain tumour not five months previously. His first impulse was to get me to Australia as soon as possible. To that end he wanted to file a motion with the US federal court asking that the arrest warrant be temporarily lifted to allow me free passage to Australia. But before proceeding with the motion, Phil said he wanted to contact Mr Turner. The former US attorney had been the intended victim and it seemed the right place to start. Phil said he would spend a couple of days ordering his thoughts and then write Mr Turner a letter. The following day I woke thinking of Peter and the grave threat to his life and the tumult of emotions that cascaded over me every day knowing of that threat. Suddenly a bolt went through me, as though I had been struck by lightning, and in that moment I knew Mr Turner must have felt just as I was feeling now when he heard of the threat to *his* life.

Suddenly I saw him as a person. I was shocked to realise that up until that moment I had never considered him to be a person. My picture of him had always been of a solid faceless menhir-like object blocking the way. Now I recognised that he was a human being just like myself. He was a human being with feelings, a human being with a wife and children and grandchildren and friends and a whole life story. And for the first time I became aware of the terrible emotional pain he and his family must have suffered when they heard his life was threatened. I had always pooh-poohed the idea that Mr Turner should have suffered at all, arguing that the plot did not come to light until after I and the conspirators had left the country. But now I knew that the knowledge of a threat was more than enough to create the same feelings of uncertainty, dread and horror that I was feeling at the threat to Peter. I was devastated to think I had contributed to such suffering.

From that moment on I began referring to him as Mr Turner instead of the brusque, impersonal 'Turner' I had always used. At breakfast I told George I wanted to write Mr Turner a letter. I knew it would not be appropriate to actually send it, but I needed to write it down. I needed to let him know that I could see him as a person now and that I deeply regretted the pain I had caused him and his family and friends. I went upstairs and wrote what was in my heart in a letter to him, and filed it in a safe place.

On 11 December, eight days after Peter's thirty-sixth birthday, Peter and Jennifer met the neurosurgeon to hear the results of the biopsy. 'We are in trouble,' was the first thing the surgeon said. Peter had an aggressive grade 3 astrocytoma, he told them. There was no known cure. His life expectancy was two to three years. That same day in America, unaware of the diagnosis, Mr Turner responded to the letter Phil had written him. Mr Turner said he had no objection to the arrest warrant being lifted in order to allow me to fly to Australia. Not only that, he gave Phil the benefit of his experience as to how he might best approach the problem.

I could not comprehend that things had taken such a turn, just when everything was going so well. It was impossible that my son should die. He was in the prime of his life. I argued passionately to George and Kylie and Gregory over the breakfast table the reasons why it just didn't make sense that Peter should die. I said categorically that he would not die. I clenched my fist and shook it at the heavens, defying the gods and shouting,

'No! Not this! Not my son!'

39

George sat at the computer researching anaplastic gemistocytic astrocytoma every spare minute he had. In Australia Jennifer was doing the same. Gregory and Kylie returned home to assist in whatever way they could. Thanks to the internet there was a wealth of information available. The majority of it agreed with the statistics which said this kind of tumour was untreatable, and fatal. However, there was a small body of knowledge centred around latest developments in medical science, and diet, which gave us hope. Jennifer contacted doctors and researchers all over the world. She discovered there was only a handful of neurosurgeons in the world who would consider operating on Peter's tumour because of the particularly delicate area of the brain it was situated in. One of those neurosurgeons was in Brisbane, a two-hour drive from where they lived. Surgery was set for 16 February 2005.

Meanwhile Phil was making every effort to get the international arrest warrant lifted. Having had the experience of this type of tumour with his mother, he felt we had to move quickly as Peter's condition could worsen dramatically at any time. When the court would not agree to lifting the arrest warrant, Phil thought another alternative would be for me to go to the States and enter a guilty plea, and have either sentencing or a surrender date postponed until such time as Peter healed, or died. But he feared the court would not commit itself ahead of time. He thought the judge might allow my free passage to court, but would want to defer deciding any conditions of release – such as being free to leave the country pending sentencing – until I had shown up for the arraignment.

'That would certainly make things scarier,' Phil wrote, 'but my thinking is that if the court were to take such a step it would be simply to test your good faith.'

Still, he was worried.

'In your case the statute on conspiracy to commit murder provides that the sentence shall be by imprisonment for any term of years or for life. In other words, at sentencing you would be facing anything from probation, to life.'

He said he was afraid that if I were to go to the States without any guarantees, it could happen that I would be imprisoned right away and might not see Peter at all.

I was reminded of my conversation with Michael before I met with the higher regional court. Again I knew that I had nothing to lose. If I did not take this chance the court would not come to know me and would have no opportunity to show mercy towards me. George and I talked the whole thing through yet again, but we both knew what I had to do. I asked Phil to go ahead and prepare a motion asking that the arrest warrant be lifted so that I could fly to America to plead guilty.

He prepared and filed the motion by the end of January, asking that I be able to appear before the court by mid-February. We were in full flight when Phil became aware that Judge Marsh, who had presided over the case since the beginning, was on leave. We both agreed we wanted to wait until he was back in town. It was his case. To go ahead in his absence did not feel right. I knew in my heart that the time had come to bring the story to completion, and after so many years we needed to take the time to do it properly. For some inexplicable reason I did not feel anxious about Peter's operation. I spoke to him on the phone and he said he would like me to come to Australia a free woman. He encouraged me to take the time needed to achieve that and said I should not worry about him. He would be there waiting to celebrate my homecoming.

Judge Marsh's absence provided the perfect opportunity for Phil to come to Germany to meet me. Up until now all our communications had been through letters and phone calls, but we had not met in person. We were both aware of a need to sit down together before I left German soil. We needed to take stock and be sure that we were clear about what we were doing.

He made arrangements and in early March sent an email,
'See you in a couple of days. If George cannot find me, I will be the tall one with the grey beard, brown fedora hat, and maybe a bow tie. I will obviously be an American. I just stick out as such, though I am told I should claim to be Canadian.'

Phil walked into our kitchen, spied the crib board on the mantelpiece and within five minutes of meeting him we were sitting at the kitchen table playing crib. It was a typically Phil way to break the ice. Dad had made the crib board from a piece of jarrah and he and Mum had played crib with it for the sixty-five years of their married life. And now it was sitting between Phil and me, helping us to get to know each other. It was a gentle start to what were to be two of the most intense weeks of my life.

If there is one thing Phil is not it is airy-fairy. He is a straight talker and he calls a spade a spade. He also has a huge heart in his chest which allows him to be brutally honest. It was he who, when I told him what had happened to Peter and Kylie, said bluntly, 'That is sexual abuse.' I had never given it that name before. To hear it called by its name was shocking, and I cried and protested that I wanted to protect the children and not speak of it in court. Phil pointed out that keeping silent about it would not make it go away, and the time had come to be honest about everything that had happened, for my sake and my family's.

He insisted that I open every dark chamber in my past and go in and turn on the light, pointing out that being human we all tend to view things in a way that makes us feel better about ourselves, but for this moment at least I was to face the facts without trying to make them nicer. I thought I had already done a lot of honest looking at myself and my motives, but Phil introduced me to a whole new dimension. It was very painful and not a day went by that I did not cry bitter tears. He helped me to see and to face the enormity of what I had done, going so far as to point out that all that 'loose talk' could very easily have led to the murder of a highly respected government official. It was only a hairsbreadth from loose talk to action as I had demonstrated on that fateful 6 July and I was very lucky, he said, that the murder attempt against Bhagwan's doctor had failed. And all the time we were talking we were both aware that Peter was deadly ill, and I must step into the void if I was to have any chance of seeing him again.

Shortly before Phil had to leave, we drove to Karlsruhe to meet with Michael Rosenthal. We spent an entire Sunday afternoon together in Michael's office while Michael explained the differences between the German and the American legal systems, and why it was that the higher regional court had refused to extradite me. Suddenly aware of the enormous cultural differences between the two systems, on the drive home Phil argued strongly with me not to go to America. He said he had more doubts than ever whether we could convince Judge Marsh that probation would be appropriate.

'You are safe and happy here in Germany with George,' he said. 'If you do this thing you will almost certainly be given a prison sentence. You will be separated from George for perhaps years, and he will be lost without you. You may never see your mother again, and you may not see Peter at all, or be there when he dies. Don't do it. It is too risky.'

I was inclined to agree with him. I had also learned a lot in the few days he had been in Germany. I had lost something of my naivety and was beginning to have second thoughts about entering the lions' den. Although Mr Turner had indicated he would write a letter to the court saying he would be satisfied with a sentence of probation for me, I no longer felt so assured about the outcome, particularly as every legal person we spoke to voiced the opinion that I would without a doubt get more time in prison.

Back in Australia Peter was doing much better. The surgery had gone well and he had been able to cut back on the seizure medication. He was to return to the hospital in Brisbane to have his blood drawn to be used to prepare a dendritic cell vaccine for the clinical trial he was to participate in. We were hopeful that this new treatment would bring healing.

Things had calmed down a lot, and as I listened to Phil I told myself he was right; I shouldn't rush into this, we should wait and see what happened with Peter. Deep down I breathed a sigh of relief. The spectre of further imprisonment had been a low-grade nightmare in the background all along, and to be able to put it on hold for a while would be a welcome respite. I said we would continue on the path we had begun but that we should take time now to try to get assurances from the court, and the prosecution, that when I came to the States, I would at least be permitted to go to Australia to see Peter before being imprisoned. I knew it would take time, but there seemed to be no great urgency now.

Unfortunately, it did not take long before it became apparent that the dendritic cell vaccine was not having the desired therapeutic effect. On the contrary, by the beginning of July Jennifer called to say Peter's condition was deteriorating alarmingly and a control MRI had shown that the tumour was growing again. Peter was at home but was completely confined to his bed. He was having frequent seizures, followed by prolonged blinding headaches.

I knew then that time was running out. A recent motion, asking the court for the appointment of a settlement judge to assist in efforts at reaching agreement with the prosecution on mutually acceptable conditions for my entry into the country, had been denied, along with an earlier motion asking that the arrest warrant be lifted to allow me to enter America. The court said I must first submit myself to the jurisdiction of the United States, before making any requests of it.

On Friday 15 July Jennifer called to say that an MRI showed the tumour to have grown from practically nothing to the size of a lemon in the two weeks since the last scan. It was pushing into the midline of the brain, causing Peter debilitating headaches and constant nausea and vomiting. Because of the explosive growth, doctors thought it had gone from a grade 3 astrocytoma to the most virulent grade 4 glioblastoma. The neurosurgeon said that unless Peter had surgery very soon, he would fall into a coma within a matter of days and die within a few weeks. Surgery was scheduled for Wednesday 20 July. The neurosurgeon said if all went well Peter could expect one to nine months of quality time before the cycle repeated itself. Jennifer said Peter was leaning towards surgery, although his weakened condition and the drugs he was receiving were making it difficult for him to think straight, let alone make such difficult decisions. He had been admitted to the hospital in Brisbane and she was with him. Kylie and Gregory would bring the children to Brisbane the following day and take an apartment close to the hospital.

There are no words to describe my feelings that day and the two days that followed. I was numb with horror and my heart felt as though it was literally breaking in two. On the morning of the fourth day I woke with the clear certainty that I must leave my safe haven and face the unknown. Peter had said to me once,

'If you don't move, Mum, nothing will change.'

I knew he was right and I knew I must go now. The time for holding back was over. I talked to George first. I told him what I had decided and asked for his support. He held me for the longest time and then said he would go with me to the end of the world if that was where I must go.

When it was morning in America I called Phil to tell him. I said that I wanted to come to America and throw myself on the mercy of the court. He again pointed out that it would be a very risky option to simply come and plead guilty to everything with no sentencing concessions, but on the other hand he thought the prosecution could not really turn down such an offer and would be compelled to assist in paroling me into the country.

'I am with you all the way,' he said.

He and I never wavered after that. Although we had no way of knowing what the court would do, I felt absolutely clear that I must bow before its sovereignty and was prepared to accept whatever ruling it made. I felt calm and peaceful. The train had left the station and there was no going back.

I called Peter the next morning and was relieved to hear in his voice that he had found his strength again. He said he had been through hell since hearing what the neurosurgeon had to say on Friday. He had fallen into a chasm of fear, but with each passing hour he had found more and more strength and clarity, and now he was ready to face the surgery. I was humbled at the way he was dealing with his reality. I told him of my decision and I could hear him smile down the phone.

'Thanks Mum,' was all he said.

Kylie called next day to say the surgery had gone well. Peter went into surgery calmly and was in recovery, she said, and he was speaking and moving all his limbs. So far, so good. He continued to make a good recovery and was home within a few days. Shortly afterwards he started a course of chemotherapy and radiation therapy.

I had been granted German citizenship in 1994 and, as it was not permitted to have dual citizenship, I was required to surrender my Australian passport. It was now necessary for me to apply for a visa to enter Australia. However, my situation posed a difficult problem for the Australian authorities. There was an international arrest warrant out for me: sufficient grounds to deny me a visa. A retired member of the immigration department in Perth who had been very kind to my parents at the time of my arrest encouraged me to persevere and suggested ways to overcome the stumbling block. Phil wrote a letter to the minister for immigration and I was given the opportunity to explain myself. I included the decision of the higher regional court and a letter from Peter's neurosurgeon with the long letter I wrote. In late August I received notification that the visa had been granted.

Meanwhile Phil was working to ensure that when I entered the United States things would go as smoothly as possible. George and I had tickets for a nonstop flight from Frankfurt to Portland, scheduled to arrive in the early afternoon of 21 September. Phil secured the cooperation of local authorities for me to be met on arrival and taken directly from Portland airport to the city courthouse for arraignment and a release hearing. With my appearance before the magistrate the arrest warrant would automatically be lifted. I was to appear before Judge Marsh five days later to enter my guilty plea.

Following very intense discussions with the prosecution, Phil was able to secure a letter of understanding from the government that it would not oppose my travelling to Australia before the sentencing hearing. The court indicated that it would go along with that, but stipulated a number of conditions, including restrictions on other travel. Phil made arrangements for me to be interviewed over the phone in Germany by the office of pre-trial services, in order that I could be released from custody without delay upon my arrival in Portland. He also asked me to submit to evaluation with a doctor of psychology in Portland before leaving for Australia. He wanted to submit the evaluation to the court prior to sentencing. The testing and interview would take a day and a half, he said. Trusting that all would go as planned, George booked us a hotel room in Portland, a ticket from Portland to Australia for me, and one for himself back to Germany, where he would have to return to work.

Not knowing if I would be away for months or years, I began putting my house in order. I cleaned it from top to bottom, including all the windows, cupboards and drawers. I washed the curtains and took rugs to the cleaners. I sorted through my papers and clothes, throwing things out and packing things away. The woodman came and filled the woodshed and I cut back the shrubs and mulched them in readiness for winter.

Then I asked myself whether there was anything else I needed to take care of. Suddenly Jorg came to mind, the German sannyasin who had paid for our tickets when Kylie and I left the commune. I had never repaid him! All these years I had taken his generosity for granted. I found where he was living in Berlin and phoned him. When I said I was sending the money and apologised for having taken so long to acknowledge my debt to him, he burst into tears. I was the first to have remembered, he said, and the money could not be coming at a better time.

Another memory surfaced then, that of the monstrous steamroller set into motion the day I had been driven away in handcuffs. I looked to see where it was. It had stopped and was completely rusted out and overgrown.

40

It was almost twenty years to the day that I had left Bhagwan and flown out of Portland airport to Europe. And it was almost fifteen years to the day that I had been arrested a second time. Now I was coming back again, of my own free will, because it was the right thing, the only thing, for me to do. It took Peter's illness and his example of facing up to things to bring me to that understanding.

A gentle giant met us at Portland airport as we disembarked with the other passengers. Showing remarkable discretion and consideration towards us, he guided us through the mass of people to his office. There were formalities to be taken care of – photos, questions, forms – but before each step he carefully explained what was to happen next, and often apologised for the inconvenience. Then we left his office in order to collect our luggage and have it searched, a formality he also apologised for. Then it was time for me to be separated from George and handed over to the FBI agents waiting to take me to the courthouse. Again, he explained what would happen in detail before setting things in motion, and everything happened in a calm, unobtrusive way. He then took George to where Phil was waiting, and the two of them drove downtown to the courthouse to wait for me.

The formalities at the airport and then the fingerprinting and formalities at the courthouse all took a long time and it was touch and go as to whether I was going to have to spend the night in prison. People seemed to care that things went well for me. Everyone I met was courteous and kind and went out of their way to ensure that I was not unduly detained, with the result that at the end of the day I was able to walk out to where George and Phil were waiting to take me to our hotel.

The next few days I spent a lot of time in Phil's office, and in between George and I explored Portland. It was disconcerting to realise that I had no memories of Portland although I had been there many times as a Rajneeshee. Everything seemed new to me, as though I was seeing it for the first time.

As we entered the courtroom on 26 September, the prosecutor stepped forward to introduce himself and I shook the hand of the man who had held me in the corner with my back to the wall for so many years. And yet it was he who had been the catalyst for me to reopen the door to my past. He was the one who had held me so firmly for so long that I had finally made the connection between my inner world and the world outside, and could untangle the knot and free my family and myself from the cords that ensnared us. In a very real sense he was a hard taskmaster, but his tenacity in pursuing his job had led me to find myself. As strange as it may sound, I had much to thank him for.

I pleaded guilty to the charge of conspiracy to murder Mr Turner and of having transported weapons across state lines. Judge Marsh set the sentencing date for early December. When all formalities were settled, he ordered that my passport be returned to me right there in the courtroom, and turning to me he added,

'We're on a trust basis from here out with this, so we'll just start trusting one another right now.'

Afterwards he invited us into his chambers, along with the prosecutor, and George too. He showed us large photos of the Big Muddy taken from the air. It was now a camp for Christian youth, he said, and thousands of young people attended summer camp there every year.

'I have shown you these photos,' he said, 'so you would know that out of darkness light can come.'

As we said goodbye he told me he was praying for me and my son. Returning to the courtroom, the prosecutor held the door open. As I walked by him he said quietly,

'I am also praying for your son. I lost a son.'

Phil suggested he drive us down to the ranch. He had never been there and he thought it might stir memories for me. We drove over Mount Hood. How many times had I driven that route? Dozens of times, and yet it was all so unfamiliar. I was shocked. It was not until we arrived in Antelope that memories surfaced: the now abandoned school, the place where the office trailers had stood, the store. The drive down the county road through the ranch property was also unfamiliar. It took me some time to realise that it was made all the more unfamiliar by the fact that hundreds of junipers whose dark green foliage had once brightened the rocky hills were dead. Their bleached skeletons stood there, ghostly reminders it seemed to me of the many dreams that had died on the Big Muddy.

The single most powerful impression I had that day was of isolation. The property was for all intents and purposes at the end of the world. When we drove through there were only a handful of people there. Bhagwan's house was gone. Apparently it had been struck by lightning during an electrical storm and burned to the ground. Everything had changed and I had difficulty orienting myself the whole time we were there. As pleasant as it was in its new role as a country retreat for city kids, I was glad to leave. For me that valley represented Hades.

The psychological tests were all standard, but there were lots of them. There were multiple choice questions, yes or no questions, and unfinished sentences to complete. I had never done anything like it before. In between doing the tests, I answered questions and talked about my life and what had happened. On the morning of the second day of testing George also participated in the interview, until it was time for him to take a taxi to the airport to catch his flight back home. A few hours later we were done, and Phil drove me to the airport to catch a flight to San Francisco, from where I would take a direct flight to Sydney. One of the men I had already met from customs and border protection delivered a document to me at the airport, ensuring there would be no hitch when I left the country. Having taken care of the formalities, he shook my hand and wished me well. I was again touched by the kindness and courteousness shown towards me since I had set foot in Portland.

For someone who had not flown anywhere in fifteen years, I was suddenly flying a lot. It was all happening so fast I could hardly take it in. At San Francisco airport passengers were required to put their passports into a machine, which then 'issued' an exit stamp. I hesitated, unsure if the machine would know it was okay for me to leave the country. It did. Someone in Portland was looking out for me and had done their work well. I didn't read or watch movies on the long flight across the Pacific. Instead I drank lots of water and slept as much as I could. I wanted to be well rested when I arrived in Australia. Mum was waiting for me at Sydney airport and together we flew on to the Gold Coast. For me it was all a miracle in motion.

Both my children were there to greet me as I walked into the airport building. They had never looked so beautiful! We hugged and laughed and cried, Mum and Jennifer and the grandchildren joining in. Then we collected our baggage and climbed into Peter and Jennifer's van for the journey home. It was the first time in almost twenty-eight years that Peter and Kylie and I were together in Australia. I was visiting my adult children and their families in their own homes for the first time in their lives. Mum and I stayed with Kylie and Gregory in the comfortable, gracious house they had designed and built together. Joshua, who had crawled all over the house in Germany, was up on his feet and running now.

Peter had a mohawk, his answer to the hair loss caused by the radiation therapy. He was following a diet that was designed to maintain stable blood-sugar levels and to avoid sudden surges that could lead to renewed tumour growth. The headaches and seizures were kept under control with the many drugs he had to take, so that one way and another his quality of life at that time was pretty good.

The tumour caused disturbance in the part of the brain that controls speech. What that meant for Peter was that he was often unable to recall nouns. He could describe the thing he was talking about, but he couldn't find the actual name of it. For example, he might say, 'It is a large, grey, strong animal used in India for logging,' when the word he was looking for was elephant. For someone who had always used language well, it irritated him to have these gaps in his vocabulary. Sometimes I would catch him standing still with a look of intense concentration on his face. 'I'm trying to think but nothing happens,' he would say wryly by way of explanation.

We regularly went for long walks on the beach in the early morning. He loved the ocean and had been a passionate surfer. Before he fell ill it was his habit to rise early to go surfing for an hour or two before coming home to open his office. But his condition meant that he could no longer drive a car and it was not safe for him to go out into the water alone, lest he have a seizure. Walking on the beach was the next best thing, although sometimes friends came by to take him surfing with them. They paddled out with him and kept an eye on him in the water. Just to be able to paddle out and sit on his board and occasionally catch the odd wave was a source of great joy to him, though he was always completely exhausted afterwards.

Following my appearance in court, Phil was given access to the masses of documents the prosecution had acquired throughout the almost nineteen-year life of the case. He was working his way through them and regularly sent me copies of documents he thought I needed to know about or to clarify for him. By the end of October he realised he needed more time to prepare for sentencing. He petitioned for a later date. The court set 30 January 2006 as the new sentencing date.

Phil had told me that I would be expected to make a statement to the court at sentencing and urged me to begin working on it. By mid-November it was clear that I must really apply myself to the task if I were to do it right. This was my one opportunity to explain myself and to say the things that needed to be said, to publicly stand up and take responsibility for what I had done. It was so important to me that I withdrew from the family. I rented a holiday apartment and Mum and I moved there. A friend of Peter's lent me his Powerbook and I began writing.

Sometimes days went by and I didn't see the children at all. I wrote and wrote, and cried and cried. Visiting the past once again to try to write it down in a coherent form opened the floodgates as never before. I wept for the young me who had lost her way so badly, and for the pain and suffering I had caused my children, Roger, my parents and our families. I wept for the fear and suffering I had caused Bhagwan's doctor, and Mr Turner and his family, and people whose names I did not even know. I wrote dozens of pages. There seemed to be so much that needed to be said. When I reduced it to what I thought was most important, it was still fourteen pages long. Too long, I knew, to read in court. Phil was up to his ears taking care of a thousand and one things in preparation for sentencing, so he asked a woman whose abilities he valued, to help me.

Deborah was in America and I was in Australia. We met on the phone. She had read what I had written. Like the emotional markswoman she is, she came to the point right away.

'You have been a victim,' she said, 'but in the arena you are about to enter, you are the perpetrator.'

In that moment I trusted her. I knew that with this woman I could clear the debris and get to the heart of the matter. But that we would do it so quickly surprised us both. In less than a week I had my statement down to four pages. Her insights fell into me like shooting stars. To my comment that my motivation at the time had been to save the world, she responded,

'Your world.' Her words exploded in my being. My world! Of course! I had been trying to save my world. Deborah encouraged me to use the opportunity to say what I really wanted to say, to apologise to those I wanted to apologise to, and even to ask for what I wanted.

George arrived for Christmas. Our little holiday apartment was out of town, on a hill in the middle of a banana grove. From the veranda we could watch the sun rise out of the ocean every morning and see the township down below. We had a direct view to Peter and Jennifer's house. We all celebrated Christmas together at Kylie and Gregory's home. It was another first and we did it in grand style. After Christmas Mum joined Sue in Sydney, leaving George and me alone for a while. We went for walks along the beach with Peter and spent time with the two families, but we also spent a lot of quiet time together at the apartment. At the end of the month we would meet again in Portland, but after that we didn't know what awaited us.

When George flew back to Germany, I returned to Kylie and Gregory's. There was not much time left. Peter's condition was stable. A recent scan showed that there had been no new tumour growth and the swelling and oedema in his brain was substantially reduced.

I spent a lot of time at the house with my son and his little family, although by now I was very focused on the sentencing. A part of me was preparing myself for what lay ahead, so that I was not always present with Peter and Kylie and the grandchildren, but was often preoccupied. Whenever possible Peter and I continued to walk on the beach in the early morning. There was something comforting about knowing that the ocean which had been lapping on that shore for millions of years was now wetting the sand beneath our feet. It gave us a sense of continuity and strength. A couple of days before I was to fly back to America I hugged Peter and Kylie and Jennifer and Gregory and my grandchildren goodbye and flew to Sydney to see Mum. When I was leaving she laid her hand on my head.

'God bless you,' she said, 'Come back soon.'

41

I returned to America five days before I was to appear in court. I wanted to give myself time to recover from the long flight, to be with George, and to be sure that Phil and I had covered everything. In San Francisco airport I was met and discreetly guided through the formalities. While my case was being searched, the cell phone on the hip of the man doing the search rang. He answered it, said,

'She'll be there in five minutes,' and hung up. 'Must be an expensive lawyer you have there,' he said. 'He's been calling all morning and now he wants you to know that he's waiting outside.'

The search was over and another plainclothes man asked me to follow him. We walked out of security and into the transit lounge, and there was Phil. My escort wished us a nice day and left. A couple of hours later we flew to Portland, where we drank a cup of coffee while we waited for George's flight from Germany to arrive.

Following a suggestion from Deborah, George and I had asked her to book a small self-contained holiday apartment for us. It was quiet and private, and I could cook our meals there. Phil dropped us off. He said his mother had always stayed there when she came to visit, and pointed out a sushi bar close by where we could have a bite to eat before going to bed. Deborah had already laid in the basics for breakfast the next morning. It was the strangest thing. A comfortable little apartment, friends to pick us up and take care of details, and a city we had come to appreciate on a previous visit. It was nice to be back! George and I felt as though we could have been on holiday together, and yet never for a moment did we forget why we were there.

Deborah came round the following day and we met in person for the first time. Although we had spoken for a total of probably only two hours on the phone, it was like meeting an old friend. Afterwards we went around to Phil's office where we discussed the recommendation in the pre-sentence report that I receive a two-year prison sentence. Phil had done his best to dissuade the probation officer responsible for the report to change his mind, but to no avail.

On the morning of Monday 30 January 2006 it was raining as we left the apartment to rendezvous with Phil. It was a bit of a walk to the tram stop and George and I held tightly to each other as we jumped the puddles. We did not talk. We were both in a place of silence, our whole attention on the task at hand.

Phil was wearing a bow tie with turtles on it that morning. I looked at him quizzically.

'Slow and steady,' he said.

We walked to the courthouse from his office. Outside the courthouse he turned to me and said,

'We have done our best. We have given it our best shot.'

It is difficult to put words to how I felt as we entered the courtroom and took our places. Perhaps 'focused' describes it best. The courtroom was my world at that moment and I was very aware of every feature: the dark wood panelling and furniture, the raised judges' bench, the wooden railing that separated onlookers from the participants. It reminded me of the churches of my childhood where an elaborate altar rail separated the people from the celebrants. In a certain way it was a holy place for me, for I had come to give an account of myself and to have judgement passed on me. I did not feel unduly nervous. I felt as though it was the right and proper thing that I should be here, and I felt very present. It was as though I had been born for this day, as if it was my destiny, the culmination of my life's work up until that point. And now at the age of sixty I was finally here, and all those of us who were destined to meet together on this day in this courtroom were also present. Phil's wife was here too. It was the first time in the almost thirty years Phil had been practising law that his wife had come to court to hear him argue on behalf of a client. She sat next to George. The prosecutor sat to the left at his table, and Phil and I sat to the right at the table reserved for the defendant. Deborah sat behind us.

Both Phil and the prosecutor had already presented their arguments in sentencing memos filed with the court a few days before the hearing. Phil had really put his heart into his memo. He told me that as he was writing it his father was looking over his shoulder and helping him. There was another opportunity now to speak to the judge directly. The prosecutor had the first word. He outlined the facts of the case, stressing the prosecution's view that I had played a major role in the conspiracy, and asked that in the interests of justice I be sentenced to an appropriate term in prison.

Then Phil spoke. He argued eloquently and passionately, pointing out the many inconsistencies in the treatment between the many different people either charged or implicated in the conspiracy. He said that I was the only one who had already served time. He spoke of the years I had been confined to Germany as having been a kind of imprisonment too. He talked about the 'manipulation of the devotion of the devoted' that led to the corruption of ideals. He outlined the way in which I had come back from the brink and put my life in order, and he asked the judge to free me on probation, arguing that I had already served time in this case when I was imprisoned in Germany for three months following my arrest in 1990.

Then it was my turn and I stood up to speak. I began by admitting my guilt and apologising to Mr Turner and his family for the suffering I had caused them. I apologised further for having taken so long to come to this point, as the wound had been kept open and prolonged their suffering. I also expressed my gratitude to Mr Turner for the enormous kindness he had demonstrated towards me. My voice broke as I spoke, but I willed it to stay strong and continued to speak.

Having given a brief synopsis of my life and how I had become involved with Bhagwan and Sheela, I went on to apologise for my lack of honesty at the time of my plea to the charge of attempting to murder Bhagwan's doctor. I admitted my guilt, and apologised to Bhagwan's doctor for the fear and suffering I caused him.

I apologised to the United States government for my disregard for the truth when dealing with its immigration laws and for lying under oath during the Helen Byron trial.

I apologised to the Dalles county commissioners for my shameful disrespect towards them and to the people of Antelope and neighbouring towns for having participated in a display of firepower that was intended to frighten and intimidate honest citizens.

I apologised to my parents, and to my brother and sisters and to Roger's family for the deep distress and suffering I had caused them.

And then I apologised to my children for having taken them away from their grandparents, aunts and uncles, cousins and friends and abandoned them to the commune, and for having denied them the benefit of parental and family warmth, guidance and protection, as a result of which both of them had become victims of sexual abuse. I acknowledged that my children had suffered immensely because of choices I had made. And I honoured the great courage and strength of character they had both displayed to grow through such daunting difficulties into the fine adults they had become.

I thanked Judge Marsh for allowing me to spend the previous four months with Peter and Kylie and their families in Australia, and I expressed my appreciation for the kind and heartfelt enquiries of so many people into Peter's condition, and for the many prayers people were offering for his recovery. I also thanked the judge for the appointment of Phil as my attorney, acknowledging that without his advice and support I might never have found the clarity and courage to take this final step.

I thanked the prosecutor, pointing out that in doing his job he had helped me do mine. And I expressed my gratitude to all those who in their own particular way had helped me come to this place of responsibility today.

In conclusion I said:

'Others have not been as fortunate as I. Many others have fared much worse, and some have even paid with their lives for their involvement with Bhagwan. Many are suffering still. I have been fortunate to have parents who waited and prayed unceasingly for my safe return, and who welcomed me home with open arms. It was their steadfast love and acceptance of me, despite everything, that laid the foundation for my rehabilitation. I have also been greatly blessed in George, my husband of fifteen years. In his quiet loving way he has walked with me on my journey into the past to face what I have done. He has listened without judgement, held me when I cried and lent me a hand when I stumbled. His steady love and support of me and my children and my mother has been a powerful healing force. I am one of the lucky ones.

'Your Honour, I now put the matter to rest before you, who has the ultimate responsibility to decide the legal punishment for my crime. Of course I would like to walk from this courtroom today a free woman, but I humbly accept your decision, whatever it may be.'

Phil would later describe Judge Marsh's response as 'probably the most anguished, articulate and profound thinking aloud' he had ever heard from the bench.

Judge Marsh began by quoting Michael Polanyi, a twentieth-century scientist and philosopher who said 'the victim of a delusion is the last to see the deception', and referred to the circle of hate that had formed in and around the commune. He said that he had been involved in the case since its inception and along the way he had gained considerable understanding of what had happened.

Referring to the many letters family and friends had written to the court in support of me, he spoke particularly of the letter from Mr Turner, who had written that he no longer wished to participate in any quest for retribution.

The judge then wondered, as if to himself, how best to balance the many factors in my favour against the severity of the charge and the mandate of the criminal code, pointing out that the code allowed for life imprisonment on the conspiracy charge. And then, as though suddenly making up his mind, he sat up very straight and continued decisively: 'I'm convinced that the defendant has seen the error of her ways, admitted to herself and to the world her complicity, suffered not only in time in prison on this very offence, the loss of family companionship for years past, some of that permanent, and that she has made a new and law-abiding life for herself.

'There is absolutely no doubt in my mind that if you would have been tried with the others you would have received a severe sentence. And there would still be justice. But there is more to breaking the circle of hate than justice alone. The prophet Micah stated it as clearly as any: "He has told you, old man, what is good. And what does the Lord require of you but to do justice, to love mercy, and to walk humbly when you die."

'Justice and mercy are both foundational thoughts in our society. Sometimes we demonstrate that with a scale. I don't think that's complete. I think there are times when justice trumps mercy. It is more necessary. There are other times when mercy trumps justice. We have such a case here.

'So stand . . . You are committed to . . . confinement for the period of time served.'

I could not move or speak. I stood motionless, as though stillness was needed for his words to penetrate. Only when he was leaving the bench did I manage to move at all, bowing my head in respect and thanks. When he had left the courtroom I turned first to Phil. Still unable to speak, I laid my head for a moment over that great big heart of his. Then I walked back into George's waiting arms. When I opened my eyes again I saw through my tears that we were surrounded by smiling faces. The probation officer who had recommended a sentence of two years approached me with his hand outstretched, his eyes smiling.

'Congratulations, Mrs Stork,' he said as he shook my hand, 'you deserve it.'

The FBI officer who had escorted me from the airport in September was there smiling broadly. Was it just because I was so relieved and happy that I had the impression everyone in the courtroom was happy too? It was completion for so many people, including the many law-enforcement officers who had worked on the case all those years. I was the last one, and now the file could be closed. And yet it was something more than that, as though we all acknowledged that we were connected through the story. Each of us had had our role in it and it touched the hearts of everyone that the story we shared should end with such an unexpected act of grace. Only the prosecutor from Washington DC remained serious, but when I approached him to say goodbye, he shook my hand and wished me well.

Phil had warned us that I might be taken into custody by border control authorities even if things went well. But nobody approached us and we walked out of the courtroom unhindered. Once outside in the corridor, the first thing I did was to call Kylie to tell her what had happened. Then we left the courthouse, where we were confronted by the press. I was completely unable to answer their questions. I had just been the recipient of an extraordinary act of mercy and my mind was still absorbing that. It could not move out to grasp things in the bigger world so quickly. All I could do was to repeat over and over how grateful I was for the mercy that had been shown towards me.

That evening we went out to dinner with Phil and his family, and Deborah and her partner. Over dinner we relived it all again and again, practically pinching each other to make sure we were not dreaming. But it was true. I was free at last.

The next day Phil came to pick us up to take us to the airport. He was wearing a yellow bow tie with little witches on broomsticks riding across it. Being the worrying type, he never quite believed that the people from border control would not show up to arrest me. He said he would stay in the airport until he saw our plane take off. George and I had boarded our flight to Frankfurt and were seated and waiting for takeoff when a steward came up to me and said a man from border control wanted to see me outside. I was not unduly concerned but took my passport and followed him to the door of the plane where passengers were still boarding. Behind them stood a man I recognised from my entry in September. As he caught sight of me he smiled and waved.

'Good! Thank you, Mrs Stork. Have a nice flight,' he called, and turned and walked away.

Once we were in the air, George called Phil. He was still in the airport. George told him we were on our way home and he should go home too.

Epilogue

42

The circle was complete. We returned to Frankfurt on the nonstop flight we had taken in the opposite direction four months earlier. We were still taking everything in and didn't talk much, sitting quietly holding hands instead and feeling as though we had been blessed.

It was deep winter and freezing when we arrived home. Nature was in hibernation. My heart jumped for joy when I saw our house again. It was cosy and welcoming as never before. Just taking a cup out of the cupboard to make tea was a joyful thing for me. At a very leisurely pace I began turning the bachelor pad into a home again – dusting and cleaning windows and baking bread and unpacking the things I had stored away. I didn't feel the need to rush around but was content to stay home and enjoy the peace and quiet of our valley in winter. Temperatures outside were well below zero and there was not a cloud in the sky. My favourite kind of weather: the world frozen white, the skies blue and the sun shining every day.

Over the coming weeks I received many letters from friends and family expressing their joy at the judgement. Many wrote that their faith in human nature had been restored.

Peter continued to do well. I applied for another visa to Australia. Although there seemed to be no need to rush back, obtaining a visa had been a long and drawn-out process the last time and I wanted to be able to go at a moment's notice. Meanwhile George and I were happy for the opportunity of the quiet time together. As it slowly sank in that I would not be taken away from him, the drawn look left his face and he began to look better and better with each passing day. Our sleep took on a deeper, more restful quality.

A month after we returned home Jennifer wrote to say that Peter was beginning to have more seizures and problems with eyesight, and the headaches had returned. A scan was scheduled. Two weeks later the scan showed that the tumour was growing again. It was spreading out from the left temporal lobe back toward the base of the skull and there was a new spreading beginning to cross over the corpus callosum to the other side of the brain. Surgery was no longer an option. The tumour would now run its course.

Although the original diagnosis of Peter's illness had told us what to expect, it was as though I was hearing for the first time that he was dying. I was devastated. There had been a part of me that wanted to believe that now I was free Peter would be all right. It was the wishful thinking of a desperate mother.

George and I flew out of Frankfurt as soon as my visa came through at the end of March.

'Thanks for coming, Mum,' Peter said as he hugged me in welcome. 'Let's enjoy ourselves.'

I was amazed and relieved to find him relatively well. He had begun taking the steroid Dexamethasone again and it had significantly reduced the oedema in his brain giving him another reprieve.

Knowing that he could not expect to feel that well ever again, Peter and Jennifer invited their friends around for one last party together. It was a gentle, loving, bittersweet evening. People brought all manner of delicious food with them. The backyard was full of children tumbling and laughing and swinging and chasing each other, while their parents and friends talked and laughed and feasted together on the veranda as they watched the children play. Peter enjoyed every moment of it. He and Jennifer's friends, some of them Peter's childhood friends from the ashram in Pune and the commune in Oregon, had offered extraordinary practical and emotional support to the family throughout Peter's illness. On this evening those who lived in this corner of the world were gathered together to share food and stories and tears and laughter.

George stayed for the entire month of April. It was a month to cherish. Although as the tumour grew it was necessary to slowly increase the amount of Dexamethasone he took in order to control the oedema-aggravated headaches, Peter was enjoying life. We undertook many excursions in the area. He wanted to show us all the places he loved to stroll through, sit under, walk along, look out from and eat at. At this point he had abandoned dietary restrictions so we indulged him wherever we could. Oysters had always been one of his favourite foods, so we went out and ordered them by the dozen. We also spent many hours playing with the children or sitting on the back veranda watching the antics of the magpies and simply hanging out together. Kylie and Gregory joined us whenever they could. It was with a heavy heart that George took his leave and returned to Germany at the end of the month.

In the weeks that followed I did what I could to relieve Jennifer of some of her load so she could spend as much time as possible with Peter. Their friends had organised rosters for cooking and shopping and child care, but even then it was often difficult for her to have uninterrupted time with Peter and to make the most of the time they still had together. No one could say how long that would be.

Most evenings someone came round with a meal they had prepared. Sometimes they just dropped it off, and sometimes they stayed to eat with us. Whenever it was my turn to cook dinner it was always a dish Peter remembered and loved from his early childhood. He was a meat-and-potatoes man and I often asked myself how he had survived all those years as a vegetarian. The Dexamethasone increased his appetite and he was eating well. For the first time in his life he began to put on weight. He developed a small paunch and began to thicken around the waist. The Dexamethasone also promoted oedema in Peter's body, and gradually his face became rounder and his neck thicker. We joked with him that he was beginning to look like a bandit out of a spaghetti western.

I had rented a caravan and had it pulled up next to the front veranda. One evening in June I was lying in bed in the caravan thinking about something my sister Sue had recently said. She had used the expression 'waiting for Peter to die' and it occurred to me that it had a negative quality to it. I realised that in a way I was there waiting for Peter to die. I was shocked. It was clearly not the right energy to bring to the situation. As I mulled over what was happening to me, I knew I had to go home for a while. After all that had happened in the past months, compounded by what was happening now, my soul was weary and needed to gather strength for what lay ahead. I knew the only place I could do that was at home with George, and the forest. The following morning I called George. He was surprised but happy to hear I was coming home. Then I talked to Peter and Jennifer. I didn't need to explain myself at all. They instinctively trusted what I had to do, even though Jennifer was at first taken aback. Strangely enough, from that day on Peter's pain levels stabilised, and remained stable for weeks to come.

43

I was home by mid-June. I walked in the forest every day, feeling held by its green canopy. It was a balmy summer. We sat on the back veranda in the evenings, eating supper and watching the butterflies enjoying the wild garden. I had days when I felt very trusting of everything, and days when I was cast into the pit of despair.

By the beginning of August there were indications that Peter was starting to falter. Jennifer wrote that his legs were giving out with such frequency that he was using a walker in the house and a wheelchair when he went out. George and I agreed it was time for me to return to Australia. I didn't feel ready yet, but then, when is a mother ready for the death of her child?

It had been a little more than two months since I had last seen Peter and the change in him was shocking. His neck and torso were heavy and bloated. His face was so swollen I did not recognise him. When I stroked his cheek the skin was stretched tight and hard over it. I sat on the bed and looked into his face, trying to see my son. It was not until he began to talk and his eyes sparkled that I recognised him. A couple of days after I arrived back, Jennifer came into my room as I was getting ready for bed and asked if I would come into their bedroom. She said Peter wanted to talk to me. He was lying in bed and I sat down on the mattress next to him. He looked directly at me and said,

'Mum, I'm going to die soon. If there is anything you would like to talk about or say, let's do it now.'

How I had dreaded this moment; the moment when I must relinquish that last tiny shred of hope I had been so resolutely clinging to.

Peter's clarity challenged me to look reality directly in the eye. In that moment I knew I had to let him go. He was no longer a child. He was a noble man with a noble woman at his side and two beautiful children, graciously treading the path laid out for him, and his family. And it was my duty as his mother to accompany them along that path, supporting them on their journey and bringing as much strength and grace to it as I could.

Silent tears rolled down my face. I told Peter I loved him and was very proud to have him as my son. He beamed. Jennifer was lying next to him crying quietly too. We talked softly for a little while, and then I left them together.

In the weeks that followed I was witness to the gradual inexorable deterioration of Peter's body. When he developed a rare steroid psychosis which made him sleepless and euphoric, he and Jennifer spent a few days in the palliative care unit at Lismore Hospital, while doctors adjusted his medication so he was himself again. When they returned home Peter had such difficulty getting in and out of bed, it was deemed necessary to bring in a hospital bed. Jennifer made up a small bed next to it. It was easier to care for Peter then, but it was a terribly hard step for both of them to take.

Soon Peter could not walk any more. Together Jennifer and I helped him out of bed into the wheelchair. For quite a while we could get him in and out of the car to drive down to the beach, or to town, or to a restaurant for lunch or dinner. The last time Peter went out was when Jennifer received her Australian citizenship. It meant a lot to him and so, with tremendous effort, and the help of a friend, he got into the car and out into the wheelchair, in order to be in attendance.

I was sick that day. I lay in bed feverish and ill with sinuses full of yellow mucus and a heavy wet cough. My voice all but disappeared. I couldn't eat. I drank gallons of lemon water and told myself day after day that I would be fine tomorrow. Peter visited me in his wheelchair. On the fifth day he said,

'This is taking too long, Mum.'

That evening it penetrated my brain that I was getting worse, not better. I was getting weaker and weaker and could literally feel the life force draining out of me. With a jolt I realised I was dying with my son. I went to find Jennifer to ask her to take me to a doctor the next morning.

She took me to Mullumbimby Hospital. I explained that I could not afford to be sick because my son was dying. While the nurse was carrying out her tests, Jennifer and I talked with her about how we were caring for Peter. When we said it was becoming increasingly difficult to move him in the bed, she ran off and came back with a slip sheet for us to borrow. I was diagnosed with bacterial sinusitis and given antibiotics, which worked wonders. So did the slip sheet.

The next day was Dylan's third birthday. Dylan and Chloe came into my bedroom first thing in the morning to show me

Dylan's presents. He had a Lego set. It made a tractor and he wasn't too sure how to go about it. Chloe asked if he would like her help. Yes, he would. I lay in bed and watched Dylan sit quietly watching while Chloe sat with one leg tucked under her and, referring casually to the building instructions, built the tractor in the twinkling of an eye. She was Peter at that age. Her posture, the way she focused on what she was doing, the way she handled the blocks, even the tilt of her head as she referred to the instructions. She was her papa playing Lego. And Dylan was Kylie, watching attentively, respectful, not moving a muscle.

Peter was now losing interest in food and eating progressively less and less. Then one evening he vomited what he had eaten and couldn't keep anything down. Jennifer called the palliative care unit. She knew if Peter couldn't keep his pain medication down he would soon be in unbearable agony. The hospital sent an ambulance to pick them up and bring them in. By this time Peter had lost all movement in the right side of his body and was beginning to lose feeling in the left side too.

Chloe and Dylan and I made ourselves a big bed on the living-room floor and slept there. We spent the days quietly at home, except once when we drove to Lismore to visit Peter and Jennifer. Peter was receiving morphine through a syringe pump, and other necessary medication in liquid form through a cannula inserted in his chest. He was very weak and unable to eat at all. He drank water through a straw. The children climbed up on the bed and snuggled into him and he smiled a gentle crooked smile with his half-paralysed face. Jennifer said they were trying to get him stable enough so he could come home to die.

On Friday evening, five days after they had left, an ambulance brought Peter and Jennifer back home again. That same day Jennifer's mother Sonja arrived from America, freeing me up completely to help Jennifer care for Peter, and for me to spend time with him. I stayed with him from dawn till dusk. Often I lay on the floor by the bed reading one of Jennifer's books on children and grief, or just stretched out on Jennifer's little bunk, while Peter lay in the hospital bed resting peacefully and Dylan drove his cars around the floor. Sometimes Chloe came and snuggled up with me, or brought a book for me to read her.

From the very beginning Peter and Jennifer addressed Peter's illness with Chloe and Dylan. They did not try to shield them from the truth of what was happening, although they were extraordinarily gentle and sensitive in the way they spoke to them about it.

I had been there in April when Peter said to Jennifer he thought it was time they told Chloe that he was not just very sick, but that he was going to die. That day Jennifer said she needed a little more time. A couple of weeks later she told him she was ready and together they went outside and sat on the couch on the back veranda with Chloe. I heard her let out a wail and cry out,

'But I don't want Papa to die!'

They were out there for a long time. When they came back inside Chloe looked quite different. She was calmer and more serene than I had seen her in weeks. It was almost as though what her parents had told her was something she already knew. Hearing it from them, being held in their strength and love, she was able to trust her feelings and was now ready to face the next step.

At first I had a real fear of talking to the children about Peter dying. It was fine talking about him being sick, but talking about him dying was a terrifying prospect. It was brought to my attention when one of the goldfish died. I came out one morning and there it was floating belly up in the bowl and I thought, 'Oh no! The children have enough to deal with without this.' Everything in me wanted to whisk the dead fish out of sight and go and buy a replacement before they woke up.

But I had been around Peter and Jennifer long enough to know that this would not be the way they would want to deal with it. I had developed a deep respect for them both by now and so I ignored the urge to make it appear as though nothing had happened. Sure enough, when Jennifer came into the kitchen she registered that the goldfish had died, and when the children came out she said to them,

'Something sad has happened. One of the goldfish has died.'

They came to see for themselves and express their regrets and sorrow. There was some discussion about the possible cause of death, and about the funeral they would hold in the garden for their dead fish, and then they had breakfast. It was not the end of the world. It was a part of life.

Jennifer had bought the children a picture book about caterpillars eating their way through leaves down in the garden. There were caterpillars of all colours and as they ate they got fatter and fatter, until each one began to spin a cocoon around itself. The cocoons hung under leaves down in the garden, until the day came when beautiful butterflies emerged from them and flew away. The butterflies settled on leaves and laid their eggs. Out of the eggs hatched caterpillars, and the cycle renewed itself.

The day before Peter died Dylan asked me to read him the book about the caterpillars. When we were about to come to the part where a butterfly would emerge from its cocoon and fly away, he slapped his hand down firmly on the book and wouldn't let me turn the page. We had a little discussion but he was adamant he did not want to see the butterfly emerge from the cocoon, and held his hand resolutely on the book to prevent me turning the page. I asked him if he would like me to read any more of the story and he replied that he wanted me to go to the end of the book where new caterpillars were emerging from the eggs.

'I don't want butterflies. I only like caterpillars,' he said.

Since the night of his last meal a week before, Peter had been unable to speak. When I said goodnight to him on Sunday evening, 1 October, he smiled up at me as I leaned down to kiss his forehead. As I moved back he looked directly at me and smiled again. He raised his left hand, opening and closing it to wave three times. It was the last time I looked into those blue-green eyes that were such a perfect mix of the vast blue skies and turquoise ocean he loved so much. The next day he drifted in and out of consciousness. He was so weak he could no longer draw water through a straw and Jennifer and I moistened his lips and his tongue with a sponge dipped in water.

44

In 1955 the photographic exhibition *The Family of Man*, created by Edward Steichen for the Museum of Modern Art in New York, opened to the public. In the catalogue accompanying the exhibition, Carl Sandburg wrote:

> *There is only one man in the world*
> *and his name is All Men.*
> *There is only one woman in the world*
> *and her name is All Women.*
> *There is only one child in the world*
> *and the child's name is All Children.*

On 3 October 2006 I woke as usual at first light. The first thing that came into my mind was this quote, and without thinking I found myself adding: There is only one grieving mother in the world, and her name is All Grieving Mothers.

I lay in bed thinking of all the grieving mothers in the world. Mothers who lost the fruit in their womb before it had time to grow into a child they could bear and suckle and hold. Mothers whose child reached full term but died at birth, or shortly afterwards. Mothers whose child drowned or died of illness or in an accident. Mothers whose child committed suicide in despair or desperation. Mothers whose sons and daughters died in wars. Mothers whose children died of starvation. Mothers whose sons and daughters died at the hands of death squads. Mothers of sons and daughters in Afghanistan and Iraq and Somalia who were dying that very moment. I belonged to a vast world community of grief-stricken mothers, and in that moment I felt held by them.

Jennifer tapped gently on the door and asked me to come to Peter. As we walked up the corridor to the bedroom, she told me Peter had been restless early in the morning. He had tried to tell her something with his eyes. Later she would realise that he had been saying goodbye. She had done what she could to make him comfortable and then his breathing had changed and his lungs had begun to rattle, so she came to fetch me.

Peter was propped up in bed. His breathing was very laboured. His whole torso was occupied in drawing breath through the liquid beginning to build up in his lungs. The air gurgled through the fluid with the sound made when you blow through a straw into a glass of water. His eyes were closed. Apart from his laboured breathing he was peaceful.

The family doctor, Dr Heyning, had talked to us a couple of weeks before about the possible ways in which death might come. Peter was already bedridden and his body was getting weaker and weaker. There was a growing tendency for mucus to build up in the lower lungs, and up until recently he had been able to cough it up and clear them. But as he grew weaker he could no longer effectively clear his lungs and the mucus stayed there, offering a perfect opportunity for infection.

Peter was on the way to getting pneumonia, Dr Heyning said, and went on to tell us that in cases of terminal illness or very old age, pneumonia is considered a blessing. So much so that it was known in the past as 'the old man's friend'. As the fluids build up in the lungs and less and less oxygen is available to the brain, the dying person drifts away gently and suffers only minimally, if at all, from the distress of drawing breath through fluid and the shutting down of the bodily systems as the life force leaves the body.

The moment I saw Peter I knew that time had come. I called Kylie to tell her he was dying. Jennifer gathered Chloe and Dylan in her arms and brought them to Peter's bedside. Today was the day, she explained to them, when Papa's spirit would leave his body and fly away. Dylan squirmed in her arms and looked down at his father in the bed. He didn't want his papa to die, he said, and why was his breath rattling? His lips trembled and he looked very concerned. He asked a lot of questions and Jennifer cuddled him and answered them as best she could.

Chloe took the purple teddy she had given Peter, with 'I love you' embroidered on its chest, and tucked it between Peter's arm and his body. Dylan watched her. He wriggled out of his mother's arms, took a beeswax rainbow from the bedside table, and a polished stone, and put them in the crook of Peter's arm, before leaning forward to kiss him. Then he left the room and strode down the hall to the kitchen where his Grandma Sonja was preparing breakfast. Jennifer turned on *Sleeping Angels*, a meditative track Peter had found especially tranquil, and pressed the repeat button. Then she took her place by his side.

The fluid built up with astonishing speed, so that by 9 am Peter's lungs were so full the liquid splashed into view in the back of his throat with each breath he drew. The gurgling, rasping sound of air being drawn through water, and the huge effort required to draw each breath, was terrible to see and hear. Jennifer was distraught. This did not seem like a blessing. It seemed like a torturous, horrible way to die, and she held Peter's hand and wept. But harrowing as it was, when I looked into Peter's face it was peaceful. Although medically speaking he was unconscious, he gave the impression he was serenely, deeply concentrated on the task at hand.

A few close friends joined us. Every so often someone refilled my water glass and, at what must have been lunchtime, Gregory's mother pressed a bowl of hot vegetable soup into my hands. There was a feeling of reverence in the room, as though we were witness to a profoundly sacred rite of passage.

At 2 pm I left the room to call George in Germany, where it was early morning. I had just hung up the phone when Jennifer sent someone to tell me that Peter's breathing had changed and I should come back. It was hardly perceptible, but he was breathing irregularly now.

I whispered greetings from George in Peter's ear. Those of us gathered around him were crying softly now. I told him we were crying because we loved him so much and would miss him, but that we were okay and he need pay no heed to us. I wished him Godspeed and reminded him to stay in the Light. Then I went to kneel on the floor at the foot of his bed. His breaths came further and further apart, and at the same time they were shallower and shallower. The gaps seemed impossibly long, and just at the point when I thought he was dead, he would gasp for the next breath, which would be so shallow it hardly counted for a breath at all. And then it was over. At 3 pm he took his last breath. I bowed my head and out of my heart rose the words: *This is my beloved Son in whom I am well pleased.*

And my mother heart broke asunder and I thought I would cry forever.

45

Peter had asked that his body not be moved for six hours after his death, and that Jennifer keep a vigil over him. It was natural that I keep the vigil with her. Kylie was pregnant and Gregory had taken her home to rest. I sat where she had sat all day at Peter's side. I was cold and wrapped myself in a woollen blanket, like an old squaw. Again and again I opened my eyes to gaze at Peter's body propped up in bed, eyes and mouth slightly open, head turned slightly to one side. He looked like a statue of an ancient Greek god I had seen in a museum somewhere. I thought he looked very beautiful and had to keep reminding myself that he was dead. Sometimes I deliberately opened my eyes to look at him as a reminder to myself to face reality.

Like Joseph Peter knew 'the important thing was to walk with courageous and willing steps the path God set under his feet'. When he heard he had a brain tumour that would kill him, he did not close his eyes or turn his face away. I, who had closed my eyes to reality most of my life, had been sorely tempted throughout his illness to squeeze them tightly shut again. I had had to make a conscious effort of will to open them and to keep them open. At times along the way they became heavy with grief at what they were seeing and fell shut, but when I realised it, I opened them again, just as I was doing now. I had to keep looking. I had an obligation to myself, and to Peter.

Chloe slipped into the room and climbed onto my lap. I wrapped her inside my rug with me. She nuzzled into me and sat quietly gazing at Peter's body. Then she looked around the room and asked why there were so many candles burning. I told her it was because Peter had died. She snuggled back down and continued to look at her papa's body lying in the bed. We sat there for a very long time. Then she jumped down and said she was going back into the light, and disappeared towards the kitchen.

Zenith, a friend and funeral celebrant, came and squatted next to Jennifer. She had talked with Peter and Jennifer many times over the past few months, giving both the benefit of her experience with natural death. Now that Peter had died she would set things in motion and guide us through the next steps of leave-taking.

Dr Heyning came to sign the death certificate. The weather was cool, he said, so there was no hurry to move Peter's body to the mortuary. He could stay where he was for now and we should simply leave the windows open.

When the vigil was over we lowered the head end of the hospital bed and laid Peter's body flat. It was already beginning to stiffen and we used pillows to prop under one side of his head to straighten it up. That night Jennifer and I slept in the room with his body.

We were in the kitchen the next morning making breakfast when I was seized with the yearning to go and be with Peter. I walked down the hall into the bedroom. There was no one there, save Peter's lifeless body. I stroked his face and arms and talked to him about how much I loved him and what a beautiful man he had become and how lovely his children were and how I would miss him, and the tears poured down my face and onto his chest and arm, and ran off onto the sheets. And then I was calm again.

Kylie came into the room and we stood on either side of Peter's body and talked quietly. She was happy, she said, to have been able to be present when Peter died. She had always feared he would die suddenly in the middle of the night and was glad he had given us plenty of notice so she could be there with him.

Friends came to help Jennifer, Kylie and me wash and anoint Peter's body, and dress him and lay him out on the flat bier Zenith provided. Then we covered him to the chest with a purple shroud, and went to the kitchen to have a light lunch.

Meanwhile other friends had cleaned and polished the van. It looked like new. Even the hubcaps were spotless. After lunch we carried Peter's body on the bier out of the bedroom, and out of the house, and put it in the van. Jennifer covered his face with the scarf she was wearing, and she and Peter's oldest friend drove away to the funeral parlour with Peter's body in the back. As they drove away I thought, 'Only in Australia!' It reminded me of *Waking Ned Devine* and I had to chuckle in spite of myself. Peter would have approved.

Before she left I asked Jennifer if it would be all right to take the hospital bed out of her bedroom and to bring the double bed back in. I thought that with all that would be happening in the next few days she would need a comfortable sanctuary to retreat to. She agreed. I called the friend who had brought us the bed and he came and dismantled it and put it back in his truck to return to the hospital. Then we placed Peter and Jennifer's bed back where it had always been, and made it up. We took out all the hospital and medical paraphernalia and put the bedside tables and rugs back. Everything was in place by the time Jennifer returned.

She walked into the bedroom and stood there with her back to the wall, taking it all in. Slowly she slid down the wall until she was sitting on the floor with her knees drawn up, facing the bed. Silent tears ran down her face. I sat down next to her and my heart wept again at the enormity of her loss.

46

The house was a hive of activity for the next few days as preparations were made for the funeral service and cremation. I couldn't understand why the world had not stopped in its path around the sun when Peter died. I was constantly shocked to register that we were all still living and moving, and it puzzled me that life went on almost as though nothing had happened.

The morning of the funeral service, I drove to the airport to pick up George, and we went directly from there to the hall where the service was to be held. The bier with Peter's body laid out on it was placed on the floor. Low chairs were arranged in a semicircular pattern around it and we took our places at the front. There were lots of children and I was fascinated to see that they were curious and interested in what was happening. They were not afraid to approach Peter's body and lay on their tummies on the floor around him, touching him gently and rearranging the flowers and fetching more rose petals to scatter over his feet. One older boy lay for some time with the top of his head touching the top of Peter's head. A little girl came up and stroked Peter's face and then came to me and said,

'Why did Peter have to die?'

I told her his body had been very sick and could not support his spirit any longer and his spirit had flown away like a butterfly. She seemed satisfied and went back for a closer look. It was a far cry from Nan's funeral when the closed coffin was kept out of reach of the family, as though it had nothing to do with us. Peter's body was lying there on a bier in the heart of his family and friends, within easy reach of everyone, allowing each person to say goodbye in their own particular way.

The service was a celebration of Peter and was full of warmth and love. Friends and family had an opportunity to speak their hearts.

When it came my turn I spoke of the enthusiasm with which Peter had embraced the role of big brother when Kylie was born, and how gentle and loving he had always been with her. I spoke of his passion for Lego, which later made way for computers and cameras, projectors and sound equipment, all of which he approached with the creativity and attention to detail that were so characteristic of him. I thanked his friends all over the world for the incredible generosity and support they had offered him and his family, and I thanked everyone who had supported us so Peter could die at home.

I said that though my own experience had taught me that Life means well with us, I did not pretend to understand why it was that Peter should have had such a long, painful illness and then died. And yet I could not help but see that in some mysterious way he had brought untold blessings upon our family, and I thanked him, saying how deeply grateful I was that I could have him as my son.

At the end of the day we loaded Peter's body back into the van and brought him home one last time.

The following morning Gregory came with the coffin he had made and we lifted Peter's body into it. Jennifer placed the letters of parting people had written to him, a few small treasures and a letter from Chloe in the coffin too. Then it was time to load him into the van for the trip to the crematorium.

At the crematorium we had one last hour with him. We drew pictures and messages on his coffin and sang over him the Celtic blessing his father and stepmother had sung over him and Jennifer on their wedding day. Then Gregory put the lid on the coffin and it disappeared behind a screen. From a small adjacent room we could watch the coffin moving along a conveyor. Suddenly a metal door opened. For a moment I registered the red-hot glow. The coffin was propelled inside and the metal door closed shut. It was a brutal shock. He was unequivocally gone. That beautiful form was no more. Chloe cried out in anguish,

'Papa! I want my Papa!' and we huddled together and cried. Then we went into the garden where Zenith had white doves for the children to release into the sky. They flew away carrying whispered messages of love to Peter.

47

George stayed for a week and then returned to Germany. Before he left he booked me a return flight ten days later. If it had been left up to me I would not have been able to leave Jennifer and the children and the house where we had fused into one unit during the last weeks of Peter's life. It felt like a violent act to tear myself away from them, and the thought of another parting was in itself unbearable, even though this one would only be temporary. As it was I almost didn't go because Kylie's son Joshua became critically ill with pneumonia and was rushed to hospital three days before I was due to fly out. I spent those last days in the hospital with Joshua and his parents and his Grandma Patricia. As the time approached when I should leave, I hesitated. I didn't want to go anywhere, but when I spoke to George he encouraged me to come home. He instinctively knew that I was running on my last reserves and they were about to give out.

Back home again I fell apart. We were driving in the car and just the sound of the tyres on the road and the vibration caused by the forward movement were completely overwhelming. It was intolerable. I needed everything to stop. My very soul cried out for stillness and calm. A part of me had died and it needed to be held in infinite silence.

When I look back I see that those first three months after Peter's death were lived in utter shock. I was functioning in everyday life but my spirit did not seem to be present. I stayed close to the house, driving out only rarely for provisions, not venturing into the garden or forest. The house was like a womb holding me.

In the fourth month after Peter's death I began going into the garden every day. I had ignored it ever since he had fallen ill and it was overgrown and wild. Now it called me to leave the house and attend to it. Although it was winter the weather was mild. I spent hours every day digging and clearing and redefining paths and garden beds. It felt good to dig in the earth and to feel the wind in my hair. And I began going into the forest again to see my tree.

My tree was a magnificent beech in the forest behind our house. Almost every day for over fifteen years I had walked up the hill to visit her. Whenever something was weighing heavily on my heart, I would tell her about it. Sometimes I cried against her like a child with its mother; sometimes I simply sat at her feet and leaned my back against her mighty trunk, drawing strength and peace from her. On a cold winter morning in the January after Peter's death, I saw as I approached my tree that she was damaged. Heavy winds had roared through the forest in the night, tearing a rent in the top of the soaring trunk. The wound was gaping under the weight of the gigantic crown. She looked as I felt – literally torn apart – and, like Peter, she was dying. A piercing wail rose out of me and I stood there doubled over in agony and sobbed and sobbed.

Painful as it was for me I was determined not to turn my face away. Every day I walked up the hill and stroked her and held her in my arms and my tears ran down her bark. And with each day the understanding that I was revisiting Peter on his path of suffering became clearer. For it was he I held in my arms and stroked, and it was his pain I sought to wash away with my tears.

The day came when my tree was so completely torn in two that I could stand at her feet and place my hand in the base of her gaping wound. One day I walked up the hill to find her crown had torn off and lay at the feet of her mutilated trunk. My heart ached. I climbed over the shattered crown strewn around her and hugged her one last time.

On my way into the forest the following morning I saw tractor tracks in the mud and knew the forester had already come to prepare for the disposal of the body. My tree had been cut through at ground level and her divided trunk lay on the ground like a great slain animal. I threw myself across it and my grief consumed me.

I have come to see that nature has her own wisdom. I am certain that were we to experience all our grief at once we would be struck dead. Instead we grieve to the degree our hearts can manage, a little at a time, slowly entering deeper and deeper into its watery depths. I do not know, but I suspect it is unfathomable.

The day came when I began writing down this story. I set off for the forest the morning after writing about Peter's coffin disappearing into the crematorium fire. Suddenly I began to cry. The deeper anguish behind the silent tears that flowed as George and I held Jennifer and Chloe and Dylan in that awful moment came pouring out. My heart was aching in my chest and I held it and wept as I walked into the forest. I had gone a few hundred metres when I became aware that the hundreds of trees all around me were like hundreds of people. They seemed to be looking at me with quiet concern as much as to say,

'Why are you crying?'

I stopped walking and through my tears I turned to them and said,

'My son died.'

I felt my heart tear asunder as I spoke the terrible words, and I sobbed loudly. I turned slowly, stopping again and again to address those standing there, repeating each time,

'My son died.'

When I had turned a full three hundred and sixty degrees, I realised they were women standing there, and they had all lost a child. They were grieving mothers like myself. I turned to them again and said,

'My son died too.' Sometimes I said,

'My child died too,' as I slowly turned to address them all again. I continued to cry but no longer so heavily.

When I had spoken to all of them I continued uphill. I felt I was walking up the hill of Calvary and all around me were other mothers who had walked the same path. I was still crying but more gently. I looked at the women lining the route and it seemed to me that now there were millions of them. They were all standing there quietly dignified, looking at me and sharing in my grief. A quiet strength emanated from them and I felt their strength enter into me. Gradually my tears stopped altogether and I walked on uphill, acknowledging the multitude of silent women who lined the way.

At the stump of my tree, I bowed deeply to my son, and to all those children who had been sacrificed on the vast altar of life. Standing upright again I sang the ancient song of the Rune Yr into the forest. It is the sound of the leaf that falls from the tree in autumn, the deep mournful sigh all life makes when it returns to the womb of the Great Mother.

END

Contents

Prologue 1
Australia 3
India 75
Oregon 107
Germany 181
Epilogue 261

Printed in Poland
by Amazon Fulfillment
Poland Sp. z o.o., Wrocław